AF794314

SERIES EDITOR

Lewis R. **FISCHER** (Canada)

MANAGING EDITOR

Margaret M. **GULLIVER**

EDITORIAL BOARD

Lars U. **SCHOLL** (Germany, Chair)
Gelina **HARLAFTIS** (Greece, Vice-Chair)
Merja-Liisa **HINKKANEN** (Finland, Secretary)

Jean-François **BRIÈRE** (USA)
Jaap R. **BRUIJN** (Netherlands)
Pin-Tsun **CHANG** (Taiwan)
Tomohei **CHIDA** (Japan)
K. **DHARMASENA** (Sri Lanka)
Morten **HAHN-PEDERSEN** (Denmark)
Gordon **JACKSON** (Scotland)
Hans-Chr. **JOHANSEN** (Denmark)
Silvia **MARZAGALLI** (France)
Keiichiro **NAKAGAWA** (Japan)
Victor **NORMAN** (Norway)
Sarah **PALMER** (England)
G. Edward **REED** (Canada)
Jeffrey J. **SAFFORD** (USA)
Edward W. **SLOAN** (USA)
David J. **STARKEY** (England)
Carl E. **SWANSON** (USA)
Malcolm **TULL** (Australia)
Jesús M. **VALDALISO** (Spain)
Paul **VAN ROYEN** (Netherlands)
Karel **VERAGHTERT** (Belgium)
Simon P. **VILLE** (Australia)
William D. **WRAY** (Canada)

INTERNATIONAL MARITIME ECONOMIC HISTORY ASSOCIATION

Yrjö **KAUKIAINEN** (President)
Frank **BROEZE** (Vice-President)
Faye **KERT** (Vice-President)
Olaf U. **JANZEN** (Secretary)
G. Edward **REED** (Treasurer)

MAILING ADDRESS

Maritime Studies Research Unit
Memorial University of Newfoundland
St. John's, Newfoundland A1C 5S7, Canada

RESEARCH IN MARITIME HISTORY
NO. 16

HARBOURS AND HAVENS: ESSAYS IN PORT HISTORY IN HONOUR OF GORDON JACKSON

Edited By

Lewis R. Fischer and Adrian Jarvis

International Maritime Economic History Association

St. John's, Newfoundland
1999

ISSN -1188-3928
ISBN -0-9681288-6-6

Research in Maritime History is published semi-annually, in June and December. The contents are copyrighted by the International Maritime Economic History Association and all rights are reserved under Canadian and international law. Copying without the written permission of the International Maritime Economic History Association is prohibited.

Research in Maritime History is available free of charge to members of the International Maritime Economic History Association. The price to others is US$15 per copy.

Back issues of *Research in Maritime History* are available:

No. 1 (1991)	David M. Williams and Andrew P. White (comps.), *A Select Bibliography of British and Irish University Theses about Maritime History, 1792-1990*
No. 2 (1992)	Lewis R. Fischer (ed.), *From Wheel House to Counting House: Essays in Maritime Business History in Honour of Professor Peter Neville Davies*
No. 3 (1992)	Lewis R. Fischer and Walter Minchinton (eds.), *People of the Northern Seas*
No. 4 (1993)	Simon Ville (ed.), *Shipbuilding in the United Kingdom in the Nineteenth Century: A Regional Approach*
No. 5 (1993)	Peter N. Davies (ed.), *The Diary of John Holt*
No. 6 (1994)	Simon P. Ville and David M. Williams (eds.), *Management, Finance and Industrial Reslations in Maritime Industries: Essays in International Maritime and Business History*
No. 7 (1994)	Lewis R. Fischer (ed.), *The Market for Seamen in the Age of Sail*
No. 8 (1995)	Gordon Read and Michael Stammers (comps.), *Guide to the Records of Merseyside Maritime Museum*
No. 9 (1995)	Frank Broeze (ed.), *Maritime History at the Crossroads: A Critical Review of Recent Historiography*
No. 10 (1996)	Nancy Redmayne Ross (ed.), *The Diary of a Maritimer, 1816-1901: The Life and Times of Joseph Salter*

No. 11 (1997) Faye Margaret Kert, *Prize and Prejudice: Privateering and Naval Prize in Atlantic Canada in the War of 1812*

No. 12 (1997) Malcolm Tull, *A Community Enterprise: The History of the Port of Fremantle, 1897 to 1997*

No. 13 (1997) Paul van Royen, Jaap Bruijn and Jan Lucassen (eds.), *"Those Emblems of Hell"? European Sailors and The Maritime Labour Market, 1570-1870*

No. 14 (1998) David J. Starkey and Gelina Harlaftis (eds.), *Global Markets: The Internationalization of The Sea Transport Industries Since 1850*

No. 15 (1998) Olaf Uwe Janzen (ed.), *Merchant Organization and Maritime Trade in the North Atlantic, 1660-1815*

Research in Maritime History would like to thank Memorial University of Newfoundland for its generous financial assistance in support of this volume.

DR. GORDON JACKSON

CONTENTS

CONTRIBUTIONS

ABOUT THE EDITORS

LEWIS R. FISCHER is Professor of History at Memorial University of Newfoundland, Editor-in-Chief of the *International Journal of Maritime History*, and Editor of *The Northern Mariner/Le Marin du nord*. He is currently working on an international comparison of port development, 1850-1939, a project suggested to him by Gordon Jackson.

ADRIAN JARVIS is Co-director of the Centre for Port and Maritime History, a joint venture of National Museums and Galleries on Merseyside and the University of Liverpool, and Secretary-General of the International Commission for Maritime History. He has published extensively on the finance, management and technology of ports. The topic of his book *The Liverpool Dock Engineers* (Stroud, 1996) was suggested to him by Gordon Jackson.

CONTRIBUTORS

FRANK BROEZE is Professor of History at the University of Western Australia and the author of numerous studies in maritime economic, social and cultural history, with a special interest in port cities, maritime ideology and containerisation. He gratefully acknowledges the inspiration of Gordon Jackson's scholarship, humour and ideas, particularly those on ports, whaling and the Grimsby Haven Company.

PETER N. DAVIES is Professor Emeritus at the University of Liverpool and President of the International Commission for Maritime History. A former President of the International Maritime Economic History Association and Chairman of the British Commission of Maritime History, his major works include *The Japanese Shipping and Shipbuilding Industries: A History of Their Modern Growth* (London, 1990, with Tomohei Chida) and *Fyffes and the Banana: Musa Sapientum – A Centenary History, 1888-1988* (London, 1990). He has known Gordon Jackson for nearly thirty years.

RICHARD GORSKI is Philip Nicholas Memorial Lecturer in Maritime History at the University of Hull. He recently worked with David J. Starkey, *et al.* on *Shipping Movements in the Ports of the United Kingdom, 1871-1913: A Statistical Profile* (Exeter, 1999). He is currently undertaking a pilot study to assess the scale and scope of the British passenger shipping industry, 1890-1914.

CAROL HILL is the final post-graduate students to undertake a PhD under the guidance of Gordon Jackson at the University of Strathclyde. Her research considers the links between regional trade; the development of port and shipping capita; commercial and economic networks, and their role in the economic development of southwestern Scotland. She has published *A Galloway Venture; The Kirkcudbright Shipping Company* and has articles in the *International Journal of Maritime History* and *Scottish Economic and Social History*.

POUL HOLM is Research Professor at the Centre for Maritime and Regional History in the Fisheries and Maritime Museum in Esbjerg, and at Aarhus University. His most recent book, *Esbjerg 1910-1998. Havneby og Storkommune*, is co-authored with Verner Bruhn. He is currently engaged in interdisciplinary research on long-term developments in marine resource utilisation.

GRAEME J. MILNE teaches economic and social history and is the Mather Fellow in the School of History at the University of Liverpool. His research interests are in port cities, trade networks and trading communities, with a particular focus on the development of the Atlantic world. He is currently completing book on trade and traders in mid-Victorian Liverpool.

LARS U. SCHOLL is an historian at the Deutsches Schiffahrtsmuseum, an external lecturer in maritime history at the University of Hamburg, and Chair of the Editorial Board of the *International Journal of Maritime History*. A specialist in nineteenth- and twentieth-century German history maritime history, his interest in North German port cities was largely stimulated by Gordon Jackson's work on British ports.

DAVID J. STARKEY is Wilson Family Lecturer in Maritime History at the University of Hull. One of the most prolific writers on British maritime history, he is co-editor of *Global Markets: The Internationalization of the Sea Transport Industries since 1850* (St. John's, 1998) and editor of *Shipping Movements in the Ports of the United Kingdom, 1871-1913: A Statistical Profile* (Exeter, 1999).

MALCOLM TULL teaches in the School of Economics and Commerce at Murdoch University. He has written a number of important articles on port history, especially in Australia, and is the author of *The History of the Port of Fremantle, 1897 to 1997* (St. John's, 1997). Gordon Jackson was an examiner of his PhD thesis.

Introduction

Lewis R. Fischer and Adrian Jarvis

It is generally conceded that biographers cannot be impartial toward their subjects: to live with the life of a single individual for a prolonged period requires a strong emotion for sustenance. For those who organize a *festschrift*, on the other hand, the choice is more limited. The only reason to undertake such a work is out of a genuine feeling of affection, which is what we, and all the contributors to this volume, feel toward Gordon Jackson. Gordon is a genuinely nice man, with a warm personality and a delightful sense of humour (that he would disagree with this characterization demonstrates that while his historical judgement is sound his self-assessment should not be trusted). Moreover, he has consistently been one of the most helpful people in the entire historical profession. The number of scholars, whether young or more established, who have benefited from his assistance, both professional and personal, is legion. It is a pleasure to be able to repay a small portion of our collective and individual debts to him by organizing this tribute.

But emotion cannot be the sole criterion for presenting a scholar with a *festschrift*. This honour retains its value only by being reserved for those few individuals whose contributions to the profession are of the highest order. By this standard there can be few maritime historians (or historians of any stripe, for that matter) more deserving of this honour than Gordon Jackson. There can be no doubt about his intellectual accomplishments. Gordon has not only produced a remarkable number of studies of importance to specialists but also a series of books that can justifiably be called seminal. *Hull in the Eighteenth Century*, for instance, has changed the way historians write about cities, and especially port cities. *The British Whaling Trade* is the single most influential volume yet written on European whaling. And *The History and Archaeology of Ports*, the obvious inspiration for this volume, has now served as an intellectual guide for a generation of scholars interested in the sea-land interface.

But it is important to underscore the fact that as important as his books have been, Gordon's other contributions have transcended them. In addition to teach - and entertaining - literally hundreds of scholars in his office at the University of Strathclyde and at his home, his service to history – and especially to maritime history – has been legendary. We will not embarrass Gordon by reciting all his achievements here, but we do think it important that maritime historians recognize what he has done behind the scenes to support our specialty. As a member from the beginning of the International Maritime Economic History Association; a member of the Executive Council of the International Commission for Maritime History; a member (and current Chairman) of the British Commission for Maritime History; and one of the most important forces behind the highly-successful series of British-Dutch seminars in maritime history, Gordon has devoted untold hours to fostering cooperation among maritime scholars. Indeed, as one of a remarkable troika of more-or-less contemporaries, along with Peter Davies and Robin Craig, Gordon has helped to ensure that the United Kingdom remains the mecca for maritime historians from around the world.

This *festschrift* was presented to Gordon is a rather unique way, but one which we hope attests to his singular role within maritime history. When we began planning this project more than two years ago, we realized that we wanted to present it to him on the occasion of his sixty-fifth birthday. But at what venue? As we were pondering the logistics, Gordon, as he has done so often, solved our problem. At a conference of the Association for the History of the Northern Seas in Esbjerg, Denmark, Gordon observed that many long conferences suffer from having too many papers. It might be better, he offered, to organize some paperless conferences, at which individuals could get together to discuss topics of mutual interest without the need to cobble together formal essays. *Voila* – Gordon had given us the idea of the "paperless conference." And it was at such a conference, suitably on port history and with Gordon as the keynote speaker, that this volume was presented in August 1999. Once again he came to the rescue of maritime historians in need. You have our eternal gratitude, Gordon.

Given Gordon's broad interests, this book could have explored a number of themes. But to provide a degree of coherence, we decided from the outset to focus on ports. And because Gordon was always exploring international linkages, it had to contain essays on British ports along with chapters on international entrepots to provide context. Initially, we envisioned a volume that would be half on Britain and half on international ports. It did not quite work out that way, but we hope that the distribution of topics still suggests the vitality and relevance of Gordon's writings.

After a personal essay by Lewis Fischer and Peter Davies that examines Gordon's life and intellectual roots, this volume features four essays on British port history. The opening piece, by Adrian Jarvis of the Centre for Port and Maritime History, uses British, and especially Liverpool, examples to try to assess where port history has been and where it might be going. It also places Gordon's contributions in context and shows clearly the seminal nature of his work. This is followed by a splendid essay by Graeme Milne of the University of Liverpool on the politics of port management and development in that port in the nineteenth century. David Starkey and Richard Gorski of the University of Hull have prepared a fascinating essay on developments in the port of Hull, a daunting task given Gordon's own work on that port. But in an analysis which can fairly be described as "Jacksonesque," they explain how the Wilsons and North Eastern Railway Shipping Company help to shape the port in the first third of the twentieth century. The final essay in this section is a useful examination of the small Scottish port of Dumfries by Carol Hill, a promising young scholar who has the distinction of being the last of Gordon's PhD students.

The final six essays in the book look at a wide array of international ports. Malcolm Tull of Murdoch University adds to his impressive body of work on the port of Fremantle with an essay that examines key developments in Australian ports since the Second World War. The focus then shifts to East Asia, as Peter Davies of the University of Liverpool contributes an essay on the rise of the port of Yokohama in the nineteenth century through an examination of the contributions of the British merchant firm Aspinall, Cornes and Company. Frank Broeze of the University of Western Australia then takes us to the Middle East and the burgeoning port of Dubai, which not only serves as an intriguing case study but also demonstrates how it is possible for a determined administration to create some significant comparative advantages where nonc had previously existed. Next, it is on the Europe, where Lars Scholl of the Deutsches Schiffahrtsmuseum looks at the port of Bremerhaven, another artificial creation designed to obviate some of the problems of the riverine port of Bremen. Close by, Poul Holm of the Centre for Maritime and Regional History in Esbjerg looks at that port's evolution from a harbour that specialized in agricultural and fisheries exports to its current role as a base for offshore development. Finally, Lewis Fischer of Memorial University of Newfoundland takes us across the Atlantic to look at a proposal for an integrated ports policy, a development which he places in a much broader North Atlantic perspective.

For the editors, this project was a joy from start to finish. But we need to acknowledge that it would not have been possible without the help of a number of others who share our affection for Gordon. That the contributors all belong in this list needs no amplification, but if we tell you that each of them committed to attend the presentation you will know how deeply they care for this very special man. We also need to thank the Director of the National Museums and Galleries on Merseyside, Richard Foster, and the Keeper of the Merseyside Maritime Museum, Michael Stammers, for providing the venue for our presentation along with their normal hospitality. We would also like to thank Margaret Gulliver, who as usual went far beyond the call of duty to coordinate the myriad of details essential to the production of this book.

But our greatest thanks go to three people without whom neither we nor Gordon would be where we are today. Margaret Hastie, long his secretary and the person chiefly responsible for transforming an often disorganized academic into someone who could achieve all the things that Gordon has done, came through as well by providing information when we most needed it. The Reverend Derek Webster, Gordon's closest boyhood friend, generously shared his reminiscences about Gordon's youth and provided some invaluable insights into his character. And then there is Hazel Jackson, without whom we, like Gordon, would have been hopelessly lost. We consulted her about this project from the beginning, and she has provided whatever we needed, including the photograph of Gordon that graces the frontispiece of this book. Perhaps one anecdote will make it clear just how far Hazel went to help us. In May 1998 Lewis Fischer and his daughter, Rebecca, visited the Jacksons in Glasgow. Hazel arranged the domestic accommodations so that Skip got to "sleep" in Gordon's study, where he had unfettered access to all of Gordon's publications, and to many of his unpublished writings as well. Hazel also undertook perhaps the most difficult task – she kept a naturally curious scholar in the dark as we put this book together. We hope that the look on Gordon's face was worth all the effort, Hazel.

Gordon Jackson: An Appreciation

Lewis R. Fischer and Peter N. Davies

Englishmen like to tell visitors that if they are bored by the current vista, all they need do is travel a few miles to experience scenery that is totally different. This amazing variety is truly one of the joys of the British Isles.. Yet even by such lofty standards, Lincolnshire is an especially diverse unit. This is true in several ways. For starters, it is spatially one of the largest of the counties. It is also highly heterogeneous economically: part of it comprises rich agricultural lands, while other areas have given rise to mining, manufacturing and fishing industries. Indeed, some geographers have questioned whether Lincolnshire forms any kind of coherent whole. While travellers who visited the region between the Middle Ages and the nineteenth century almost always commented on the diversity of topography and economy, most tended nonetheless to see a kind of unity in its people, who were most often described as "pious," "industrious" and, most typically, "independent." These attributes perfectly describe Gordon Jackson, Lincolnshire born and bred.

Gordon is proud of his Lincolnshire roots, yet if you ask him where he is from, his answer usually is far more specific: he will tell you that he is from Cleethorpes, where he was born on 14 April 1934. If you listen carefully, however, you will soon discover that what he really means is that he is from the northeastern part of Lincolnshire. For a maritime historian who, like Gordon, has written with a special passion about whaling and ports, there is perhaps no more fitting birthplace, for this area includes Grimsby, long the largest fishing port in the country, and across the Humber, where Lincolnshire blends into Yorkshire, is Hull, historically one of Britain's most important ports (and a centre of whaling as well). A boy growing up in this region in the years spanning the Second World War could hardly avoid being touched by the sea.

Gordon, in perhaps this way alone, was typical. It must be admitted, though, that Cleethorpes was a very special kind of maritime town. A quiet backwater until the 1860s, it was transformed into an important tourist destination by the arrival in 1863 of the Manchester, Sheffield and Lincolnshire Railway, which brought holiday makers down the coast from Hull and Grimsby. By the time Gordon was born, seaside tourism was the town's number one industry, and in summer at least, Cleethorpes was a bustling centre, attracting as many as 30,000 visitors over holiday weekends.

Although it was no port, Gordon nonetheless learned early in his life about port functions. When he was very young, one of the most popular attractions along the Cleethorpes foreshore were the so-called "Land and Sea Cars." Developed locally, these were thirty or forty foot boats mounted on the chassis of a Model T. They were constructed so that when the car entered the water, the road wheels stopped spinning and a propeller took over. While it would be a stretch to call this the precursor of intermodalism, it certainly suggested to an impressionable lad that the boundary between land and sea was highly permeable. It is this interface between landward and seaward activities that Gordon has explored throughout his scholarly life, and he has done so with "industry, piety and independence," just as one would have expected from a good Lincolnshireman.

But Gordon would not have been limited in his youth merely to Cleethorpes. His father was a bookbinder who worked at Burnetts in Grimsby, and the site of his work provided opportunities to learn about Britain's leading fishing town at the height of its prominence. And although it was across the Humber, there was Hull, still one of Britain's most lively ports. Gordon Jackson imbibed information about a variety of maritime activities virtually from the day he was born.

It is a Lincolnshireman, albeit one who has spent most of his adult life on the shores of the Clyde, whom his friends wish to honour with this *festschrift*, presented on the occasion of his "retirement" from the Department of History at the University of Strathclyde, a place that has been his intellectual home for close to thirty-five years. During that time he has been many things to many people, but his most over-riding characteristic has been yet another Lincolnshire quality: a generosity of spirit. Gordon has been willing to share not only his immense knowledge but also his humanity with a wide range of students, friends and colleagues. While we will say something in this appreciation about his achievements, which have been both many and impressive, we also want here to try to unravel several of the threads that explain why this complex, modest and influential man developed the way he did.

It might not be a bad idea to approach this task by treating Gordon as the quintessential Lincolnshireman. And a good place to start might be by examining his piety, which is at the root of the kind of man and the kind of scholar he became. Gordon was raised as a Methodist, hardly unusual in the part of Lincolnshire from which he came. By all accounts, his parents were devout adherents and inducted Gordon and his younger brother, Derek, into the faith at an early age. Methodism as a religion was all-encompassing, providing moral and ethical guidelines for every facet of life. And in his youth, Gordon embraced the religion. In so doing he was not influenced solely by his parents. There was also his church at New Clee, where a young minister reached not only his intellect through sermons but also his social awareness through organizing arguably the best youth group in the area.

In grammar school Gordon focussed on English history and theology. At this point in his adolescence, history and theology formed a kind of dialectic, and one of his intellectual challenges was to reconcile his spirituality and intellectuality. But on the practical side, even as a teenager this was more than an abstract struggle, almost as if Gordon recognized that at some point he might have to make a choice between the two. At the Humberston Foundation School (also known as the "Clee Grammar School") Gordon encountered two teachers who represented the twin sides of this conflict. Mr. Jones, the history master, fanned the flames of Gordon's love of the past, while Mr. Lawley, his theology teacher, made that subject fascinating. In the sixth form, Gordon made a choice, announcing to friends his intention to become a Methodist minister.

But the battle within him was not yet over. To try to be loyal to his twin passions, Gordon decided to enter the University of Hull to do a first degree in history. If his undergraduate years did not really dent his faith, he did discover that Clio could be a relentless seductress. Several things happened to Gordon between the time he entered the University in October 1952 and the time he graduated in the summer of 1955 with his honours degree in history. First, he came under the influence of some remarkable teachers. One was Ralph Davis, arguably the most influential maritime historian of the twentieth century, who eventually became Gordon's doctoral supervisor. The other, perhaps more important, albeit in a less visible way, was an historian named Freddie Brooks. Brooks was a scholar of the old school, by which we mean that he was a man who was incredibly learned but who was devoted to teaching and service rather than writing. By all accounts, Gordon was impressed by Brooks' teaching, but he also developed a habit of skipping classes, which suggests that another part of Brooks' arsenal had an even greater impact. Freddie Brooks was active in the Hull Workers' Education Association (WEA), an organization devoted to making knowledge available to working people who lacked the opportunity to continue their formal education. While not everyone joined the WEA out of a sense of Christian duty, Gordon quickly saw it as a possible way to reconcile his twin passions. He would work with this group in a few years at an especially critical time of his life.

A second thing that happened to Gordon as an undergraduate was that he fell in love. While it might seem strange to mention this fact in a discussion of piety, we can assure you that in this case love and religion were inextricably linked. Gordon first met Hazel Kirk on a ferry crossing the Humber in 1952, his first year at university. Gordon was standing by the rail with Derek Webster, his closest friend and the man who eventually would be best man at his wedding. In Hazel's words, she was "attracted by his university scarf," but contemporary photographs suggest that she might also have noticed that it was wrapped around the neck of a very handsome young man. Gordon, on the other hand, once admitted in an uncharacteristically candid moment that he noticed immediately that the Kirk girl was an incredibly attractive young woman.

But there was more to the relationship than merely a physical attraction, and an understanding of the way in which Gordon approached it will reveal a lot about his basic views. Despite admitting that he was attracted to her - and despite the fact that, as Derek Webster says, Gordon "always had his eyes on girls" - the two did not start dating until Christmas in Gordon's last year in university. Why this delay? The answer is simple: Hazel was going out with someone else and Gordon refused to ask her out as long as her previous relationship had not ended. Since Gordon was (and still is) a shy man, preferring a small group of good friends to a large number of acquaintances, it is tempting to see this as a kind of defence mechanism against rejection. Yet within the context of his continuing battle with his spiritual and secular natures, it clearly was more than this. A man had to have principles, and Gordon was not about to traduce his, even in so important a matter.

Yet almost as soon as they started dating it became clear that theirs was a very special relationship. Hazel was his soul mate in a variety of ways. One of the most important was that she, too, was a devout Methodist; indeed, during the years before they started to date the two had frequent contact through a Methodist student group. Because she shared his beliefs, she was the perfect sounding board for his doubts, which crystallized in this period. The denouement was shaped by two events. One concerned a woman with whom he boarded during the first year of his doctoral programme, an elderly widow fond of telling her boarder that she was tolerating life on earth only so that she could go to heaven to sing hymns with her deceased husband. She was clearly looking for spiritual comfort and validation from a man whom she knew to be thinking about the ministry, yet Gordon's evolving views about the role of religion as a set of guiding principles for life (rather than death) meant that he felt he had little to say to her. And if he could not offer spiritual comfort to such a woman, could he be an effective minister? The doubts began to increase.

The other event that drove him away from the ministry was internal – he found himself head over heels in love with Hazel. As Methodists, there were no religious barriers to such a union, even for a man destined for the ministry. But there were temporal ones: the road to wearing a clerical collar was long, and for a man like Gordon, marriage could not be countenanced until he could support a wife. In the contest between a religion about which he was having increasing doubts and a woman without whom he could no longer envision living, there was only one choice: in 1958 they were wed in Goxhill Methodist Church. In his toast at the reception, Derek Webster reminded Gordon that he had paid for his ticket on the ferry that day in 1952 when he first met Hazel. No one who knows Gordon will be surprised that to this day the Reverend Derek Webster claims that he has not been reimbursed.

While his marriage and work on his doctorate signified the triumph of scholarship over theology, they did not quell completely the inner battle. Gordon's relationship with religion had been no short-term infatuation, and he could not turn his back on something that had been so important to him for his entire life. He solved this in the first instance by becoming a lay preacher, a role he has continued to play for more than four decades in both England and Scotland. Influenced by Freddie Brooks, he also joined the WEA and began to teach night classes to workers, thus finding yet another avenue along which to marry his religious and secular beliefs. In 1958, even before he completed his doctorate, he also began work on educational qualifications. This was not because he saw himself as a teacher in the schools – his eyes were firmly set on a career in academic life – but because his religious beliefs had left him a confirmed pacifist. In those days, when national service was still compulsory, teaching offered a way around the moral dilemma of having to make a difficult choice between ideals and civic duty. Gordon chose pragmatism in the service of his firmly-held beliefs.

In short, Gordon Jackson fits the Lincolnshire definition of piety. And understanding this will help readers to understand a number of things that have made him such a special human being. There is in Gordon's writing an authority that derives from his solid spiritual base. Nowhere in the vast output that is documented in the bibliography at the end of this volume will one encounter an historian unwilling to judge the actions of those he studies. Gordon has no time for impostors or those who behave in immoral or unethical ways. While he never forgets that in capitalist societies making money is an acceptable goal, he can be scathing in his judgements of those who ignore the fact that there are other imperatives in life. And his wrath for those who take themselves too seriously, whether historical subject or contemporary, is legendary.

Deriving from these same beliefs is the explanation for why no matter how busy he may be Gordon will never turn away anyone who comes seeking help. We both have seen Gordon explain to a visitor for the third (or fourth) time a difficult concept, and we have wondered sometimes at his willingness to go far beyond what seem to us like reasonable bounds to help someone in need. The answer as to why he does this, of course, is that he has no choice: he has been gifted by his creator with certain abilities, and he has an obligation to use them in the service of his fellow man. Gordon would of course not put it so crudely, but that in the end is what it boils down to.

But piety, you will recall, is only one of the characteristics of the quintessential Lincolnshiremen. Men from that part of the world, our travellers also tell us, are industrious. Gordon has followed this precept all his life, whether in his study or doing some of the fine woodworking that visitors to his home in Pollokshields have admired (or, it must be said, in working in the garden under Hazel's careful supervision). But it is perhaps useful to go back a bit farther to see how this attitude evolved. Part of the explanation no doubt is religious; it is hard to imagine a Methodist who does not recognize that life is a serious undertaking that requires a good deal of effort. But for Gordon it was more than this: some of his drive clearly came from his family. Gordon came from a comfortable, but not a well-off home. His father was in a sense a role model, working long hours to ensure that his family had what it needed. This attitude was reinforced by his mother, whom one friend described as a pleasant, but meticulously organized, woman with fixed priorities, one of which was that both her sons should work hard and be successful. By all accounts she was not overbearing, but on the other hand she left no doubt that one was expected to do one's best. Gordon has never let her down.

This attitude about the worth of work would have been reinforced by his experiences in school. But here, as with religion, his school years were marked by struggles. Although he excelled at history and theology, he was less apt in two other fields: maths and sports. Anyone who has ever heard Gordon discuss econometrics (or even less rigorous forms of quantitative history) will not be surprised by his dislike for maths, which he avoided as soon as he could (interestingly enough, though, Gordon, in an understated way, often uses numeric data in a highly sophisticated fashion). Sports, however, presented a different problem in an age in which it was still considered important not only that a young person exercise but also that he or she engage in organized activities on the playing fields. As a young man with intellectual rather than sporting interests, he was forced to opt for a variety of "deceits" to avoid participation (we will say no more here, but readers who encounter Gordon might wish to ask him about them). Yet, firmly schooled in the gospel of work, Gordon felt some guilt over his desire to avoid both.

The same kind of struggle carried over into university. There the crisis was stimulated by a required course in Latin, which Gordon failed. He had not worked very hard at it, to be sure, but here was the rub: imbued with the creed that one could accomplish anything through hard work, Gordon could find no way around the problem except intensive study. In those days, if you failed a course you could re-sit the examination in September; after a summer spent ruing his luck and reading more of Catullus than he would care to remember, he managed to pass the exam and save his year.

A similar struggle involved his intellectual interests. Once it became clear that Gordon was a special student, Ralph Davis began trying to recruit him to do a PhD. Gordon, as we have seen, was torn between scholarship and theology, but even as he drifted ever closer to history, there were the related problems of what and where to study. Hull was by no means his first choice. Nor was he set on his eventual topic, "The Economic Development of Hull in the Eighteenth Century." But in the end Ralph Davis got his man, in more ways than one. In retrospect, this was fortunate for both of them: in Gordon, Davis got an excellent student whose intellectual interests were still not fully shaped. On Gordon's side, he had the privilege of working under someone who truly qualified as a "great man." Moreover, since Ralph was an economic historian interested in maritime history, the field got a dynamic young historian who well and truly qualified as Ralph Davis' successor.

Completing his PhD in 1960 did not, however, guarantee a job, even in those days when, at least according to most current postgraduates, there were "far more jobs than qualified people." In fact, the effects of the postwar baby boom were still a few years away from transforming universities, and in the absence of any significant increase in the post-secondary participation rate, posts were exceedingly scarce. While he applied for university lectureships, he kept busy with other things. He continued his work with the WEA in the evenings, as well as doing some part-time teaching for the Hull University Department of Adult Education. But the discovery soon after he completed his thesis that Hazel was pregnant with their first child, Helen, meant that these part-time posts were not enough. Fortunately, after completing his Dip.Ed. in 1959 he had accepted a post as Senior History Master at the Frederick Gough Grammar School in Scunthorpe. Even before he completed his doctorate, then, he had squared the circle by going back to Lincolnshire.

But no one with Gordon's work ethic was going to stop applying for that elusive university post that he so much wanted. At Christmas time in 1962, while celebrating the news that his family was soon to be augmented by a new addition, Nicholas, Gordon had an interview at the University of Strathclyde. Although he did not get the job, he did make the acquaintance of a man who was to become a close friend and in some ways a new mentor – the Head of the Department of History, Edgar Lythe. The reason that Gordon was not hired says something about Edgar Lythe: the post was only part-time, and Lythe did not want to hire a man with a wife, a small child and another baby on the way in a part-time capacity. It also says much about Gordon Jackson that he not only understood but agreed with the decision.

Having met Gordon, though, Edgar Lythe recognized that here was a man whom he would like to add to his staff. The opportunity came three years later, and in January 1965 Gordon joined the staff at Strathclyde. He never left. The transition was made easier by the close relationship he established with Lythe. Here was a man who could be a new mentor while simultaneously sharing many of Gordon's most salient characteristics. Like Gordon, for example, Edgar hated small talk, and the two quickly became fast friends. When Edgar left in 1976, Gordon found the loss irreplaceable.

Still, he thrived at Strathclyde. He was barely ensconced in his post when he received news that he had won the John Nichols Prize in English Local History, awarded by the University of Leicester, for his essay "The Grimsby Haven Company, 1786-1846: A Study in Local Economic History." Not even the arrival in 1967 of a third child, Adrian, prevented him from revising this manuscript into his first book, *Grimsby and the Haven Company, 1796-1846*, which appeared in 1971. While working up an arduous series of lecture courses, he still found time to revise his doctoral thesis into *Hull in the Eighteenth Century*, a seminal work brought out by Oxford University Press that has affected not only maritime history (just look at the way that David Starkey and Richard Gorski analyze nineteenth-century Hull in their essay in this volume) but also English economic, urban and local history. The enduring nature of this volume can be seen by the fact that sixteen years after its initial appearance the University of Hull Press re-published it in a paperback edition. The publication in 1975 of a third book, *The Trade and Shipping of Eighteenth-Century Hull*, led to his promotion the next year to Senior Lecturer.

Gordon is fond of telling people that he has never worked too hard, yet the prodigious effort chronicled immediately above should suggest that on such subjects Gordon's views are not to be trusted. Indeed, while he was in the process of doing all this, he had also contracted with David and Charles to be Editor of a new series of scholarly monographs entitled "The Ports of the British Isles." Gordon, with characteristic modesty, does not even list this on his *curriculum vitae*. While only one volume appeared before the publisher ran into difficulties, it was an important book: Francis Hyde's *Liverpool and the Mersey. An Economic History of a Port, 1700-1970*. In hindsight it is easy to see that the failure of more volumes to appear became a stimulus for Gordon's own *magnum opus*, *The History and Archaeology of Ports*, about which more below.

If there are any doubters left about Gordon's industry, it should be admitted that while he was producing everything detailed thus far he was also turning his attention to a different subject: whaling. Here the catalyst was a suggestion by Ralph Davis in the last years of his life that Gordon should write such a volume. It appeared in 1978 as *The British Whaling Trade*. It says much about the quality of this work that two decades later it remains the seminal study on the subject and probably the most widely cited work on whaling history not only in Britain but also internationally. His hard work was rewarded in 1981 with a well-deserved promotion to Reader.

Two years later Gordon brought out his most famous work, and the one in particular that suggested the theme for this *festschrift* - *The History and Archaeology of Ports*. People outside the area of port history may not appreciate the breadth and depth of its influence, but those who have worked on ports well recognize its importance. The term "paradigm" has in the past few decades become one of the most overused (and misused) words in the historical lexicon, but there is no doubt that in this book Gordon Jackson created a new paradigm for the study of ports. It would be hard to find a significant study that has appeared on ports in the past decade and a half that does not specifically acknowledge its intellectual debt to Gordon's book. For those who have not read it, Adrian Jarvis' essay in this volume suggests a little about the power of the way that Gordon has taught us to think about this subject.

At the same time that he was accomplishing all this, Gordon was also turning his efforts ever more to administration. In part this was beyond his control; as most academics will know, it is expected that everyone will pull their weight in university administration, and given his intellectual background, it would have been totally out of character for Gordon to have refused. The list of his university committee work would daunt even the most inveterate committee-goer, and success begat success: the more he undertook, the more he was asked to do. Moreover, he also became an extremely effective spokesman for junior colleagues and for his department. The result was that for a few years - and especially while he served as Head of Department from 1986 to 1990 - he concentrated on articles and chapters in books rather than full-fledged monographs. But he never shirked his duty, and he never stopped writing.

This might be a good place to shift gears and say something about the third attribute of Gordon's, independence. One of the joys of being around Gordon, or of hearing him lecture at conferences, is his unpredictability: he is never boring or less than stimulating, and the connections that he sees between often disparate topics are often both insightful and startling. In short, in things intellectual Gordon, as his friends well know, has always marched to his own drummer.

The first evidence we can find of this trait came when he was a child. Gordon had an uncle, named Albert, who is described as a genuine eccentric; Gordon idolized him. A childhood friend notes that even more than most independent boys, Gordon was always ready to take the side of the underdog and to befriend those who somehow did not fit in. In university he was perfectly willing to befriend the unfashionable and, as we have seen, his choice of topics for investigation was not always in the mainstream of historical interest.

But perhaps nowhere was this trait more clear than in the direction his scholarship took after he stepped down as Department Head in 1990. Gordon had long been collecting materials for a "big" book on the maritime history of Scotland (it is a guarantee that it will appear before long and that it will make the wait worthwhile). Yet the direction in which he headed in the early 1990s reflected his sense of what needed to be done rather than what might bring him the greatest accolades. *The Trade and Shipping of Dundee, 1780-1850*, which appeared in 1991 under the authorship of Gordon Jackson with Kate Kinnear (his research assistant on the project), brought to life a crucial period in the history of what, charitably, was what Gordon once called a "minor port." Yet a complex port system like Britain's could only be understood if the role of the smaller ports was clear. The Dundee book won him few academic kudos, but it was a necessary brick in the wall that he hoped to build. So too was his next book, an edited volume with Edgar Lythe entitled *The Port of Montrose: A History of Its Harbour, Trade and Shipping*, which appeared in 1993. For an edited volume Gordon wrote an incredible amount of the text. The subject was even more modest than Dundee, but Gordon gave it his all and produced an extremely good result.

His most recent major contribution has come in the essays he has written for a two-volume history of Glasgow (1995-1996), the first of which he co-edited. In particular, his two chapters in the first volume show the mature scholar at the height of his powers. "Glasgow in Transition, 1660-1740," though, fits especially well into the theme of independence. As most readers will know, the obvious transition in this period was commercial and, to be fair, Gordon does deal with this. But he discusses much more, thus making it clear once again that he was conceptualizing history in his own way, oblivious of the expectations of mainstream historians or their unadventurous conventions.

It is all these things that have made Gordon Jackson the scholar he is today. If there is a muse looking out for true sons of Lincolnshire, he or she must be watching Gordon's every move. But we need to mention a few more points about Gordon before closing. First is the fact that, as Gordon has acknowledged in all his books, much of his success belongs to his wife Hazel. It may be a cliche for scholars to thank their significant others, but in Gordon's case it clearly is sincere. To see the two of them together is to see a couple in which each clearly cares for the other in a very special way. Indeed, it is possible without too much imagination to look in Gordon's eyes and see the reflection of Hazel as she much have appeared to him on that Humber ferry in 1952. The second point is that, just as he had an eye for girls at an early age, he has been extremely fortunate in the women who have been closest to him. Besides Hazel, there was first his mother, who set him firmly on life's journey, even if he did not necessarily select the path that she would have chosen for him. And then there is a very special woman known to a generation of his friends and admirers as the person who kept him functioning, especially when he was Head of Department, Margaret Hastie. As Gordon has often acknowledged, if Hazel did not dress him and Margaret remind him of what he had to do each day, he would have been hopelessly lost. In at least some respects this might not be one of Gordon's characteristic overstatements.

Finally, we need to say this: if anyone deserves the serenity of retirement, it is Gordon Jackson. His contributions, as we have tried to outline briefly here, have been immense - maritime, economic, British and urban historians (among others) are all in his debt. But having said this, if anyone is unlikely merely to tend his garden and take long walks through the Scottish countryside, it is Gordon Jackson. The fires that have made him such an important scholar - and such a beloved friend - to all who contributed to this *festschrift* and to so many others - have hardly been quenched. Enjoy Lochgaire, Gordon, but be ready for the multitudes who will beat a path to your door to tap your incredible knowledge and to seek your wise counsel. And please do not forget that there are a legion of scholars waiting in eager anticipation for you to throw down the next next intellectual gauntlet and to continue to delight us with many more wonderful books in the years ahead.

Port History: Some Thoughts on Where it Came from and Where it Might be Going

Adrian Jarvis

There comes a time later in most historians' lives when there is a sudden rush of blood to the head which convinces them that the time has arrived to summarise the knowledge about their subject. A yellowed card index, perhaps initiated for a long-forgotten thesis, is exhumed in the quest for the beginnings of a synthesis which merits that accolade "magisterial." Somewhere in the background there probably lurks the hope that perhaps this will be the piece which finally earns some royalties to supplement the pension. Gordon Jackson, undoubted master of British port history, cannot follow this perhaps pretentious path, for in 1983, when he was a long way from retirement, he produced his *History and Archaeology of Ports*, one of those very rare works which combine a broad overview with a detailed and incisive insight and thus genuinely deserve to be called "magisterial."

Obviously a great deal of work on port history has been done since 1983. In Liverpool, for example, a huge amount of detailed information has come into the public domain.[1] Similar changes have benefited the histories of many other ports in the UK and elsewhere. The work of Natividad de la Puerta Rueda on Bilbao; Frank Broeze on the ports of Asia; and Malcolm Tull on Fremantle might be expected to damage the underlying assumptions of a *History and Archaeology*, which is both comparatively general and limited to British ports.[2] Moreover, Gordon did

[1] I refer chiefly to the Mersey Docks and Harbour Board (MD&HB) material at Merseyside Maritime Museum (MMM), but there have been other significant accessions as well. The transfer of the Liverpool Ship Registers and the Customs Bills of Entry to the Museum makes their use in conjunction with the MD&HB material much less daunting. Nor should we forget the improved access to the Port of London Authority Archive.

[2] See, for example, N. de la Puerta Rueda, *El Puerto de Bilbao come Reflejo de Desarollo Industrial de Viscaya, 1857-1913* (Bilbao, 1994); F. Broeze, "Dubai: From Creek to Global City" *this volume*; and M. Tull, *A Community Enterprise: The History of the Port of Fremantle* (St. John's, 1997).

not have access to the detailed records of port authorities that have become available over the last few years, and he did not extend his attention to ports overseas. Nor could his research benefit from the power of the personal computer, which was in its infancy in the early 1980s.

If I turn to my own yellowing card index, I can find plenty of things of which Gordon could not possibly have been aware in 1983. They challenge basic assumptions on which some earlier work on the port of Liverpool rests.[3] Yet there are few instances in which they lay any of Gordon's work open to question, much less invalidate it. There is a simple reason for this: Gordon Jackson's book is an incisive, seminal work.

The Philosophy of Ports

There are few, if any, areas of history where the mere collection of large volumes of information is a valid end in itself. It is the construction of a philosophy and an interpretive framework which turns antiquarian fact-gathering into history. In some cases which are either fortunate or inspired the philosophy may be built on comparatively limited data and yet have the discovery of further information actually strengthen it. So it was with Gordon's underlying assumptions of what ports were about.

Ports have always been about bringing things and people together. Goods converge into ports from inland and then diverge across the seven seas. Because Gordon recognised that, he also realised that old docks in prime town centre locations could be more attractive to customers than one might expect. The reason was simple: old-fashioned naive technological determinism suggested that the biggest and newest docks were the best. So they were for some purposes, but convenient access to the merchant quarters of the town was another desirable attribute, and one which other historians have neglected. Those docks which continued, atypically, to thrive in obsolescence, were known in Liverpool as "pet docks." Princes Dock, opened 1821, with an entrance only forty-five feet wide, and with about twenty-one feet of water on its sill at mean high tide, was an outstanding example, remaining very busy, and "profitable," until

---

[3]One example is F.E. Hyde's assumption that shipowners had an inalienable right to expect port authorities to pander to their every whim; for further details see A. Jarvis, "The Port of Liverpool and the Shipowners in the Late Nineteenth Century," *The Great Circle*, XVI, No. 1 (1994), 1.

the turn of the century.[4] What Gordon will not know until he reads this is that in the Mersey Docks and Harbour Board Archive there is one volume surviving from a run kept by the Harbourmaster's Department which is a register of "Vessels Requiring to Enter the Dock[s] when the Flags are up." The flags referred to are those which were flown at entrances to indicate that particular docks were full, so the docks most frequently entered in that book were the ones most sought after by the customers in numerical (not tonnage) terms. The winners in this popularity poll were, by a large margin, Canning and Princes, both obsolescent "pet docks" close to the town centre. This is eminently predictable from Gordon Jackson's work and substantiates his dictum that "in the final analysis, a port is not a place but a community of merchants."[5] That statement points the way to the comparatively recent realisation that mercantile networking is an important topic about which we know remarkably little.

Behind a simple statement that ports are a multi-purpose interface lies a host of issues for historians, and over the years they have been addressed in many ways at different levels. At the simplest, we may record the rising or falling volume or value of trade in a particular port. Next we may relate that to the trade of the whole port services industry in whatever country we are concerned with and decide whether our port is doing well or badly compared with the others with which it is notionally competing. Then we may look for reasons.

There used to be two main schools which considered these issues, although to both they were relatively peripheral. Economic historians looked at the trades a port served and evaluated its effectiveness, while engineering historians wrote narratives about port and harbour construction and beatified the engineers for these marvellous works.[6] When their

---

[4]Between 1844 and 1924, MD&HB compiled a tabular summary of the trade of each dock: for the latter part of the last century this was published as an appendix to the *Annual Accounts*.

[5]G. Jackson, "Do Docks Make Trade?" in L.R. Fischer (ed.), *From Wheel House to Counting House: Essays in Maritime Business History in Honour of Professor Peter Neville Davies* (St. John's, 1992). A key argument is the importance of good access to the mercantile network.

[6]F.E. Hyde, *Liverpool and the Mersey* (Newton Abbot, 1971), is an example of the former, while Samuel Smiles' account of John Rennie in his *Lives of the Engineers* (London, 1862), is the type-specimen of the latter.

interpretations are thus over-simplified – caricatured even – it is obvious that both were wrong and each was right. That is exactly what one might expect when both were taking at best a partial view of the process of port development. But who knew that in 1982? What was happening historiographically was simply a reflection of the celebrated "two cultures" divide. Engineering historians did not worry too much about where money came from, so long as there was plenty to pay for the works they described.[7] Even less did they worry about docks once they were completed and in use. Economic historians were largely concerned with paper transactions and saw little need to understand engineering arcana.

This points to the second achievement of *History and Archaeology*: it recognised that port engineers, whether in-house or consultant, were by far the largest single spenders of British port authorities' money and therefore subjected them to the critical scrutiny to which that expenditure rightly exposed them. Gordon was the first fully to recognise the dock engineers for what most were: a weird, perhaps random, mixture of greatness and incompetence. Some were great in what they achieved and incompetent in estimating how much it would cost, while others exhibited extraordinary variation in performance between one development and another.[8] A really bad engineering job could be a major factor in the decline or even complete failure of a port, since it left the port authority encumbered with long-term debt without providing a sufficient increase in revenue either to service that debt or to allow the incurring of new debts to rectify the mistakes.

These insights were, and remain, important. To some, they may be felt to encourage us to stray beyond the legitimate boundaries of history, to investigate what ports were *actually* for rather than what people said at the time they were for. Who wanted them to do what, and why? The easy answer is that shipowners wanted them to discharge ships rapidly and at an uneconomically cheap rate (loading export cargoes was less

---

[7]In so far as we may make any clear distinction, people who considered themselves technological, rather than engineering, historians generally took a wider view.

[8]From the time of Thomas Steers, engineer of the first commercial wet dock in the world, completing a dock to budget was the exception rather than the rule. As an example of variation we may compare James Meadows Rendel's very competent work at Garston with the shambles he created at Birkenhead (though he was shamefully messed around by his clients in Birkenhead).

critical).[9] It was Gordon's remarks along these lines which led me to the frivolous invention of "The Kind Dock Fairy," who would provide expensive facilities at no cost to anyone. But behind this lay a complete failure to view ports as a national industry in the way that railways had been since government first started trying to regulate them in the early 1840s. While the pressure to nationalise the railways in the 1860s came to nought, the telegraph system was nationalised partly on the grounds that it was, by its nature, a national system.[10]

This was quite extraordinary, since ports were of far greater national importance than either the railways or the telegraphs, even before one takes into account the "naval reserve" and "harbour of refuge" functions thrust upon some civilian port authorities in areas such as the provision of dry-docking. Is it the legitimate business of the historian to think out issues in the past which the past did not bother to think out for itself?[11] Before one answers too rapidly in the negative, it might be worth considering whether or not a couple of millennia of Biblical exegesis have or have not added anything to the understanding of the original subject.

My own spare-time interest is the writings of Samuel Smiles, a much-misunderstood man. One such misunderstanding is the suggestion

---

[9]The financial disasters of the early years of the Manchester Ship Canal originated with the idea that Liverpool was a rip-off and Manchester could do it cheaper. This delusion left the ratepayers of Manchester subsidising the users of the port to the tune of the interest on a little over £5 million, approximately the original total estimated cost of construction. Just about every large general cargo port was attacked in this way, and the result for the shipowner was higher port costs as, for example, Liverpool had to bail out Birkenhead.

[10]For railway intervention, see the recital at the beginning of Great Britain, Parliament, *Parliamentary* Papers (*BPP*) (1867), "Report of the Royal Commission on Railways" (3844), XXXVIII part 1, 32. For arguments in favour of nationalising telegraphs, see BPP (1867-1868), "Report of the Select Committee on Electric Telegraphs Bill" (435), XI, 333.

[11]This refers to the *official* view;: individuals were clearly capable of greater insight, as this quotation from the dedication at the opening of Sir John Rennie, *The Theory, Formation and Construction of British & Foreign Harbours* (London, 1854), shows: "The vast commerce of Great Britain, which pervades every quarter of the Globe, and her powerful Naval Armaments, so indispensable to her protection and to the maintenance of her high position among the Great Nations of the Earth, render it imperative that the utmost attention should be devoted to the perfection of her Harbours – those invaluable Asylums for her mariners and promoters of her Trade."

that the good Victorian *paterfamilias* who practised the thrift on which Smiles was so keen would fail to consume enough to pay the just rewards of those who sought to prosper through self-help.[12] This argument fails to understand the purpose the Good Lord had in mind when He created those people generically known as "foreigners." Foreigners were there to supply the hub of the universe - Britain - with raw materials it lacked, and then pay it lots of money for the resulting manufactured goods. Herein lies not just the resolution of the apparent conflict between thrift and self-help but an important part of the rationale of "The First Industrial Nation."[13]

This rationale would not work if we adhered entirely to the old historiography, which depicted the industrial revolution as the interaction between manufacturing and inland transport technology on the one hand and a new spirit of enterprise backed by improved financial mechanisms on the other. These factors alone would cause an industrial revolution, but sooner or later they would also produce torrents of unsaleable manufactured goods, and a point would be reached where the product had to go overseas. To do that, it needed effective shipping and port services industries. Although the Latin American Bond Bubble of the early 1820s was largely driven by foolish dreams of endless supplies of precious metals, those metals were chiefly significant as a convenient way for foreigners to pay British merchants for British credit and British goods.[14] A high proportion of British "credit" was in fact dispatched in the form of manufactured goods, chiefly weapons and hardware.[15]

---

[12]Advanced in R J. Morris, "Samuel Smiles and the Genesis of Self-Help: The Retreat to a Petit-Bourgeois Utopia," *Historical Journal*, XXIV (1981), 89-110.

[13]Whether imperialism actually produced net gains is another matter and a highly contentious one; see, for example, P.K. O'Brien and L. Prados de la Escosura, "The Costs and Benefits of European Imperialism from the Conquest of Ceuta, 1415, to the Treaty of Lusaka, 1974," in Clara-Eugenia Nunez (ed.), *Debates and Controversies in Economic History. Proceedings of the Twelfth International Economic History Congress* (Madrid, 1998).

[14]Though, of course, there were also British-owned or funded mining companies looking to exploit Latin American mineral wealth directly. See F.G. Dawson, *The First Latin American Debt Crisis* (New Haven, 1990).

[15]Some cynical souls might connect this statement with recent allegations that less-developed countries which were good customers of the British arms industry were more likely to receive overseas development grants than those which were not.

The importance of shipping was recognised at an early stage, but unfortunately it was assessed in terms other than the ability to serve industry. Many thought that Britannia could rule the waves only if its warships were backed by a strong merchant marine. The manner for doing this was two-fold: the merchant marine was there to provide a supply of skilled and experienced seamen in time of crisis and to transport soldiers and supplies to anywhere in the Empire with trouble that needed sorting out.

While such perceptions were dubious, this does not alter the fact that they existed or that they were exploited by shipowners, who did not hesitate to play the patriotism card when they saw fit. What is doubly unfortunate from an historical perspective is that they also concealed the importance of what was really happening in shipping. In general terms, and ignoring short-term cyclical variations, the industry in the last third of the nineteenth century tried to avoid the negative consequences of an over-investment in new, expensive and constantly-changing technology. In the process, the industry imposed quite impossible demands on the small number of major ports which could invest enough to try to remain at the ever-shifting forefront of port technology.[16]

A Few Words on Progress

Because the Whig interpretation has been so long and so comprehensively discredited in British political and constitutional history, it is possible to assume that any notions of definable progress in the design and construction, or even operation, of ports or the ships that use them is necessarily invalid. There are at least two reasons why, certainly since the Napoleonic Wars if not before, this assumption may not be invariably correct.

First, the Whig interpretation was a construct of historians rather than an integral part of the period under consideration. Even if the Anglo-Saxons really did bring to Britain some underlying ideas of democracy which were traceable through to the nineteenth-century British constitution, there can be no ground for claiming that they did so consciously, with the intention of progressing towards that distant state of constitutional bliss. When, on the other hand, an engineer designed a new dock to suit

---

[16]Jarvis, "Liverpool and the Shipowners." For a broader view, see G. Jackson, "Ports, Ships and Government in the Nineteenth and Twentieth Centuries," in P.C. van Royen, L.R. Fischer and D.M. Williams (eds.), *Frutta di Mare: Evolution and Revolution in the Maritime World in the 19th and 20th Centuries* (Amsterdam, 1998), 161-175.

more or larger ships, he did do so with a clear vision (whether or not it was correct is another question) of how things would be when it was in service. That is what he got paid for. Engineers themselves thought and wrote in terms not only of achievement or excellence but of progress. A famous example is the advertisement for the Rainhill Locomotive Trials, where the prize was offered not for the "best" locomotive, but for the one representing the most "decided improvement."[17] That term is indicative of the understanding not just that locomotives were improving very rapidly but that they would continue to do so. The idea of progress was not an anomalous interpretive device superimposed on events by historians but the underlying assumption of the engineers and their paymasters at the time. A clear case, to contrast with the ludicrous suggestion about Anglo-Saxons, is to be found in stationary steam engine technology: James Watt calculated and published the maximum theoretical thermal efficiency attainable by a perfect engine. This figure of Watt's remained a long-term aim of engineers for many years - but in 1835 the famous Fowey Consols engine achieved a "duty" some five times higher![18] That did not, however, prevent engineers from seeking further improvements in thermal efficiency. It was why they were there.

The second reason is that while it is impossible to define the ultimate end to which "constitutional progress" is directed, or measure the extent of the progress achieved, it may well be possible to do so in the case of ports. This is certainly what port authorities had to attempt to do when preparing the evidence for enabling acts: the entire process was geared to establishing the unsatisfactory nature of the *status quo*; conjuring a vision of an ideal future; and then spelling out a course of action which would effect noticeable progress from the former towards the latter. It may be objected that the process of "progress" itself makes the definition of an ideal state impossible: a dock designed in 1900 for the general cargo liner trade might closely approach perfection in that trade and yet be virtually useless for container traffic. But that is simply a case of setting

---

[17]This expression came from the report of Rastrick and Walker on the means of propulsion to be used, in which the holding of a trial was first suggested. For the background, see R.H.G. Thomas, *The Liverpool & Manchester Railway* (London, 1980), 63-64.

[18]For a summary of progress in thermal efficiency at this period, see D.S.L. Cardwell, *From Watt to Clausius* (Ames, 1989), 158-159.

the objective too narrowly and assuming it must necessarily be static. If one speaks instead of transferring the maximum tonnage of goods per linear yard of quay per unit time at minimum cost, then a moving target is created towards which continuing progress is and continues to be possible. This, of course, is how port authorities measured their own efficiency at the time and it is why their officers and members could talk so confidently of progress: they knew where they were going and they knew how to measure how far they had gotten. If we ignore notions of progress, we will fail to identify their effects.[19]

If this belief in progress, with its implication of continuous obsolescence and repeated heavy investment in modernisation, ever penetrated the corridors of government, it had little effect. As Gordon has pointed out, there simply was no government policy on ports, or even any demonstrable recognition that there might need to be a policy.[20] There were major government enquiries into port-related issues, including harbours of refuge, local charges on shipping and tonnage measurement, and there were innumerable Select Committee enquiries into individual enabling bills, but there was no general investigation of the industry as a whole until after the Great War. The nearest approach was the Royal Commission which investigated the management of the Port of London - and the localisation which was explicit in its warrant - serves only to reinforce the message that government did not view port services provision as a national industry. This was followed in 1903 by a detailed and extensive national "Return of Harbour Authorities," which seemed to show a new concern but led to no action.[21]

The Way for Port History to Go Next

It is a distressing characteristic of relatively new historical specialties that their devotees are often so occupied with archival research, establishing a basic narrative and fitting it into some sort of intelligible interpretive framework that wider linkages and contexts get neglected. There are two

---

[19]At the risk of pedantry, it may be added that some worked by tonnage per unit area of quay, a method I think less reliable.

[20]See Jackson, "Ports, Ships and Government."

[21]*BPP* (1902) (1151), XLIII, 222; and (1903) (325), LXIII, 189.

ways of approaching this problem, of which the first, and perhaps the more generally favoured, is the creation of economic models. If one can find patterns in the development of ports for which research has been done, this provides useful shortcuts in researching the others – the model can tell us what to look for and probably where to look as well.

A colleague of mine once challenged me to produce a typology of ports. This is an impossible task, because there are simply too many different parameters for the result to be meaningful. But we may divide ports according to their principal traffics, for example: mineral exports; general cargo liners; passengers; or bulk imports. Alternatively, we may classify them according to their form of ownership or administration: central government; local or provincial government; statutory trust; joint-stock company; or private. We may group them according to the nature of their trade: mainly importing; mainly exporting; or distributive. Or we may approach them from a more demographic point of view: capital city ports; metropolitan ports; or wilderness ports. In the long run, possibly the most important typology relates to the physical difficulties of constructing the port in the first place, for this determines the extent of its debt charges; the amount of capital debt per yard of quay is an infrequently calculated but very useful index. Thus, we might have excellent natural harbour; passable natural harbour; completely unnatural harbour, or large tidal range or high-wave energy ports.

This list, which is nowhere near exhaustive, gives nineteen different attributes of ports in five categories. Few ports could be adequately described in less than three of the terms and few would need five, but the permutations are still numerous and when we have got our heads round them, what will they teach us? To answer this let us take an example beloved of Gordon: the parallel between Birkenhead and Grimsby.[22] Neither port deserved to exist in terms of the accepted normal rules of economics at the times of their respective births. But what brought about their initial failure had nothing to do with any of the typological criteria above: it was that they were conceived in avarice rather than need. No typology or model derived from the histories of *proper* ports – the ones people wanted, used and paid for – could tell us anything useful about the relative performance of these two ventures. In fact, it is much worse than

---

[22]Jackson, "Do Docks Make Trade?" The idea is further developed in his paper "Docks and Railways: An Overview," in P. Rees (ed.), *Docks, Railways and the Movement of Goods* (Liverpool, 1996), 5-16.

that, for most British ports were atypical by the standards of ports of the rest of the British Empire, and *vice versa*. That is not a direction in which there seems much mileage: comparisons need to be stretched and strained to achieve even a tenuous result. The Bird model, the leading example of its kind, was a good idea, but we must remember that when Bird created "Anyport" he had not had the benefit of reading Gordon Jackson's work or, indeed, mine.[23] For example, in "Anyport," oil terminals are established downstream of large and elaborate docks which are themselves downstream of the central docks of the early dock-building phase. In some places they are, but on the Mersey - which is, after all, one of the major oil-importing centres in the UK - they developed in five identifiable phases between 1882 and 1962 on sites which are without exception upstream of the site of the original docks. There is not a single downstream oil facility. That is not a minor "exception which proves the rule:" it is a sequence of exceptions which calls into question the validity of one of the "eras" upon which the model of "Anyport" depends.

An economic model does not need to be precise, but it must work, even if only imprecisely, most of the time. Otherwise, it becomes dangerously like a way of trying to fit known events into a framework which is the wrong shape and size. It can even be an invitation to look for new evidence to fit that framework, and that would lead us away from economic and technological interpretations and back towards the geographical ones which Gordon's work has shown to be over-rated.

Financial Crisis and the Port of Liverpool in Mid-Century

Having offended a few colleagues, I shall now do worse by having the impudence to suggest to the recipient of this *festschrift* how he should spend his time once he has moved into a bijou retirement residence. There are still, despite his labours thus far, further separate cultures to be united. Consider, for example, Boot's substantial pamphlet on *The Commercial Crisis of 1847*.[24] I am not trying to write a concordance of it, but I did

---

[23]The "Anyport Model" is developed in J. Bird, *The Major Seaports of the United Kingdom* (London, 1963). The idea is partly foreshadowed in F.W. Morgan, *Ports and Harbours* (London, 1952).

[24]H.M. Boot, *The Commercial Crisis of 1847* (Hull, 1984); the same is true of D.M. Evans, *The Commercial Crisis 1847-1848* (1849; reprint, New York, 1969).

notice that the word "dock" did not appear. Yet in 1844, the year the railway mania really began to rumble, the capital expenditure authorised for new construction under the Liverpool Dock Act equalled about five percent of the entire railway industry, at a time when substantial expenditure on the works under the 1841 Dock Act, including the Albert Dock, its warehouses and associated ensemble, was still in full swing.[25] These were not trifling undertakings even when viewed on a national scale.

When confidence collapsed, and everyone decided they needed a shoe box of gold under the bed, banks defaulted, companies failed by the cartload, Mr. Merdle committed suicide and eventually even George Hudson fell. In Birkenhead, the infant port went bankrupt and the population of the town is said to have fallen as a result by two-thirds within a year. The cotton and woollen industries suffered severe recession and half of Europe wallowed in a heady mix of bankruptcy and revolution - except Liverpool, where Jesse Hartley calmly continued to build docks. As railway projects ground to a halt and the price of labour and building materials fell, one can even imagine a flicker of a smile crossing that stern Yorkshire visage as he brought works which had been running over budget in 1846 back into line by 1848. There has been a debate over whether railway investment was cyclical or counter-cyclical: Hartley did not use those terms, but he certainly understood the benefits of counter-cyclical spending.[26] As we shall see, his employers supported him.

It is clearly a matter of some importance. Liverpool banks were severely, and probably rightly, criticised for the rather paltry reserves they held, the fact that even those small reserves were not always very liquid; and for allowing too much credit to too few clients.[27] There were indeed

---

[25]For works under the 1844 Act, see A. Jarvis, *Liverpool Central Docks 1799-1905* (Stroud, 1991), chapter 3; for Albert Dock and associated works, see N. Ritchie-Noakes, *Liverpool's Historic Waterfront* (London, 1984).

[26]This description begs the question one must ask about many of the great engineers: at what point did they cease to be craftsmen and become engineers? But it is here begged deliberately, or rather sidestepped, because becoming an engineer *added* attributes to a man: it did not remove the ability of Hartley - or Telford - still to think like a stonemason where appropriate.

[27]*BPP* (1847-1848), "Secret Committee of the House of Lords to Inquire into Causes of Distress among the Commercial Classes" (565), VIII, part 3, 1, 537. See also Evans, *Commercial Crisis*, 94, for comments on the Royal Bank of Liverpool which, with

three major local bank failures in the 1847 crisis. Liverpool was the pre-eminent home of the cotton trade, which was among the heaviest sufferers in the brief recession which resulted from the commercial crisis, and the revenues of the port suffered accordingly. According to Ellison, three shipowners and twenty merchants failed in October alone.[28] We must enquire how Hartley could carry on as though nothing had happened, and how the Dock Trustees could let him. On 28 October, for example, the Committee confirmed Hartley's employment of an extra ninety-four men at Albert Dock alone, at rates from eighteen shillings per week for labourers to forty shillings for foreman coopers.[29]

The first reason is easily found. While the overall revenues of the port did indeed decline in the accounting year ended July 1848, they did not fall by nearly as much as we would expect from the general doom and gloom of the textile industries.[30] This was partly because Liverpool's trade was very broad-based and some trades, notably timber, had a good year.[31] In some cases, Liverpool positively profited from the misfortunes of others, for it was a good year for corn importing. In the event, there was actually an over-supply of imported corn, prices fell and merchant houses fell with them, but that was *after* the dock dues on the corn had been paid. Bad news for the working classes, such as the potato famine or sky-high corn prices, was good news for the migration trade. In the first quarter of 1847, over 90,000 "poor Irish" arrived in Liverpool, trying to escape death in the famine.[32] Exactly how they arrived is immaterial, but we may

---

a paid-up capital of £600,000, had advanced £500,000 to a single customer.

[28]T. Ellison, *Gleanings and Reminiscences* (Liverpool, 1905), 168. Ellison was an insider and is generally considered fairly reliable.

[29]MMM, MD&HB, "Dock Committee Minutes," 28 October 1847.

[30]The published *Annual Accounts* give the following totals: 1845, £223,247; 1846, £213,423; 1847, £244,435; 1848, £197,617; and 1849, £224,617. The fall was also partly due to an extraordinarily bold decision to cut the rates of dues from 25 June 1847.

[31]Braithwaite Poole, *The Commerce of Liverpool* (Liverpool, 1854), shows cotton falling from a record total of 276,000 tons in 1845 to 182,000 in 1847, while timber rose from 234,191 in 1845 to 321,495 in 1847. It may be significant that when cotton recovered in 1848, timber fell again.

[32]*Gore's Annals*, 17 April 1847.

be sure they did not walk, so someone made money even out of them. The ruin of the railway investor produced a surplus in rail production which quadrupled exports of railway metal from Liverpool to the USA.[33] The Dock Trustees got their money and Hartley spent it.

The Trustees showed a much sharper appreciation of what the "crisis" really was than did many people of whom one would have expected better judgement. Faced with a total revenue down twenty percent on the previous year, they did not panic or withdraw from their expansion programmes. Many were old enough to remember the panics of 1825-1826 and 1839, and they judged correctly that this was another such problem arising from wild speculation which, over the long terms in which they were accustomed to thinking, would prove transient in the extreme. They ran down their bank deposit account from a normal level of around £130,000 to around £12,000 and found another £10,000 by running down stocks of construction materials in the dockyard, and carried on building. The glut of building materials on the market, caused by the suspension of railway and other projects, made the holding of stocks less necessary. This rundown may have done little for the state of the Liverpool banks, but it did more than keep the building programme rolling: it ensured that when most of the country was scrambling for cash, the Trustees were still easily able to borrow money on bond.

The minutes of the Sub-Committee of Finance make astonishing reading. Approached in late 1846 by James Bromfield of Whitchurch, offering to procure loans in return for a commission of 0.25%, they replied haughtily that they were not in the habit of paying to raise money.[34] Offered £20,000 on bond at five percent, when their current rate was 4.5%, they summarily declined the offer.[35] They continued to borrow what they wanted on the terms they chose. Near the peak of the panic, their meeting of 7 October 1847 heard applications from bondholders seeking repayment of £2000 - and accepted renewal proposals for £4150 and authorised the sealing of £1750 worth of new bonds. This was a poor result: the previous week had seen £4200 in renewals and new money of £3230, so they asked the treasurer to look into the estimated expenditure

---

[33]From 12,635 tons in 1847 to 50,188 tons in 1848. Poole, *Commerce*, 53.

[34]MMM, MD&HB, Sub-committee of Finance, 5 November 1846.

[35]*Ibid.*, 4 October 1846.

between then and January 1848. Receiving his report on 14 October, they decided the arithmetic was unfavourable, raised the interest offered by 0.5%, and were rewarded with £2400 in new money within a week. Charles Turner distinguished between that and the previous trough: April had been "pressure" while October was "panic," so we may assume that public confidence in the Dock Trustees was not merely high but quite exceptional.[36] It is perhaps worth noting that if the Sub-Committee of Finance seems rather laid-back in its approach, the Sub-Committee of Works (to which Jesse Hartley reported and which was responsible for virtually all major expenditure) was positively recumbent. There is literally not a word in its minutes for October 1847 from which one could deduce the existence of any financial difficulties whatsoever. It was, however, spending sums fluctuating between £5000 and £9000 per week on construction.[37]

If a relatively small body like the Liverpool Dock Trustees was able to stand through the 1847 Crisis like a rock surrounded by quicksand, its achievement was not unique, for the same had been done in 1825. The fever then for foreign bonds (mainly, though not exclusively, Latin American) created a highly volatile financial climate. This had comparatively little direct effect in Liverpool, but led indirectly to a classic outbreak of over-speculation in several commodities, notably raw cotton, whose price spiralled although no actual cotton shortage existed. Predictably, once word got around that it was fetching bonanza prices in Liverpool, cotton poured in from all over the world, prices collapsed and the spate of wilder speculators was ruined.[38] The Dock Trustees' successor body, the Mersey Docks and Harbour Board, spent freely during the multiple collapses which followed the failure of Overend Gurney in 1866-

---

[36]*BPP* (1847-1848), "Secret Committee on Commercial Distress" (395), VIII, part 1.1., evidence of Charles Turner, q. 656.

[37]Hartley's expenditure was vetted and confirmed at each weekly meeting as a matter of normal procedure, so these figures may be found in the minutes.

[38]*BPP* (1847-1848), "Select Committee on Commercial Distress," (395), VIII, part 1, q. 95, opined that the actual losses had been heavier in 1825 than in 1847, but that despite thirty years in business, "I have never witnessed the feeling of helplessness and hopelessness so strong as in the last year." On the other hand, Harold Littledale, when reminiscing in old age on such difficulties, jovially remarked "Why, I have lived on the top of a volcano half my life." Ellison, *Gleanings,* 109.

1867. That was when the Royal Bank of Liverpool (which had been given mouth-to-mouth resuscitation in 1847) collapsed for the second and final time, and it was also when Lyster, Hartley's successor, had massive construction programmes continuing at Herculaneum and Waterloo Docks at the same time he was spending heavily in Birkenhead.[39]

The ordinary rules of financial collapse clearly did not apply in Liverpool dock construction. During the 1847 crisis, the Trustees were able to borrow easily at a time when both the gold and currency reserves of the Bank of England were haemorrhaging at a worrying rate and consols fell from around ninety-five in October 1846 to about eighty in October 1847. Liverpool's docks might be said to have been perceived as safer than the Bank of England. The odd thing is that the reason we do not know why this incredible state of affairs existed is that we have not asked.

It is easy enough to establish that dock construction was loosely counter-cyclical, simply because design, obtaining Parliamentary approval and construction took so long. A few good trading years produced hideous congestion in the docks and sufficient income to remedy it, but by the time the legal and engineering proprieties had been completed the chances were that recession had arrived. A long-term view demanded that one go ahead anyway, on the grounds that by the time construction had finished good times would probably have returned. Yet the same was true of railway projects, and it was estimated that in 1847, 50,000 railway labourers had been put out of work.[40] Had the long-term view exhibited by the Dock Trustees been acted upon in other industries, the economic history of the nineteenth century would have been smoother and happier. So what was special about the port of Liverpool and the men who ran it?[41]

One is tempted to answer that there was nothing special about them. Nearly all the individuals in the governing body were also involved

---

[39]The *Annual Accounts* show capital expenditure for the year ended 24 June 1867 as £401,659 and revenue expenditure (Engineer's Department) £95,525. The previous year's expenditures had been comparable, but were swollen by the payment of £546,000 to the Corporation of Liverpool, the Nominees of the Birkenhead Dock Trustees and the Birkenhead Dock Company. This was the final settlement of the millstone of debt with which the MD&HB was encumbered at birth.

[40]*BPP* (1847-1848), "Select Committee on Commercial Distress," q. 1024.

[41]Different, that is, from other lines of business; some other ports, including Hull and Glasgow, were spending heavily in 1847-1848 as well.

in banking, railways, insurance and other sectors notorious for domino-effect collapse in adversity. John Bramley-Moore, for example, was a merchant in Brazil, which was about as volatile a trade as one could find. Something made him behave differently when he was acting as Chairman of the Liverpool Dock Committee, and this difference in behaviour bears crucially on the way nineteenth-century business worked.

The time for public self-criticism in the Maoist mould is arrived. Because my chosen field contains well over two hundred tons of almost virginal archival material, I find it difficult to broaden my view sufficiently to place things fully in their context. Ports may be studied and compared, but they are part of a much bigger picture, and the problem is that, with one notable exception, the people with the wide-angle lenses have often been as deficient in studying ports as I have been in raising my gaze from the minutiae. There really are some big questions involved in the port services industry which could have a bearing on our whole view of the way the nineteenth-century economy worked. This is not an appeal to dismember the historiography but rather a plea for a realisation that there are still gaps which pose questions that need careful examination.

Taking a Long-Term View

One of those questions is a broader version of that posed in relation to John Bramley-Moore: what was it that modified the normal commercial behaviour of individuals when they were acting as members of a port authority? The answer is a matter of considerable importance, for it may also explain the surprising financial stability of the Liverpool Dock Trustees and of a number of other port authorities in the face of change and adversity which might have been expected to cause serious damage.

To get an enabling act to build a canal in eighteenth century Britain it was necessary to prove, normally before a Parliamentary Select Committee, five things: that the *status quo* was unsatisfactory; that the proposed undertaking would benefit "the public;" that feasible engineering solutions existed; that the undertaking would be sufficiently profitable to attract investors; and that it would not lead to the unfair exploitation of users. Many who subscribed for shares in canal companies did so either because they thought it was a good investment as a canal or because they thought they could sell their "scrip" at a profit before they had paid it up.[42] The former group were willing to take a long view: few canals, even minor ones, were completed in less than five years, and in the exceptional case of the Leeds and Liverpool, completion took forty years. During this time, the shareholders were almost completely dependent on the engineer: they could only back him or sack him. The latter course might well (as in the case of the Leeds and Liverpool) delay even further the happy day of the opening and the prospect of a first dividend. There was, of course, the possibility of great profit, and it was this prospect which induced some investors to risk long fallow periods before the money rolled in. This recognition, which dawned only slowly and painfully on some canal investors, was part of the background to that phase of port construction where costs first began to get counted in the millions. It was always going to be years between the first expenditure on the professional services of lawyers and engineers and the earning of the first revenues.

This meant that bodies such as the Liverpool Dock Committee were not being peculiarly wise in planning well ahead: if they waited until a problem of under-capacity or overcrowding actually occurred, the "problem" would most likely disappear during the drawn-out process of financing, designing and constructing a new facility, as some of the customers took their trade elsewhere. The extent to which it was necessary to plan ahead was a matter of acute controversy. Those who took the long view considered that Liverpool's trade had grown strongly and steadily in volume and value over the last fifty years. There might be good years in timber or bad years in cotton, or years when interest rates rose and increased the debt charges of the port, but overall there was no doubt that the port could tough it out and plan for continuing growth. In retrospect we can see that they were right, for until the Great Depression, Liverpool never had a surfeit of berth space or high-tech oceanic berths accommodating coastal colliers or Irish cattle boats. But we can also see that there was really no alternative: they had to plan or fail. The short-term "solution" of piecemeal modernisation or building new facilities only to the size required by vessels already in service was no solution at all.

Those willing to take the long view generally looked about twenty years ahead, of which anywhere from two to five years would be occupied with design, obtaining Parliamentary powers, and construction. By the end

---

[42]Some, of course, invested for the benefit of their principal business interest, such as Wedgwood in the Trent and Mersey.

of the twenty years, obsolescence often was setting in. This was a remarkably long time ahead to be trying to look in a period of financial instability and rapid change. Consider, for example, a few things that happened in the twenty years after 1845. The railway mania rose to its peak and collapsed, as did Chartism; the Irish Potato Famine briefly put tens of thousands of starving paupers into Liverpool's workhouse and outdoor relief system; emigrants left Liverpool at the rate of over 100,000 per year for several consecutive years; the width of the largest dock entrance in the port doubled; the port was drastically re-organised by an Act of Parliament and made to incorporate Birkenhead Docks; Jesse Hartley died; and the Navigation Acts were repealed. As well, the Crimean War disrupted the grain trade, shook up everybody's idea of logistics and firmly established the daily press as a power in the land. The Indian Mutiny, by wiping out the last residual of the East India Company, eventually opened new markets for Liverpool. The American Civil War threatened disaster in the short term through a shortage of cotton and in the long because Liverpool had backed the losing side. All these things had important effects on the prospects and profitability of the port.

Through this scene of constant change, the management of the port of Liverpool sailed serenely on. Few of the events or changes listed above attracted even passing mention in the official documents. These men had their eyes fixed on their own long-term future and, undistracted by the need to pay dividends or face an angry electorate, seldom deviated. In railway companies, bad trading conditions were followed by strings of excuses and sometimes panic-stricken actions. The port authority was able to exhibit greater constancy and stability than probably any other body in the country - the Anglican Church, riven by the Tractarian controversy and attacks on the Mosaic cosmogony, included.

This, I suggest, is what enabled them to ride out the financial crisis of 1847 with apparent nonchalance. It was quite an extraordinary achievement for a port authority whose total "capital" was only in seven digits, and most of it impossible to liquidate, to be seen as safer than government stocks or the Bank of England. No existing interpretive framework of technological, economic or geographical determinism has even identified this question, much less answered what is obviously in part a question of mercantile behaviour. Each approach can provide some understanding of what went on in managing a port, but none is complete; because we do not know how many pieces the jigsaw has, we do not know whether the next piece to be fitted will complete the picture or not.

Mercantile Determinism

What we do know is that one missing piece is what I shall temporarily dub "mercantile determinism," which is simply a tentative development of what Gordon has already written. We may take another breach of the "Anyport" model as an illustration. The programme of construction enabled by the 1873 Liverpool Dock Act was the biggest yet, at an estimated cost of £4.1 million. It was specifically geared to the construction of docks for the larger ships using the port. Toxteth and Harrington Docks had their sills as deep as any of the new works at the downstream end of the port and totalled over twenty acres. They were built upstream, unlike Bird's suggestion, because they could be closer to the commercial infrastructure than if they were built downstream.

No source has yet come to light which reveals the exact number of messengers in nineteenth-century Liverpool, but it clearly grew to several thousands, and by the 1891 census may possibly have exceeded 10,000.[43] The mileage covered by these people was one of the costs of using the port, so the shorter the distances they travelled, and the less time they spent doing it, the better. It was to unite the extremities of the dock estate with the town centre that the Board played an important part in the promotion of the Liverpool Overhead Railway (opened 1893). Its intended role is made abundantly clear by the spacing of the stations: at the extremities they were relatively widely spaced, whereas at Pierhead, James Street and Custom House they were within about three minutes' walk of each other. As originally built the railway did not serve residential areas, and its first enabling act was passed in 1878, during the early stages of the construction of the works under the 1873 act.[44]

Birkenhead docks, as Gordon has shown, initially failed partly through ignoring mercantile determinism. The Mersey Railway under the river was at first a disastrous venture which envisaged interchange of freight between the two dock railway systems. It ended up by being part of the salvation of Birkenhead, not by carrying freight but by providing a passenger connection between the Birkenhead docks and Liverpool. The handling of goods was not the central problem.

---

[43]Messengers were, unfortunately, aggregated with two other occupations.

[44]See A. Jarvis, *Portrait of the Liverpool Overhead Railway* (Shepperton, 1996).

The annual reports of the overhead railway company never make happy reading and are full of excuses for poor financial performance. Among the whinges for 1914 is one which is genuinely informative: it cites the growth of telephone usage as a reason for the decline in passenger revenue, establishing the previous importance of the messenger.

In 1894, Liverpool had easily the largest number of telephones outside London and the highest proportion of lines per capita (one per 119 people); the busiest exchange on the National Telephone Company's system was Liverpool Royal, with an average of 96,644 calls per day. Perhaps more significant is that the third densest provision, at one line per 131 people, was not, as one might expect, in Manchester, Birmingham or Glasgow, but in Birkenhead.[45] "The one-eyed city," as Liverpudlians called it, had begun to overcome the disability with which it was born.

It may be that we should investigate the feasibility of a new kind of port history in which the success of a port development, its nature and location, even the need for it in the first place, is partly determined by the ease of urban transport and communication, by the cost of transmitting mercantile information? It may be difficult to measure these factors, but it is not impossible that we could produce a new model in which port development is still divided into eras, but that the temporal divisions are based on communications technology. For example:

> Era 1: Development of paved streets in vicinity of waterfront
> Era 2: Employment of full-time messengers
> Era 3a: Arrival of rudimentary telecommunications: flag systems, semaphores; first electric telegraphs, urban passenger railways
> Era 3b: international electric telegraph, telephones, electric trams
> Era 4: W/T, ship-to-shore, motorcycles for telegram boys
> Era 5: Fax machines, networked PCs

As with the Bird model, not all ports will exhibit every characteristic of every era: few, for example, used semaphore telegraphs and by no means all started in Era 1. In some railway-built ports Eras 1-3a occurred

---

[45] *BPP* (1898), "Select Committee on Telephones" (383), XII, 1, appendices.

simultaneously, as Grimsby or Silloth were constructed where nothing had stood before. A more serious criticism might be that the overall importance of communications will vary greatly from port to port, being greatest in large ports with long internal routes and with significant commodity exchanges. A small port like Workington or Garston, dominated by a single coastwise export trade, would be a different matter. But if one believes in the model, then the fact that these ports did not grow and diversify in the way that Cardiff, almost another single-traffic port, did may have been exactly because of their failure to follow the model by improving communications.

There is a lot of spadework needed here, but one may certainly question whether Gladstone Dock in Liverpool (first designs 1906; completed 1927)would have been built nearly five miles from the city centre without the availability of the overhead railway and telephones: there were alternative plans to build a giant new dock on the sites of Albert and Canning, adjacent to the site of the Old Dock, and the idea of building inland of existing docks was repeatedly examined in the pre-telephone era. Dare one suggest that the movement of dock facilities downstream was affected not only by physical considerations but also by mercantile ones? The initial failure and subsequent success of other downstream moves, like Avonmouth and Tilbury, may have been affected by an information dimension as well. One would never claim universality for such an approach, only that it might be another piece of the jigsaw, but if it should prove a useful research framework, we could perhaps dignify it with the title of the "Jackson Model."

Certainly every reputable published work on port history contains elements of economics, technology, politics, and social and demographic context, albeit in widely varying proportions. The question is whether enough of the basic research has now been completed for us to embark on the completion of the integrative task, to which Gordon has made such a distinguished contribution, of taking port history out of its pigeon hole and placing it in its wider context. In the process, we shall probably make some difference to the understanding of that context. If we do not, port history has no meaningful future anyway. Have we, in Mr. Churchill's words, reached the end of the beginning?

Port Politics: Interest, Faction and Port Management in Mid-Victorian Liverpool

Graeme J. Milne

How can we measure the success or failure of port authorities? In his classic *History and Archaeology of Ports*, Gordon Jackson pointed to the accommodation of diversity as a key indicator. The specific context of the remark was the mid-century building programme of the Liverpool Dock Trust. Its great achievement in the 1840s and 1850s, Jackson argued, was to create and operate a dock system capable of handling the full spectrum of trades, from bulk timber to luxury spices, carried in a range of vessels from coastal ketches to Cunard liners.[1]

The historian studying Liverpool shortly after this period is bound to wonder what went wrong. Evidence from the early years of the new Mersey Docks and Harbour Board (MD&HB, founded in 1858) reveals a port struggling to balance the interests of competing factions and slipping into inertia and poor management. The local press adopted a weary tone when reporting Board meetings, like the one in 1863 during which "a long and exceedingly desultory discussion took place relative to providing accommodation for the steam trade, but nothing of the slightest public interest was elicited."[2] Later commentators have been equally critical. Recalling the Board's activities in his youth, William Forwood claimed that the 1870s were marked by bitter disputes between different trades for representation and widespread manipulation of the election process.[3] The Board's own historian pointed to the mid-century era as a rough patch, although he argued that the controversies helped to mould the

[1]G. Jackson, *The History and Archaeology of Ports* (Tadworth, 1983), 80.

[2]*Gore's Advertiser*, 8 October 1863.

[3]W.B. Forwood, *Recollections of a Busy Life, Being the Reminiscences of a Liverpool Merchant, 1840-1910* (Liverpool, 1910), 37-38.

organisation into a more effective body, with its mind set "not on sectional interests but on the commerce and trade of the whole Port."[4]

Of course, historians have reason to be suspicious of some of this evidence. Men like Forwood had every interest in highlighting early failures because they claimed credit for reforming the work of the Board later in the century. When Forwood wrote early in the twentieth century that "there is no branch of the public service of which Liverpool people are more proud," his case was helped by the contrast he drew with the earlier era.[5]

Nonetheless, more recent scholars have also identified divisions and factionalism as real and dangerous issues in the management of the port. The last major study of the port of Liverpool attempted to analyse the factional dimension of the Board's activities, but struggled to distinguish between internal divisions and external threats. Francis Hyde devoted much discussion to internal divisions which, he conceded, could be "harmful to the interests of Merseyside's growth as a port." On the whole, however, Hyde argued that external pressure was by far the more serious threat to the Board's work.[6]

Part of Hyde's problem was that the internal/external dichotomy is not very helpful for understanding such disputes. The decision-making processes of mid-century England rarely allowed local issues to stay local. Dock building and port management regularly came under Parliamentary scrutiny and internal issues rapidly acquired wider implications. Efforts to define internal and external disputes obscure rather than illuminate the issues.

Yet the mid-century period has enormous potential for casting light on the operation of a major port. Three factors coincide to make mid-Victorian Liverpool a particularly important laboratory for change. First, there was the considerable growth and diversification in the port's trade. Second, there were significant changes in the profile of the port's trading community, in particular the rise in influence of the specialised Liverpool shipowner. Third, there was a shift in the way the port was administered:

---

[4]S. Mountfield, *Western Gateway: A History of the Mersey Docks and Harbour Board* (Liverpool, 1965), 26.

[5]Forwood, *Recollections*, 39.

[6]F.E. Hyde, *Liverpool and the Mersey: An Economic History of a Port, 1700-1970* (Newton Abbot, 1971), 121 and 132.

constitutional changes leading to the creation of the MD&HB brought the dock systems of Liverpool and Birkenhead together under a port authority elected by the users of the port.[7]

This essay analyses port management in mid-century Liverpool using divisions within the trading community as an investigative and explanatory framework. The first section highlights the important changes in Liverpool's trading profile in the period. It is not enough simply to cite figures for the *growth* of trade and shipping; a more sophisticated account of the increase in *diversity* of the port's traffic is necessary to understand the pressures on the Board. The rest of the paper addresses the changing relationship between the port authority and a range of factional interests and considers the evolving dynamics and internal tensions of the trading community.

Growth and Diversification

The middle decades of the nineteenth century were crucial to the development of Britain's ports. Economic historians have long recognised this as an era of major growth in the global economy, and particularly in international trade. The period between 1840 and 1870 was marked by trade expansion which far outstripped the growth of industrial production.[8] As well as growth, there was change – in transport systems, the rise of steam placed great strains on port authorities; reductions in shipping costs made bulk transport of relatively low-value goods more profitable, requiring new handling and storage facilities; and shifting official attitudes toward tariffs and protection created new demand for luxuries, requiring additional security in docks. This section offers a brief overview of the changing context of trade in the port of Liverpool.

The relative importance of change and growth is demonstrated by a number of indicators: patterns in tonnage using the port are a useful starting point. Figure 1 shows the sail and steam composition of overseas trades arriving in Liverpool in the third quarter of the nineteenth century.

---

[7]For general accounts of the port in this period, see Mountfield, *Western Gateway*; and Hyde, *Liverpool*.

[8]S. Kuznets, "Quantitative Aspects of the Economic Growth of Nations, X-Level and Structure of Foreign Trade: Long Term Trends," *Economic Development and Cultural Change*, XV, No. 2 (1967), 1-140.

The logarithmic scale highlights the rate as well as the absolute level of change: the much steeper line of steam tonnage demonstrates a dramatic rise from a low base. Steam caught imaginations and headlines, particularly with the rise of high-profile, publicity-conscious joint-stock steam companies in the early 1860s. The Liverpool press noted with some understatement in 1864 that if all the new lines recently launched on paper were actually realized, "the Dock Committee will be required to make some large alterations for their accommodation" - between them the companies claimed to have more than 100 ships on order.[9] Worse, the timetable was often so short as to be ridiculous, with companies announcing new services and demanding berths a matter of days in advance of their commencement.[10]

Figure 1
Sail and Steam (Arriving Tonnage), 1855-1869

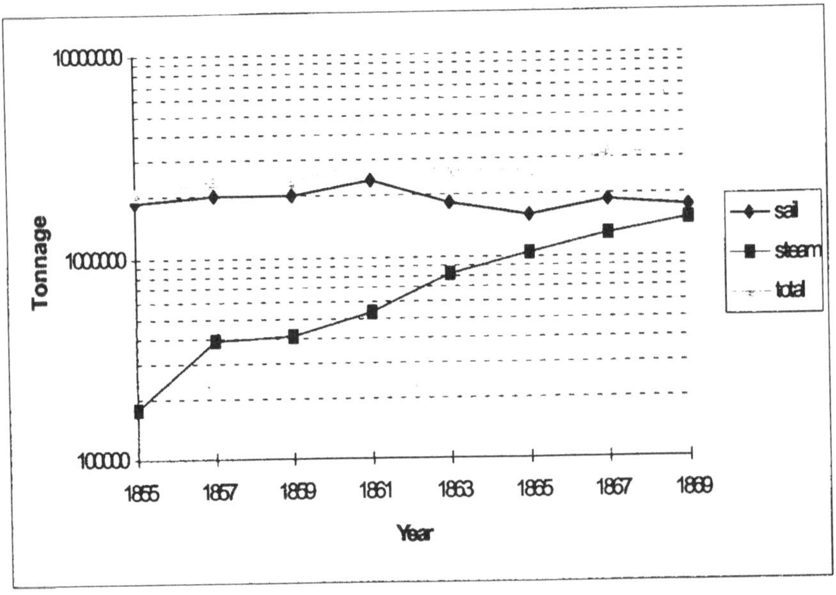

Source: Great Britain, Parliamentary Papers, Annual Returns of Trade and Navigation.

[9] *Gore's Advertiser*, 14 January 1864.

[10] Merseyside Maritime Museum Archives (MMM), MD&HB/Leg/A/7/11.

There are other lessons to be learned from the figures, as well. The historiographical preoccupation with steam tends to disguise the fact that sailing tonnage using the port remained broadly steady in mid-century. This is crucial because during its first decade, the MD&HB was faced with a considerable rise in steamship traffic *with no corresponding drop in sailing tonnage*. Only the Mediterranean and northern US trades made a significant transition from sail to steam in Liverpool before 1870, while sail tonnage expanded in other trades, such as to East Asia and the west coast of South America. These sail operators feared that the Board would be unduly influenced by the high-profile demands of the steamship promoters, and that huge expenditure would be undertaken for the benefit of a few steam companies.[11]

It is important to consider the implications of the sail/steam transition for ports like Liverpool. Economic historians have tended to stress its gradual and evolutionary nature, tracing the decline of sail and the rise of steam over the long term.[12] Nonetheless, it is also well-known that each major trade in turn made the transition rapidly. Contemporaries therefore had to live through decades during which sail and steam operated side by side, being used for different and changing purposes. Shipowners and merchants often had the best of both worlds in this period, having a range of choices and opportunities before them in making the most efficient use of old and new technology.[13]

---

[11]For example, MMM, Liverpool Docks Bill (1855), evidence of John McNicholl, 188-189.

[12]C.K. Harley, "The Shift from Sailing Ships to Steamships, 1850-1890: A Study in Technological Change and its Diffusion," in D.N. McCloskey (ed.), *Essays on A Mature Economy: Britain After 1840* (Princeton, 1971), 215-237; Harley, "Ocean Freight Rates and Productivity, 1740-1913: The Primacy of Mechanical Invention Reaffirmed," *Journal of Economic History*, XLVIII (1988), 851-876; and G.S. Graham, "The Ascendancy of the Sailing Ship, 1855-1885," *Economic History Review*, IX (1956-1957), 74-88.

[13]For useful work on particular trades, see P.L. Cottrell, "Liverpool Shipowners, the Mediterranean and the Transition from Sail to Steam during the Mid-Nineteenth Century," in L.R. Fischer (ed.), *From Wheel House to Counting House: Essays in Maritime Business History in Honour of Professor Peter Neville Davies* (St. John's, 1992), 153-202; and M. Lynn, "From Sail to Steam: The Impact of the Steamship Services on the British Palm Oil Trade with West Africa, 1850-1890," *Journal of African History*, XXX (1989), 227-245.

Figure 2
Rate of Change in Tonnage Handled
by the Liverpool Docks

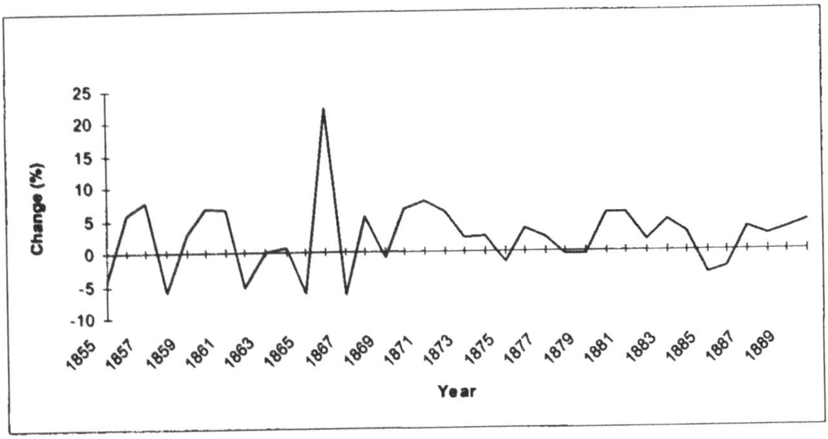

Source: MMM, MD&HB Dock Revenue Statements.

For port authorities, of course, such choices meant trouble because any dock-building programme was likely to be overtaken by events. Worse still, the rise of steam coincided with an era of marked short-term fluctuations in shipping. Figure 2 demonstrates the volatility of Liverpool's shipping during the 1850s and 1860s compared to more regular patterns later in the century. Especially during the American Civil War in the 1860s, the port authority's ability to plan was hampered by the unpredictable development of shipping patterns. There were always voices opposed to new dock building, and they gained credibility in an era which saw such marked gains and slumps in traffic; it was tempting to wait for a more recognisable pattern to develop.[14]

Other indicators of the port's activity show increasing predictability and conformity across the third quarter of the century, but this was hardly a comfort to the MD&HB. By 1870, Liverpool's dock system operated on a much less seasonal basis than in earlier decades, increasing pressure on facilities and reducing the opportunity for maintenance and

---

[14]Mountfield, *Western Gateway*, 25.

alterations during quieter periods. Figure 3 shows the fluctuating patterns of monthly arrivals in Liverpool; the 1870 series is clearly smoother than those of earlier years, with a much less pronounced winter trough and summer peak. The total number of overseas vessels arriving in the port increased by almost 1000 between 1855 and 1870, but the difference between the busiest and quietest month dropped dramatically from 347 in 1855 to only 206 in 1870.[15]

Figure 3
Monthly Variations in Arriving Shipping

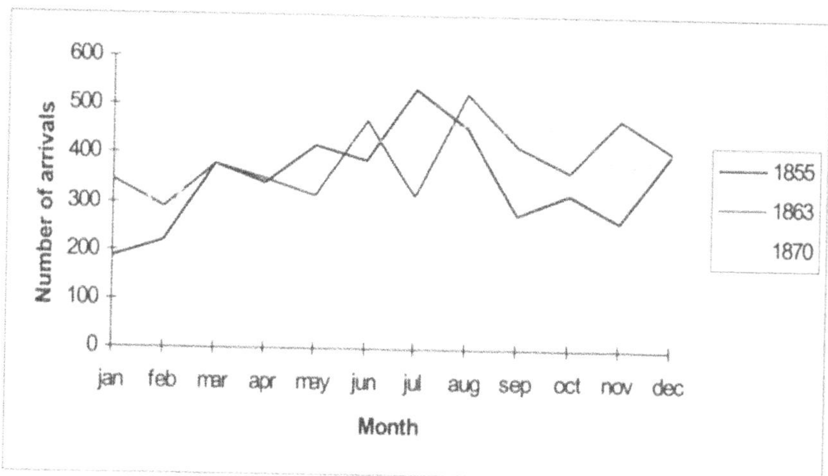

Source: Calculated from Liverpool Customs Bills of Entry, 1855, 1863,1870.

Much of this shift was due to a combination of steam transportation and diversification of supply. Cotton, for example, began to be imported in quantity from India, as well as from the southern US, which had dominated Liverpool's markets in the first half of the century. Even in the American cotton trade, an increasing volume was transported internally to northern ports and then carried in steamships to Liverpool, resulting in a different pattern from the old direct sailing routes.

[15]Incoming voyages in Liverpool *Customs Bills of Entry*, 1855, 1863 and 1870.

The MD&HB was therefore confronted with increasing pressure on its facilities during its first decade that was no longer easy to define or anticipate. How did it cope? The most obvious solution was to continue with the old Jesse Hartley strategy: build more docks, of varying sizes and functions, to accommodate diversity. In the 1860s, this would have required the construction of steam docks. The received wisdom was that steamers could only be efficiently accommodated in specialised docks, separated from sailing traffic. Not only was there a perceived risk of fire, but the pressure of steam liner timetables was such that owners worried that vessels would be boxed in or made to wait for berths.[16]

Like other ports, Liverpool began building specialised steam docks in the second quarter of the century - the first was Clarence (1830).[17] There followed a succession of docks built to accommodate ever- larger steamers: by the mid-1850s, Liverpool's steam traffic was concentrated in Nelson (1848) and Huskisson (1852). Between them, these docks handled eighty-two percent of Liverpool's steam tonnage in 1855.[18] More space for steam was created with the opening of Hartley's last Liverpool dock, Canada, in 1858. Canada is an important illustration of the "accommodating diversity" theme. It was built not only with wide entrances to cater for the then-fashionable Atlantic paddle steamers but also with large flat storage yards for the benefit of the timber trade. Although their owners frequently argued over the details, timber ships and transatlantic liners coexisted in Canada Dock effectively enough from the Board's perspective.

Thereafter the pattern breaks down, however. The Board devoted most of its building efforts in the 1860s to the Birkenhead docks rather than to the Liverpool system. As figure 4 demonstrates, however, while Birkenhead absorbed some of the increase in shipping during the 1860s, the bulk of its traffic was sail rather than steam. The rise in steam was accommodated, in the main, by the existing steam docks on the Liverpool side, particularly Canada, Huskisson and Nelson. There is one exception: Wellington made a transition from sail and was a busy steam dock by 1870. Small amounts of steam shipping began to appear in much older

---

[16]Jackson, *History*, 74-75.

[17]Docks mentioned in this paper have their date of opening in brackets.

[18]Calculated from Liverpool *Customs Bills of Entry*, 1855.

docks, like Prince's; the smallest steamers working the European trades could fit physically into older docks, and the port authority forced them to use such facilities rather than mix with the large steamers in the new, deeper docks. This was not popular; Mediterranean steam traders working from Queen's were clearly offended by being assigned to "what was always a sailing dock."[19]

Figure 4
Proportion of Sail/Steam Tonnage Using Key Docks

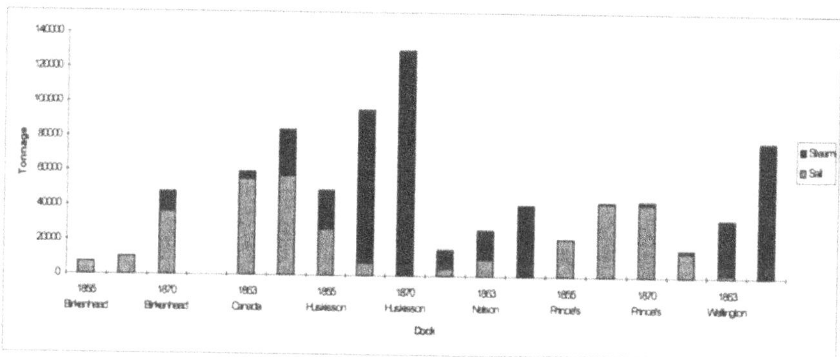

Source: Calculated from Liverpool Customs Bills of Entry, 1855, 1863, 1870. (Canada did not open until 1859).

It is clear therefore that the MD&HB managed to maintain sail/steam segregation across a large part of the system even during the sharp rise in steam traffic after 1860. It is also clear, though, that both sail and steam vessels were having to work more intensively. The Board's investments on the Liverpool side during the 1860s were targeted at accommodating steam: an extension to Huskisson in 1861 undoubtedly helped with the rising steam tonnage using the dock, but there were no equivalent extensions to the other steam docks, and no new, large docks. On the other side of the Mersey, Birkenhead did useful work accommodating sailing ships on the long-distance routes. It catered for a considerable expansion in the guano trade during the 1860s, served as an ideal

---

[19]MMM, MD&HB (No. 1) Bill (1873), evidence of Walter Glyn, q. 778.

export point for Cheshire salt, and played host to emigrants leaving for Australia on sailing clippers.

The Birkenhead docks did not, however, meet the needs of the more vocal steamship operators, who became an effective new force in the port at mid-century, in some contrast to the influence of sailing ship owners in earlier decades. It seems bizarre to argue that shipowners were slow to emerge as a major interest group in Liverpool, but it is clear that much of the port's prestige trades relied on foreign sailing ships in the first half of the nineteenth century. As late as the mid-1850s, forty-eight percent of sail tonnage arriving in Liverpool was American-owned.[20] Of course, these vessels relied on a large number of Liverpool merchants, agents and brokers, but only at mid-century did Liverpool *shipowners* begin to operate a majority share of the ocean shipping using the port. Much of this depended on the rise of steam, as merchants of all kinds began to use British steamers rather than foreign sailing ships, thus giving Liverpool's shipowners a higher profile in the trading community.

The rise of steam and the diversification of supply in key commodities had implications both for the trading community and trade. Commodity specialists were less identifiable with particular regions or types of shipping as the port's staples, like cotton and grain, were imported from an increasing number of countries in a range of vessels; "cotton trader" and "American trader" were no longer synonymous. As well as having to deal with rapidly changing trades, the port authority confronted a diversified mercantile community, with a wider range of vested interests, all demanding recognition, representation, and specialised accommodation.

Interests and Influence

The diversification of trade and traders would have been complex in any case, but it happened in a period when the Mersey port authority was being significantly redefined. Exactly how members of the trading community brought influence to bear on members of the port authority remains unclear, as does the level of influence considered appropriate by contemporaries, given that a number of individuals were leading traders *and* members of the Dock Board. This section highlights some general principles and patterns.

[20]Calculated from Liverpool *Customs Bills of Entry*, 1855.

The first point to be made is the extent to which members of the trading community came to dominate decision-making in the port by mid-century. Looked at superficially, the changing face of the port authority was almost a Whiggish stereotype of the inexorable progress of the mercantile and commercial classes. Liverpool's pioneering efforts in dock building during the eighteenth century were driven by the port's traders, who used their influence on the Town Council.[21] By the beginning of the nineteenth century, however, trading interests doubted that the Liverpool Dock Trust - effectively the Council wearing a different hat - was fully representing their priorities. The various regional trade associations began to argue for more representation. By 1825, eight of the twenty-one member Dock Committee were being elected by the port's users. It was under this constitution that the Committee, chaired by South America merchant John Bramley Moore, drove through the dramatic period of dock planning and building in the 1840s. In 1851, another reform bill increased the size of the Committee to twenty-four, of whom twelve were elected by port users and the remainder nominated by the Council. Finally, in 1858, the mercantile classes seemingly emerged victorious when all but four of the members of the new Dock Board were elected by users. In addition, this was to be a new port authority for the Mersey as a whole. The MD&HB would continue the trend established by the old Dock Committee of gradual separation of port finance and management from the town of Liverpool, and it would apply the skills and competence demonstrated in Liverpool over a number of decades to salvaging the less- than-successful docks at Birkenhead.[22]

How was the changing profile of the trading community reflected in the composition of the new Dock Board and the decision-making processes of the authority? These are not straightforward issues. Members of the Board generally denied that they were there to represent various interests: they did not explicitly speak for the Corn Trade Association, the Steamship Owners Association, or any of the other groups. On the other hand, there is ample evidence that at least some of these interests expected a certain number of Board members to be drawn from their trade.

---

[21]M.J. Power, "Councillors and Commerce in Liverpool, 1650-1750," *Urban History*, XXIV (1997), 301-323.

[22]For an outline, see Mountfield, *Western Gateway*.

The Steamship Owners Association offers useful evidence. Formed in 1858 explicitly to lobby the new Dock Board, the Association was already complaining in 1862 that its representation on the Board was too small. It was to be hoped, the Association stated in its annual report, that there would shortly be restored the "former recognised status, that four parties connected with the steam trade should have seats on the Board."[23] The Association's concerns were caused by the retirement of William Inman and its failure, despite some effort, to persuade any other leading steamship owner to stand for election in his place.[24]

It should not, however, be assumed that the Steamship Owners saw the remaining members of the Board as opponents. There was, in fact, a remarkable level of agreement across the trading community as to whom should sit on the Board. When the Steamship Owners and the Chamber of Commerce both published slates of twenty-four candidates approved for election in 1858, there were only four discrepancies, and the great majority of candidates were elected.[25] Even in 1862, when the Steamship Owners were complaining about their representation, they congratulated themselves on the fact that twenty-two of the twenty-four men on their approved list for that year had been elected.[26]

Given that the Chamber of Commerce represented the widest range of traders of every scale and specialty, and that the Steamship Owners represented a much narrower interest, there was clearly a fair consensus about the leading men of the port. Particular factions did not, it seems, object to having a wide range of interests on the Board, as long as unwritten rules about the "appropriate" level of representation of some trades were observed.

This is reinforced by the uncontroversial nature of elections to the Board in the early years. Members tended to be re-elected without opposition, and if factions did jostle for places, they did so at an earlier point in the process which remains invisible to historians. The 1859 election, at the end of the Board's first year of operation, was by far the

---

[23]MMM, D/SS/2/1, "Annual Report" (1862), 7.

[24]MMM, D/SS/1/1, 78-79.

[25]*Ibid.*, 1-4.

[26]*Ibid.*, 29-31.

most widely contested, with eight candidates failing to be elected. Thereafter, however, the Board settled into a comfortable routine. During the 1860s, only three sitting members failed to be re-elected, and while there were several retirements and resignations, no fewer than sixteen men sat on the Board for at least ten of its first dozen years.[27]

It seems unlikely, therefore, that the influence of particular trades and interests on the Dock Board will be readily uncovered by a Parliamentary-style analysis of elections and candidates. Rather more promising is an analysis of some of the key issues facing the port authority in mid-century, and the extent to which particular trades wielded an influence in their resolution. The legal framework of the MD&HB held it accountable to scrutiny and gave interests every opportunity and encouragement to raise objections. In addition, trading interests by definition worked in a wider world; both competition with other ports and the involvement of central government in the planning of port infrastructure were vital issues in this period, creating still more potential for conflict. Research that focuses narrowly on the internal workings of the Dock Board is likely to miss the point.

Within this broader framework, traders had two key tactics in bringing pressure to bear on the Board. First, they were well aware that Liverpool was not the only port in Britain. A favourite ploy was to threaten to move to another port if facilities were not provided in Liverpool. Major players used this tactic throughout the period, and opponents of the Liverpool port authorities claimed that various trades would leave the port. In the mid-1850s, Birkenhead's dock engineer, James Rendell, argued without much evidence that the American trades would abandon the increasingly congested Liverpool docks.[28] Rendell was scaremongering and trying to promote Birkenhead, but the tactic was taken up a decade later by leading Liverpool steamship owners such as James Bibby, who threatened to move his operations to Southampton or London if accommodation in Liverpool was taken away from him.[29]

---

[27]Figures derived from membership lists in the Dock Board's minutes, MMM, MD&HB/MP/9.

[28]MMM, Liverpool Docks Bill (1855), 213.

[29]MMM, MD&HB Bill (1867), evidence of James Bibby, q. 890-892.

The Board did not take such threats too seriously. It judged correctly that Liverpool's hinterland was far more important to traders than any problems with dock space; however impressive the railways might be, they could hardly carry bulk staples effectively enough to make Southampton a sensible entrepot for the northwest of England. Board members accepted that there would be competition from southern ports in the passenger trades but were not intimidated by the cargo-handling capabilities of such places. Southampton, argued Ralph Brocklebank, was "a tea-cup as compared to Liverpool."[30]

The Board was a great deal less secure in dealing with the other key tactic of its opponents, opposition to Parliamentary Bills. It is important to stress that the Board was severely limited in the decisions it could take. In particular, it had to secure Parliamentary approval for major borrowing and expenditure. This immediately moved questions of port management onto a wider and more complicated stage. The process of securing a Private Act was complex enough without having to deal with opposition from within the port, and the experience of the Mersey port authorities led prominent members of the Board in the 1860s to question the whole Private Bill process.[31]

Confusion between strategic planning and day-to-day operation was at the heart of the Board's difficulties in securing Private Acts. Traders who felt disadvantaged by operational decisions recognised that the Private Bill system gave them power and influence far out of proportion to their role in the port. The nuisance value of a petition against a major dock extension scheme was such that the Board would often make concessions to those who threatened to object. In addition, the frequency of new schemes in the 1850s and 1860s meant that there were regular opportunities to threaten a Parliamentary petition rather than negotiate with the Board through more normal channels. All manner of groups took advantage of this ploy, from individuals to major trading associations. In 1855, while facing some of the most complex negotiations of the period, the Dock Trust had to reach a compromise with five local

---

[30]*Liverpool Daily Post*, 30 October 1861. Brocklebank was soon to be Chair of the MD&HB.

[31]MMM, MD&HB Disc/1/17, J.A. Tobin's comments at the Dock Board regarding the 1867 Act.

men who wanted a road built more quickly.[32] In 1863, an entire Bill was withdrawn because the Steamship Owners Association lodged an objection in Parliament.[33] The Board argued, reasonably enough, that Parliamentary committees were suspicious of dock schemes that attracted local opposition, especially from the very people the projects were supposed to help.

The interaction of factional interests with the scrutiny procedures of central government is therefore at least as important to understanding change in the port as the composition of the Board or the behaviour of its members. Three key issues from mid-century will serve to illustrate the questions at hand. They highlight the changing nature of factional division in Liverpool and its impact on the direction of the port. The first is the debate over warehouse docks conducted in the late 1830s and early 1840s, which resulted in significant success for the Dock Committee. This is discussed very briefly, not only because it demonstrates the relative ease with which the pre-1858 port authority was able to balance interests and pressures but also because it raises themes which were to prove more fraught in subsequent circumstances. The second considers the much more serious dispute over the use and development of Birkenhead in the 1850s and 1860s, an issue that dominated the period before and after the creation of the MD&HB in 1858. The third considers the rise to influence of the steamship owners as a vocal and powerful faction in the 1860s, and their conflicts with more established trades for dock space.

The Proper Role of Port Authorities: Warehouse Docks

Warehouse docks offered port authorities an important means to improve efficiency and to generate new income. Some of Liverpool's existing trades, already expanding in the 1830s and early 1840s, were demanding better facilities if they were to develop further; cotton merchants, for example, often complained about their bales lying in the rain on the quaysides. The port was also keen to attract new trades, some of which required more sophisticated handling and storage than the bulk staples. The East Asian trades had been a London monopoly during Liverpool's rise to prominence in the eighteenth century, but by the mid-nineteenth

---

[32]MMM, MD&HB Leg/A/7/11, Letter from Dock Solicitor's Office re: James Jack, *et al.*, 5 June 1855.

[33]MMM, D/SS/1/1, 116-117.

such lucrative traffic was open to the provincial ports if they could encourage their merchants to exploit the opportunity. Liverpool accordingly cut its dock dues to attract long-haul shipping from the region and began to plan the sort of secure warehouse docks needed by high-value commodity trades.[34]

The idea of warehouse docks brought the port authority into conflict with important elements in the trading community. Objections fell broadly into two categories. The first came from trade associations which had no need for warehouses. The Canadian traders, for example, needed flat space for timber and the Shipowners Association needed space to unload and load its vessels quickly; neither body had any interest in the secure storage of luxury commodities. The second set of objections came from a well-organised lobby of private warehouse owners and road hauliers. This group feared that the convenience and security of dock warehouses would prove attractive to traders who up to that point had been forced to incur three unwelcome costs: warehouse fees, cartage charges and extensive pilfering. Port authority warehouses might lower the first and eliminate the others, leaving the private warehouse owners unable to compete. Arguments naturally tended not to be made in such stark terms, but were dressed up as a more serious discussion of the proper role of port authorities. Port authority funds should provide a lowest common need, it was argued, and trades with more expensive requirements should seek specialised facilities in the private sector. By the late 1830s the authorities had lost patience with such arguments, believing that their opponents were motivated solely by the pursuit of profit at the expense of the trading community as a whole. The Liverpool Council Finance Committee argued that opposition from private warehouse owners was the best reason for Albert and similar docks to be built without delay.[35]

Despite such well co-ordinated opposition, the Dock Committee was able to go ahead with Albert (1846) and Stanley (1848). This is remarkable because such facilities were extremely expensive: the warehouses at Albert doubled the cost of building the dock.[36] The Dock

---

[34]MMM, Birkenhead Docks Bill (1848), evidence of John Bramley Moore, 139.

[35]MMM, Report of the Finance Committee of the Town Council...Docks and Warehouses, 21 November 1839, 8-15.

[36]N. Ritchie-Noakes, *Liverpool's Historic Waterfront* (London, 1984), 49-54.

Trust's success in taking warehouse docks forward stemmed from a combination of internal and external factors. It was able to enlist official support for the view that warehouses should be an integral element in the port's facilities. The Trust was also helped by the behaviour of some of its opponents, who managed to alienate government officers charged with taking a strategic view of port facilities. The Admiralty Surveying Officer, James Abernethy, found himself at the centre of a typical Liverpool brawl when he supervised an inquiry into plans for the 1848 Dock Bill. After announcing relatively broad terms, he rapidly realised his mistake and struggled to curtail the efforts of warehouse owners and Birkenhead advocates to turn the inquiry into a forum for their complaints. Abernethy's conclusions backed up the earlier decisions of the Dock Trust that warehouses should be a matter of public interest, not private profit, and were a perfectly legitimate venture for a port authority.[37]

The Trust was also able to reassure most of its critics. Its plans for dock development in the 1840s were so extensive that they offered something for almost everyone. Traders who had no use for Albert's warehouses would have facilities in the new complex of docks to the north, due to open in 1848. In acreage terms, warehouse docks comprised less than one-third of the dock space already in the planning stages when Albert opened; traders feeling left out did not have long to wait.

With such powerful friends, the Trust could afford to make a few enemies. Private warehouse owners Richard Harbord and Thomas Dower claimed to reflect a "strong anxiety at Liverpool" about the new powers inherent in allowing the Dock Committee to manage warehouses.[38] The warehouse owners could also be politically astute, and contemporaries wrote with some admiration of their Machiavellian approach to Council business.[39] It was all too easy, however, to caricature people like Dower as reactionaries with vested interests - later accounts refer to his refusal to ride the new-fangled omnibus - and a decade after Albert's opening he

---

[37]MMM, MD&HB/Parl/15, 23, appendix.

[38]MMM, Liverpool Docks Bill (1848), evidence of Harbord and Dower, 29-32.

[39]J.A. Picton, *Memorials of Liverpool, Historical and Topographical, Including a History of the Dock Estate* (2 vols., London 1873), I, 570.

was still raising the warehouse issue with tedious lack of effect at Town Council meetings.[40]

The port authority of the 1840s therefore was working in an environment of expanding resources, with support from government officials, and opponents who hardly represented the future of the port and its trade. In such circumstances, the accommodation of diversity was not particularly difficult. Conflicts in subsequent decades were to be conducted against a very different backdrop.

The Enemy Within and Without: Birkenhead

It has already been noted that the MD&HB's early record of dock building in Liverpool was not as impressive as that of its predecessor, and that much of the Board's spending in the 1860s was directed at the Birkenhead docks. This would not have been the Board's favoured approach given a choice; instead, it was forced by Birkenhead's advocates, who were able to insist on extensive remedial work for the failed Birkenhead dock system. They achieved this largely by marshalling forces in Parliament and the Board of Trade, and by successfully creating a perception that Liverpool was profiteering from the nation's trade. The greed of the town should be curtailed by preventing further expansion and by encouraging a competitor port across the Mersey in Birkenhead. In 1855, the Board of Trade urged Parliament to stop Liverpool's "improvident extension in a northerly direction," and this became, in effect, the official position until the 1870s.[41]

Contemporary Liverpool opinion was fond of casting the battle as between progressive merchants and reactionary landholders. While the Dock Board as a whole was elected by the trade of the Mersey, the Birkenhead lobby represented landed interests on the Cheshire bank, and conflict was obvious.[42] Birkenhead's promoters ("extensive land speculators") had secured the aid of the "Cheshire nobility and landed

---

[40]H. Shimmin, *Pen and Ink Sketches of Liverpool Town Councillors* (Liverpool, 1866), 61-63.

[41]Great Britain, Parliament, *Parliamentary Papers*, "Communications from the Board of Trade to H. Labouchere, respecting the Birkenhead and Liverpool Docks Bill, (1854-1855), L, 333, 5, Letter from James Booth, Secretary to the Board of Trade.

[42]MMM, MD&HB Disc/1/3, 16.

gentry, probably the most aristocratic and feudal in their ideas of any in the kingdom."[43]

The Birkenhead question also had more subtle aspects which reveal important issues in the Dock Board's ability to deal with faction and interest. One key point was the changing face of the Birkenhead question over time. By the mid-1850s, when the companies building and running the Birkenhead docks had run out of funds and were demanding to be rescued by Liverpool, some leading Liverpool figures saw this as a lesser evil than continuing disputes in the port. Charles Turner, Chairman of the Dock Committee, argued in March 1855 for the amalgamation of the Liverpool and Birkenhead docks under a single management which would operate them much more efficiently by developing specialised facilities for particular trades. Turner's thinking was driven by the "constant squabbles...which are very injurious to the trade of the port," and which were provoked by the Birkenhead lobby.[44]

Amalgamation, however, did not solve the problem. The Birkenhead interest did not fight only in Parliament and did not rest when the failed docks were taken over. Indeed, it was the only formally recognised faction within the new Dock Board. Continued trouble was written into the Board's constitution: four seats went to government nominees rather than being open to election by the trading community in general. The government used these places to ensure that advocates of further expansion in Birkenhead had guaranteed seats on the new Board, and its nominees took their role as watchdogs seriously. During the 1850s and 1860s, the nominated members hampered the Board's strategic planning at Parliamentary level and obstructed its operational decision-making locally. Until the mid-1860s, the lobby's priority was to get Birkenhead "finished." Unless harassed at every opportunity, feared the Birkenhead lobby, the new Dock Board would be tempted to write off the partly-built docks on the Cheshire bank and continue developing Liverpool. This would have represented a serious defeat for key individuals, motivated partly by their own financial investments in Birkenhead, but

---

[43]Picton, *Memorials*, I, 575.

[44]MMM, Liverpool Docks Bill (1855), evidence of Charles Turner, 22-29. Turner was Chair of the Dock Committee in its later years and went on to be the first Chair of the new Board.

also by a real commitment to the development of industry and trade on the Cheshire bank of the Mersey.

Harold Littledale, for example, was a tireless agitator for Birkenhead, although given to playing down his role with some inspired understatement. In 1855 he remarked to a Parliamentary Committee that the subject of dock accommodation had been "a sort of hobby" of his.[45] Littledale sometimes went to bizarre lengths. The Dock Trust's lawyers gleefully noted that a petition against the 1855 Dock Bill had lain unsigned in the Liverpool Exchange, forcing Littledale to carry it door-to-door to Birkenhead's tradesmen. He then attempted to pass it off as a petition from the "Merchants, shipowners, masters of vessels and others interested in the Port of Liverpool." Littledale was responsible for another petition at the same time, which was indeed from "Holders of Bonds on Liverpool Docks," albeit only two of them; almost three thousand others somehow neglected to sign.[46]

Such a record on the Birkenhead question made it easy for the Board to discount Littledale's views on other issues, especially when he began raising uncomfortable truths about the work of the Engineer's Department later in the century.[47] Other Birkenhead partisans would also have played a more positive role in the Board's proceedings if they had been less identified with that single issue. John Laird, for example, was a valued member of the Board, but even he found himself sidelined for his frequent, nit-picking efforts to bring the Birkenhead question into almost any matter under discussion. The first Board meeting in 1858 was well-covered in the press and supposed to be a celebration of the new era. Laird, of course, took the opportunity to disrupt proceedings by opposing the election of Charles Turner to the Chair; Turner, he claimed, had been instrumental in obstructing the progress of Birkenhead. Typically, though, Laird did not nominate an alternative candidate and his actions only served to alienate Board members.[48] By the mid-1860s, Laird's constant complaints about the Birkenhead question had long since proved counter-

---

[45]MMM, Liverpool Docks Bill (1855), evidence of Harold Littledale, 157.

[46]The petitions and commentary are in MMM, MD&HB/Leg/A/7/25.

[47]A. Jarvis, "Harold Littledale: The Man with a Mission," in H.M. Hignett (ed.), *A Second Merseyside Maritime History* (Liverpool, 1991), 5-16.

[48]*The Times*, 7 January 1858.

productive, serving only to irritate his colleagues and embarrass the Board in the local press. Some of the most forceful condemnations of the Birkenhead enterprise – warmly endorsed in the editorial columns – were provoked by Laird's repetitive interventions on the issue.[49]

Laird's most important work for Birkenhead was done in Parliament. Elected MP for Birkenhead after his retirement from business in 1861, Laird used his influence in the Commons to thwart plans for further expansion in Liverpool. By the later 1860s, though, even Laird had trouble arguing that Birkenhead's development had been neglected. Almost two-thirds of the Board's works expenditure between 1858 and 1867 went to Birkenhead. Such figures were enough for the Chair of the Board's Parliamentary Committee: "I ask any impartial man whether we have not performed our duty by Birkenhead."[50]

At this point, the Birkenhead lobby moved the goal posts and the question took on yet another dimension. If the docks were finished, and some sheds and other facilities put in place, the Board could not just sit back and preside over a system of free choice; it had to force certain elements in the trading community to use Birkenhead. Laird urged a coercive pricing policy on the Board, arguing that if Liverpool's steamship lines insisted on cramming themselves into the Canada and Huskisson Docks they should have to pay dearly for their berths, thus encouraging them to move to lower-rated docks in Birkenhead.[51] Laird claimed that Birkenhead offered excellent facilities and that failure to use them was motivated only by prejudice; his family's shipbuilding yard was a demonstration of the economic success that could be achieved in the place. This was very much the exception that proved the rule, however. While shipbuilding might have been at home in Birkenhead, mainstream trading was not. Those who expressed approval in principle for Birkenhead were disinclined to lead any business migration across the Mersey, and their actions reflect a more acute business sense than their words.

---

[49]See for example Turner's speech at the Dock Board meeting on 1 October 1863, *Liverpool Chronicle*, 10 October 1863.

[50]£1,561,485 was spent on works in Liverpool, £2,731,423 on Birkenhead: MMM, MD&HB/Disc/1/1, 11-12.

[51]MMM, House of Commons, MD&HB (No. 1) Bill (1873), evidence of John Laird, MP, q. 2599.

Traders were afraid to move their operations away from the established commercial infrastructure of Liverpool. Laird could not even persuade his own business partner to relocate.[52] A leading Australia merchant thought that his trade could move to Birkenhead, but when pressed bemoaned the lack of storage and handling facilities, which were just as vital to traders as the docks. Birkenhead, he argued, was "a perfect Balaclava, no sheds or anything."[53] Two of the Mersey's largest trades, timber and cotton, were often mentioned as being ideal for Birkenhead, although rarely by the people who actually traded in them. Those timber or cotton merchants who did approve of Birkenhead (including Harold Littledale) usually argued that the whole of a given trade should move, and did not volunteer to relocate their own businesses for a trial period.[54] In such circumstances, it was easy for critics to argue that Birkenhead partisanship had more to do with inflating property prices than serious mercantile thinking; Liverpool partisans never tired of pointing to Littledale's extensive landholdings in Wallesey, adjacent to the Birkenhead docks.[55] In a final, fitting demonstration of the true focal point of the Mersey trading community, when the Birkenhead Dock Company held its final meeting in 1864, it met in the Clarendon Rooms – in Liverpool.[56]

Partly to cover its back and demonstrate that it was making an effort, the Board did indeed encourage traders to move their operations to Birkenhead. It approached individual merchants and shipowners and advertised the availability of Birkenhead berths in the local press.[57] Yet such efforts did not satisfy Birkenhead's advocates and only served to sour relations between the Board and leading traders in Liverpool, who complained that even the Board's low-key measures were far too much.

---

[52]MMM, MD&HB (No. 1) Bill (1873), evidence of L.H. Parr, 470.

[53]MMM, House of Lords, MD&HB Bill (1867), evidence of Edward Thompson, q 1767.

[54]See for example, MMM, Liverpool Docks Bill (1855), evidence of Harold Littledale, 160-162.

[55]MMM, MD&HB/Leg/A/7/25.

[56]*Gore's Advertiser*, 24 November 1864.

[57]MMM, House of Commons, MD&HB Bill No. 1 (1873), evidence of Thomas Hornby, q. 1716.

William Lamport claimed that "individual members of the Board have worried me out of my life to go to Birkenhead." Corn merchant Henry Tunnicliffe felt he had been blackmailed into taking some warehouse accommodation in Birkenhead because only then would the Board also give him some space on the Liverpool side.[58]

Such tensions became more pronounced in the 1860s when the pressure for dock accommodation in Liverpool grew dramatically. With no prospect of new docks in Liverpool, thanks to the success of Birkenhead's voice in Parliament, traders recognised that they were competing for shares of a finite system, rather than the expanding dock estate of the 1840s and 1850s. As a result, they began to fight among themselves. This was perhaps the most invidious effect of the Birkenhead issue: it drove divisions between groups of traders who had no particular interest in the Birkenhead docks. Shipowners and merchants desperate for dock space began to suggest that particular trades should be moved to Birkenhead. When some merchants in the Australia trade conceded that their business could in principle be managed from Birkenhead, the Liverpool Shipowners Association pounced. Writing to the Dock Board, the Association urged that the trade's berths in Liverpool should immediately be taken away and reassigned "to those who so urgently require and prefer accommodation on the Liverpool side."[59]

While it helped create a climate in which Liverpool's traders fought among themselves, the Birkenhead question became a less tendentious issue in the later 1860s because the Board's considerable investment in the Cheshire docks could not reasonably be denied. Even the manufacturing interests of East Lancashire and Yorkshire began to support the Dock Board's plans, recognising that an efficient port of Liverpool was in their interests.[60] This was, of course, only a brief truce before they changed their minds and agitated for the Manchester Ship Canal, but it is clear that they no longer saw Birkenhead as a useful stick with which to beat Liverpool. John Laird's death in 1874 was another important milestone, and while others continued to accuse the Board of neglecting

---

[58]MMM, House of Commons, MD&HB Bill (1867), evidence of W.J. Lamport, q. 1406; evidence of Henry Tunnicliffe, q. 1831.

[59]MMM, MD&HB Discl/1, 2, Shipowners Association to MD&HB, 3 July 1867.

[60]MMM, MD&HB Disc/1/1, 27, list of supporters of 1867 Bill.

the Cheshire side, no one could muster the same combination of local and Parliamentary influence. Despite his claims to the contrary, Laird was always recognised as the dominant force among the four nominated members of the Board.[61]

The collateral damage from the Birkenhead question, however, was felt for years. By the time major dock building in Liverpool began to be approved again by Parliament in the 1870s, the port had to catch up with almost two decades of expanding and diversifying trade. More important, though, is the culture of conflict that the Birkenhead issue helped create. As will be seen, this was further exacerbated by the arrival on the scene of the new, powerful steamship lobby.

The New Elite: The Rise of the Steamship Owners

Sharply rising steam traffic in a period of stalled dock building was bound to create a vociferous new lobby within the Liverpool trading community. Steamship owners felt particularly aggrieved by the lack of new docks on the Liverpool side of the river during the 1860s, arguing that Birkenhead was even less suitable for them than for the sailing trades.

There is good evidence to support the steamship owners' case. Liners handling passengers and consignments of cargo operated in a quantifiably different mercantile framework from sailing ships carrying bulk goods. Handling a large number of small cargo consignments made steam operations more complex than sail, which generally handled a small number of large consignments. In 1863, the median number of merchants listed as consignees for sailing ships arriving in Liverpool was four, while the figure for steamers was twenty-nine.[62] In other words, steam voyages required significantly more interaction within the trading community and steamship agents had to be at the hub of complex networks of merchants, passengers and inland transport systems. The implications for business structures and management are significant, but for the purposes of this essay, the most important point is that steam operators could legitimately argue that they had to be based as close as possible to the physical focus of Liverpool's trading infrastructure and networks.

---

[61]See statements by G.H. Fletcher to the Manchester Chamber of Commerce, *Manchester Guardian*, 10 June 1871; and Laird's obituary in *The Times*, 30 October 1874.

[62]Calculated from Liverpool *Customs Bills of Entry*, 1863.

Such requirements made steam a belligerent interest group, increasingly likely to take a hostile attitude to other port users. Liverpool's town centre docks were heavily used by sail, as they had been since they were built in the eighteenth century. They were also, of course, ideally situated at the hub of the landward infrastructure so necessary for steam operations. In addition, coastal steamers worked in competition with railways on some routes and had an equally valid, if rather different reason, to demand central dock facilities. Either way, while sail trades could and did claim greater priority over each other because of the value of goods handled, steam companies injected a new dimension, claiming that their operational requirements were inherently different and deserving of special attention. At a meeting in 1858, leading steam operators resolved to lobby the port authorities for exclusive accommodation in Liverpool's North Docks, but argued that they should be no further north than the new Canada Dock. The implication was clear: sail traffic would have to be moved to the margins and the city centre docks modernised to make way for steam in the heart of the system.[63]

The rise of steam therefore brought as large a shift in the factional profile of the trading community as it did in any technological or economic sense. It created an interest based on the type of shipping used, although there was no unified sail lobby. In the longer term, of course, steam became divided into different commodity trades and between liners and tramps, but in the crucial mid-century period it was a powerful, united group, predisposed to disputes with older users of the port.

Like much else in an age fascinated with statistics, the disputes over steam accommodation became a battle for information. It was no secret in mid-century Liverpool that some parts of the dock estate worked more tonnage or made appreciably more money than others. Particular trades often tried to exploit such numbers for their own ends, and successive Parliamentary Committees were regaled with figures from members of the trading community keen to demonstrate how important their traffic was. In 1855, a representative of the American Chamber of Commerce painted a glowing picture of how American traders in

---

[63]MMM, Leg/A/22/22, account of a meeting of the steam trade, 11 October 1858.

Waterloo (1834) worked three times the tonnage per acre handled in King's (1788) or Queen's (1786, extended 1816).[64]

Such figures could be concocted by any trade given an appropriate spin and a willingness to neglect inconvenient facts. The American trader just mentioned, for example, forgot to add that other docks handling the US trades had earnings well below those of Waterloo. Most trades had peculiarities that made comparisons difficult. The timber trade pointed to the high density of its unloading practices; being able to unload from the front rather than over the side meant that timber achieved a uniquely high tonnage to quay length ratio. In the autumn of 1863, with timber imports at their annual peak, it was claimed that 1155 tons of timber were being handled every day in Canada Dock. This, argued timber's representative, would compare well against figures for the steam trade.[65]

The steam trade naturally disagreed, but by this point the Board realised that it would be opening a Pandora's box by debating statistics with particular interests in the port. The Board refused a series of requests from the Steamship Owners Association in the early 1860s for statistics that would reveal the relative contribution of sail and steam to port revenue.[66] Moving beyond the needs of propaganda and into the domain of management, it rapidly became clear to the Board that breaking the system's earnings down by trades was a futile and self-defeating exercise.

The disparity in revenue across the dock system was indeed considerable, but this did not necessarily mean that some docks were working less efficiently. Some parts of the dock estate, like graving dock entrance basins, only existed to service others, and the fact that they earned any income at all on shipping and cargo was a bonus. It was also true that the system worked as a whole in some ways. Even the steam magnates accepted that they could not operate without sailing ships. Five hundred coastal colliers supplied Cunard's liners with South Wales coal every year in the mid-1850s.[67] Cunard's David MacIver cited that figure on a number of occasions to underline the scale of his firm's operations,

---

[64]MMM, Liverpool Docks Bill (1855), evidence of William Barber, 20 April 1855, 150-154.

[65]MMM, D/SS/1/1, 135.

[66]See, for example, MMM, D/SS/1/1, 101.

[67]MMM, Birkenhead Docks Bill (1856), evidence of Charles MacIver, 351.

but it stood equally well as a reminder to the Board that pitting sail against steam was unlikely to yield a coherent port management strategy.

If steam's attitude to the Board remained tense over operational issues, it was further complicated by the sense of collective responsibility felt by the trading community toward the Board. Individual trades were reluctant to criticise the Board, and this encouraged their existing tendency to attack one another instead. The timber trader Hilton Halhead's criticism of Cunard's David MacIver is the clearest expression of this at mid-century and is worth quoting because of the range of subtle points being made. According to Halhead, MacIver had complained that the Board was failing to keep up with expansion in the steam trades, but because

> it was inconvenient or impolitic to say all that he wished against the Board direct, he made the most unjustifiable attack on the timber trade by which he sought to mislead the public as to the true merits of the case, and by imputing to the Board undue partiality to the timber trade induce the conclusion that improper influences were at work, an inference unworthy of Mr. MacIver and alike insulting to the Mersey Docks and Harbour Board and to the timber trade.[68]

It is clear, therefore, that the conflict between steam and sail had two key threads stemming from the genuine differences in their operational requirements. But this was exacerbated by the trading community's attitude toward the Dock Board. Having gained ownership of the port authority through the 1858 reforms, the trading community was restrained in its direct criticisms; obviously, if MacIver were too vocal in his condemnation he would have to explain why his Association routinely approved of the great majority of those elected. An elaborate game was being played, in which various trades accused each other of trying to influence the Board to gain unfair advantages. Even when adopting the well-proven tactic of opposing strategic plans for dock extensions in retaliation for perceived local grievances, the trades were cautious. The Board withdrew its 1863 Private Bill following opposition from the Steamship Owners, but the Association denied that its objection had been

---

[68]MMM, D/SS/1/1, 134, Halhead to Steamship Owners Association, 13 November 1863.

an attack on the Board, claiming instead that it wanted wider questions of steamship tonnage measurement aired in Parliament.[69]

The Board in the end got the worst of both worlds. It had to referee public conflicts between trades that in part were fighting not to appear disloyal to the Board. At the same time, it could not rely on the steamship owners, who were rapidly becoming the best organised and most vocal lobby. The expansion of steam and the rapid growth in the size of steamships guaranteed that the relationship between the steam owners and the Board would be a central element in the management of the port for the rest of the century. That relationship was defined by patterns already visible in the 1860s. In particular, the issue of the steam trade's contribution to the port's revenue became ever more contentious.[70]

Conclusion

The implications of the rise of steam were therefore profound for the port of Liverpool. Steam gave the port's shipowners and merchants far greater control over the traffic using the port than had been the case for half a century. But if the rise of steam made the port of Liverpool rich, it also threatened to make it unmanageable. The steam trade created a new kind of factional interest that was dependent neither on sharp practice in Council elections nor on the landed classes of Cheshire. In contrast to the port authority's earlier opponents, steam symbolised the future rather than the past, and its demands were therefore much harder to counter. The new Dock Board's great tragedy was to be created just as these demands reached an unprecedented level and with a legacy from Birkenhead that forced it to divert crucial resources from its primary mission.

[69]MMM, D/SS/1/1, 116-117.

[70]For the situation late in the century, see A. Jarvis, "The Port of Liverpool and the Shipowners in the Late Nineteenth Century," *The Great Circle*, XVI (1994), 1-22.

"Our Little Company:" The Wilsons and North Eastern Railway Shipping Company Limited, 1906-1935[1]

David J. Starkey and Richard Gorski

Gordon Jackson has identified "the need to connect trains and ships in a sensible manner" as one of the more important factors that conditioned the development and organisation of Britain's ports in the nineteenth century.[2] Some places made this connection with more alacrity than others. While there were ports such as Grimsby and Birkenhead that were purposely built or redeveloped to facilitate the movement of cargo from railway truck to ship's hold as efficiently as possible, there were many instances of port authorities, dock owners and local government institutions adapting existing provisions to accommodate and exploit the arrival of the railway.[3] Yet the response of some ports to the opportunities presented by the new transport mode was decidedly slow, usually as a consequence of political in-fighting between entrenched vested interests. Hull was one of these stragglers. Indeed, such was the intensity of the disputes that engulfed dock construction and railway links that Hull was poorly served in both respects until the mid-1880s – forty years after the opening of the city's

[1]We are grateful to the University of Hull Research Support Fund for financial assistance for the research effort that contributed to this paper. Thanks are also due to Brian Dyson and his staff in the Archives Office, Brynmor Jones Library, University of Hull, for their help as curators of the Wilson Line archive. Neil Ashcroft and Robin Craig offered valuable advice on the business accounts consulted in our research; in acknowledging their help, we claim responsibility for any errors made in the interpretation and presentation of these data.

[2]G. Jackson, "Shipowners and Private Dock Companies: The Case of Hull, 1770-1990," in L.M. Akveld and J.R. Bruijn (eds.), *Shipping Companies and Authorities in the 19th and 20th Centuries: Their Common Interest in the Development of Port Facilities* (Den Haag, 1989), 50.

[3]See Gordon Jackson, "Docks and Railways: An Overview," in Paul Rees (ed.), *Docks, Railways and the Movement of Goods* (Liverpool, 1994), 5-16.

first railway connection – when a consortium of port users promoted the Hull and Barnsley Railway. As Jackson observed, "while many railway companies built ports, Hull appears to have been the only port which built a major railway in self-defence."[4]

A further dimension to the relationship between trains and ships and ports lay in the ownership and operation of steamers by railway companies. Such integration of services was a common and logical feature of Britain's transport provisions from the 1860s, especially in ports where packet services across the English Channel and the North and Irish Seas were based. While Hull did not pioneer such enterprise, in the 1890s the North Eastern Railway Company (NER) began investing in steamship services between Hull and the "near-continental" ports, an interest that developed significantly in 1906 with the incorporation of the Wilsons and North Eastern Railway Shipping Company Limited (WNERSC). Jointly promoted with Thos. Wilson Sons and Co. Ltd. (TWSC), this was an unusual form of railway steamship enterprise in which shipping expertise and railway capital were combined in a mutually-beneficial alliance.

The WNERSC was a modest venture. Often referred to by Oswald Sanderson, chairman from its birth until his death in 1926, as "our little company," the firm operated independently until 1935, experiencing many of the crises and rewards that marked British shipping during this era.[5] In examining this company we focus on three facets of its development. First, we consider why it was established and why it took the form it did. Second, its earnings, expenses and profits are assessed. And, third, we seek to identify the principal factors that conditioned the fortunes of the WNERSC during the thirty years it operated as an independent concern. It is intended that the analysis will shed light not only on railway steamship enterprise, a subject largely neglected by transport historians, but also on some of the opportunities and operational problems that confronted shipowners in Britain's home trades in the first third of the twentieth century.

---

[4]G. Jackson, "The Ports," in M.J. Freeman and D.H. Aldcroft (eds.), *Transport in Victorian Britain* (Manchester, 1988), 226.

[5]For examples, see University of Hull, Brynmor Jones Library (BJL), DEW (2) 41/48, Oswald Sanderson to Sir Ralph Wedgwood, 3 November 1923; and DEW (2) 41/50, Sanderson to Sir John Ellerman, 9 December 1926.

"A Purely Shipping Concern"

The WNERSC was the product of a union between TWSC, Hull's leading shipping firm, and the pre-eminent railway enterprise north of the Humber, the NER. When it formally commenced in 1906, this collaboration must have seemed odd to those old enough to have witnessed the discord that had impaired the physical and commercial development of the port of Hull over the preceding forty years. The TWSC and the NER were two of the chief protagonists in the long and frustrating battle over port improvements. As the city's shipowners and merchants, led by the Wilsons, demanded better docks, improved communications with the interior and reduced rail rates and dock dues, the NER was condemned for diverting traffic from Hull to West Hartlepool, where the under-utilised port facilities were owned by the monopolistic railway company. So deep was the rift over this issue that in 1870 Charles Wilson, one of the principals of TWSC, invested £20,000 in an unsuccessful attempt to launch the Hull and South West Junction Railway Company.[6] A decade later, the Wilsons were instrumental in forming the Hull and Barnsley Railway, which in 1885 linked the South Yorkshire coalfield to the Alexandra Dock, its new deepwater facility at Hull. At long last, Hull's shipping interest had broken the entrenched monopolies of the Hull Dock Company and the NER.[7]

From the early 1890s, a number of factors encouraged TWSC and the NER to forget past grievances. In 1893, the railway absorbed Hull Dock Company and so acquired a major dock estate that had grown fitfully over the previous 120 years under the stewardship of a private owner more concerned to pay dividends than provide a public utility. Now possessing a much greater stake in Hull, the NER sought to improve traffic flows to, through and from its docks. Accordingly, whereas it had spent just £1.76m on Hull between 1854 and 1892, the NER invested more than £4m over the next twenty years, much of it on a collaborative undertaking with the Hull and Barnsley to build a massive, deepwater "Joint Dock," which eventually opened as King George Dock in 1914. With the spirit of co-operation now abroad in the city, the railway

---

[6]R.J. Irving, *The North Eastern Railway Company 1870-1914: An Economic History* (Leicester, 1976), 120.

[7]See Jackson, "Shipowners and Private Dock Companies."

company began to invest in Hull's steam shipping to entice cargoes to its docks via its railway network.[8]

An important stimulus to such investment arose from the competition offered by Grimsby and Goole. Though neither rivalled Hull in the Baltic, Mediterranean and transoceanic routes, these rival Humber ports were extremely competitive in trades with Europe between the Elbe and Brest, the so-called "home trades." Indeed, during the late nineteenth century, Hull was increasingly eclipsed by its Humber rivals in the carriage of general cargo, coal and passengers on these short-sea routes. In this competitive environment, one important advantage that Grimsby and Goole held was the high degree of integration of ownership and operations that existed between land and water modes of transport in both ports. While the docks and port facilities at Grimsby had been built as the eastern terminus of its rail network, the Manchester, Sheffield and Lincolnshire Railway (MSL) extended its interests in 1864 when it commenced operating its own steamers from Grimsby, co-ordinating their departures with the arrival of passenger and goods trains from London, Liverpool, Manchester, Sheffield, Leeds and Huddersfield.[9] Likewise, the port of Goole, though established by the Aire and Calder Navigation Company in the 1820s, was largely developed by the Lancashire and Yorkshire Railway (L&Y), which also engaged in steamship enterprise as principal shareholder in, and ultimately sole proprietor of, the Goole Steam Shipping Company.[10]

The NER's response to this situation was to seek to bolster Hull's home trades by emulating its rivals and investing in steamship enterprise. This move was made in two stages. First, in 1894 the NER coaxed the two remaining firms in Hull's struggling Dutch trade, C.L. Ringrose and W.H. Hutchinson, to amalgamate to form the Hull and Netherlands Steam

---

[8]Irving, *North Eastern Railway*, 169.

[9]George Dow, *Great Central, Volume 2: Dominion of Watkin, 1864-1899* (London, 1962), 156. The Manchester, Sheffield and Lincolnshire Railway in 1898 became part of the Great Central Railway (GCR), which was itself absorbed into the London and North Eastern Railway (LNER) in 1922.

[10]Baron F. Duckham, "Railway Steamship Enterprise: The Lancashire and Yorkshire Railway's East Coast Fleet 1904-14," *Business History*, X (1968), 44-57. The Lancashire and Yorkshire Railway was absorbed into the London Midland and Scottish Railway (LMS) in 1922.

Shipping Company. Purchasing a majority shareholding, and then in 1900 acquiring Parliamentary approval to run the new company, the NER proceeded to subscribe at least £180,000 to the Hull and Netherlands before the First World War.[11] The second step was taken in 1905 when the NER and TWSC joined forces to found the WNERSC. To some extent, this was precipitated by the difficulties the TWSC was encountering in its near-continental trades. Like Hull's Dutch interests a decade earlier, TWSC's French, Belgian and German trades were suffering at the hands of railway-supported competitors in Grimsby, Goole and Manchester. The NER therefore intervened to support the shipping concern as a means of retaining the rail and dock traffic that it generated.[12]

The shipping company's records confirm that the firm's home trades were far from the most lucrative branch of its business. In 1904, for instance, TWSC steamers made 361 sailings to Antwerp, Ghent, Hamburg and Dunkirk, twenty-seven percent of the 1339 voyages undertaken by the company that year, but these routes yielded just £5307, a mere 5.7% of the firm's annual voyage balance of £93,848.[13] But TWSC was far from a passive agent, a point implicit in the assertion of H.S. Holden, a director of the WNERSC, that the Wilsons had reacted positively to the challenge posed by the steamers of the joint-stock railway companies:

> the original reason for throwing the old Wilson Line trades to the Continental ports into a separate company...was because...(First) Lord Nunburnholme and...Arthur Wilson felt that Wilsons as a private company were unfairly handicapped by having to fight the services owned by the GCR from Grimsby and the L&Y from Goole.[14]

More explicit was TWSC's response to the NER's efforts to gain Parliamentary approval for its own steamship services in the home trades.

---

[11]Irving, *North Eastern Railway,* 232-233.

[12]*Ibid.*, 172-173.

[13]BJL, DEW (2) 3/126, Summary of Trade Results, 1903-1904.

[14]BJL, DEW (2) 41/88, H.S. Holden to Wedgwood, 12 January 1931.

No stranger to protecting its interests against railway encroachment, as its successful opposition to the MSL's plans to enter the Grimsby-Gothenburg trade had demonstrated in 1891, TWSC gave notice that it would object to the passage of the North Eastern Railway (Steam Vessels) Act unless the railway company agreed to refrain from establishing services to near-continental ports.[15] A compromise was reached before the Bill went to Parliament, and it was on the basis of the ensuing formal agreement, signed on 3 November 1905, that the WNERSC was born.[16]

At this time, it was widely believed that railway companies were prepared to run their steamship services at a loss, as the provision of an overseas connection attracted sufficient traffic to more than make up any deficit on sea freights. This was a source of unease to railway customers and shipowners alike. At a Parliamentary Enquiry into the matter in 1911, witnesses complained that "when railway companies get possession of a line of steamers they sacrificed their steamers," thereby running independent shipowners "off the road" to leave the way clear for the integrated concern to charge excessive through rates.[17] While such contentions were disputed by railway managers, to H.S. Holden it was an "obvious fact that certain railway owned shipping services are run (and...naturally so) more with the idea of benefitting rails rather than ships."[18] This judgement was largely based on the character of railway steamship enterprise in the Humber ports. Since 1864, the MSL/GCR's wholly-owned fleet of steamers had worked as an integral facet of a rail-oriented transport network.[19] Likewise, the L&Y's takeover of the Goole Steam Shipping Company, a firm that continued to return profits under

---

[15]Dow, *Great Central,* 157-158.

[16]Great Britain, Parliament, *British Parliamentary Papers* (*BPP*), 1911, XXIX (2), q. 1835, Departmental Committee on Railway Agreements and Amalgamations (Departmental Committee); and BJL, DEW (2) 4/60.

[17]*BPP*, Departmental Committee.

[18]BJL, DEW (2) 41/88, Holden to Wedgwood, 12 January 1931.

[19]See Dow, *Great Central*; and Gordon Jackson, "Do Docks Make Trade?: The Case of the Port of Great Grimsby," in Lewis R. Fischer (ed.), *From Wheelhouse to Counting House: Essays in Maritime Business History in Honour of Professor Peter Neville Davies* (St. John's, 1992),17-42.

railway ownership, and the NER's rescue of Hull's Dutch services, which remained a loss-maker, were essentially designed to maintain outlets for traffic carried by rail.[20] The WNERSC, however, did not conform to either model. It had been founded by partners eager to counter the competition on land and sea of the GCR and the L&Y, whose services "were obviously run more from a rail point of view than that of shipping." As a partnership in which the NER's capital was deployed to buttress a branch of TWSC's business, thereby indirectly benefiting rails, "the peculiar position of the Wilson and North Eastern undertaking as a purely shipping concern" was well understood by both parties.[21]

As far as the NER was concerned, investment in the new company, which was to be administered by experienced, professional shipowners, promised to improve its competitive position in relation to rival railway services at Grimsby and Goole at a time when the L&Y and the Hull and Barnsley were seeking to extend their shipping interests at Hull.[22] From TWSC's perspective, this joint initiative was a means by which external capital could be injected into a struggling facet of its business without surrendering any control over the more important and profitable lines. A convenient device for both partners, the WNERSC emerged into the commercial world of Edwardian Hull as a distinctive form of railway steamship enterprise.

The "Wilson Amalgamation Agreement Company"

The WNERSC was a "private company limited by shares" with an initial paid-up capital of £100,000 - extended in 1907 to £165,000 - divided into £100 shares, with TWSC and the NER the major investors. From 1907, each firm owned 821 shares, with four belonging to TWSC directors and four being purchased by "railway directors." Reflecting the symmetry of shareholding, the Board of Directors of the WNERSC comprised equal numbers of Wilson and railway representatives. Initially, two were

---

[20]Duckham, "Railway Steamship Enterprise;" and Irving, *North Eastern Railway*, 232-233.

[21]BJL, DEW (2) 41/88, Holden to Wedgwood, 12 January 1931.

[22]Though both the L&Y and the Hull and Barnsley received Parliamentary approval to operate steamer services from Hull, neither developed this to any extent.

nominated by each partner - Oswald Sanderson (chair) and E.K. Wilson from TWSC, and William Gray and Alexander Kaye Butterworth from the NER - the number rising to three by 1910 when the second Lord Nunburnholme and Sir Hugh Bell joined the Board. Despite changes in personnel, and in the ownership of the two corporate shareholders, this equitable structure remained in place until the WNERSC became part of Associated Humber Lines in 1935.[23]

The NER, though an equal partner in terms of shareholding and directorships, played no part in the day-to-day running of the WNERSC, which was entirely undertaken by TWSC in line with an agreement signed by the two parent firms on 20 March 1906.[24] By this contract, TWSC was appointed the loading and forwarding agent, as well as manager and ships' husband of the new company at rates of £5 percent of gross sea freights and passenger fares; £150 for each vessel; and £1500 per year towards the costs of management. In addition, the WNERSC paid for the supplies and services provided by TWSC's administrative and cargo-handling departments. Such charges were carefully audited under three headings: printing, stationery, advertising, telegrams, telephones and postage; stevedores' superintendence, inward and outward foremen's wages, detectives, etc.; and stevedores' stores, repairs and renewals of gear. While some expenses were incurred in goods and labour deployed solely for the WNERSC, many were calculated on a proportionate basis, according to the consumption by WNERSC of supplies and services used in common with TWSC. In 1926, for instance, the auditors reported that the equivalent of thirty-five of TWSC's 250 administrative staff worked full-time on the business of the "Home Trades Company." The salary costs of these workers, together with an apportionment of the expense of office accommodation and allowances for the use of equipment - down to minutiae like the wear and tear on seven typewriters and "pens, ink, blotting paper, pencils, india-rubbers, typewriter supplies etc. issued to the staff engaged in connection with the Home Trades steamers (estimated

---

[23]BJL, DEW (2) 41/2, Company Act Returns, 1906-1934. While TWSC was purchased by Ellerman Lines in 1916 and operated thereafter as Ellerman's Wilson Line, the NER was absorbed into the LNER in 1922.

[24]BJL, DEW (2) 41/89, Agreements.

at the rate of 1s. per week per man)" – amounted to a management charge on the WNERSC of £10,995.[25]

Table 1
Voyages by Destination, 1906-1935

Year	Ham-burg	Ant-werp	Ghent	Dun-kirk	Ant-werp/ Ghent	Dunkirk/ Antwerp/ Ghent	Total
1906	145.5	150	73	51	-	-	419.5
1907	137.5	155	93	54	-	-	439.5
1908	105.5	125	66	53	-	-	349.5
1909	103.5	109	68.5	51	-	-	332
1910	103	104	67	51	-	-	325
1911	104.5	101	63.5	48	-	-	317
1912	114.5	106.5	70	53	-	-	344
1913	111	127	69	52	-	-	359
1914	61	61	34	43	-	-	199
1915	-	-	-	64	-	-	64
1916	-	-	-	86	-	-	86
1917	-	-	-	70	-	-	70
1918	-	-	-	47	-	-	47
1919	2	-	-	54	54	0	110
1920	24	-	-	42	79	-	145
1921	59	0	0	37	84	-	180
1922	52	0	0	34	87	0	173
1923	46	-	-	30	86	0	162
1924	61	-	-	-	-	108.5	169.5
1925	52	-	-	-	-	99.5	151.5
1926	59.5	-	-	-	-	107.5	167
1927	52	-	-	-	-	110	162
1928	52	-	-	-	-	103	155
1929	53	-	-	-	-	118.5	171.5
1930	51	-	-	-	-	129	180
1931	52	-	-	-	-	115	167
1932	52	-	-	-	-	103.5	155.5
1933	52	-	-	-	-	101	153
1934	53	-	-	-	-	103	156
1935	22	-	-	-	-	45	67

Notes: Dunkirk includes four voyages to Dieppe in 1917; thirty-two voyages to Dieppe in 1918; and fifty-four voyages to both Dunkirk and Dieppe in 1919.

Source: University of Hull, Brynmor Jones Library (BJL), DEW(2) 41/21-61, Trade Analyses, Wilsons and North Eastern Railway Shipping Co. Ltd.

[25]BJL, DEW (2) 41/52, Audit of Managerial Services, 1926.

Year	Outward General	Outward Coal	Outward Horses	Outward Passage	Homeward General	Homeward Animals	Homeward Passage	Voyage Earnings
	Voyage Earnings by Cargo Type (£ Rounded)							
1906	73931	-	-	778	51853	-	532	124021
1907	55228	37250	-	705	56109	-	505	142378
1908	46339	28423	4902	713	48686	0	445	124653
1909	50447	19470	5537	669	48723	0	485	122763
1910	51508	17315	6830	633	47974	0	483	121482
1911	57633	15227	6849	551	48212	0	450	125303
1912	74735	15289	7282	563	58061	0	435	153739
1913	67136	21530	8156	703	71651	0	586	164750
1914	30787	12950	4280	270	35645	-	263	82123
1915	39509	12072	-	-	6746	-	-	59442
1916	122164	15556	-	-	13863	-	-	154716
1917	154917	2501	0	0	2570	-	-	163153
1918	126037	3011	-	-	2804	-	-	136321
1919	228367	-	2551	494	35034	-	309	271841
1920	203679	1814	26408	918	107289	-	387	340216
1921	85693	259	20629	1043	87539	-	427	195946
1922	67170	8085	4649	997	72395	-	608	150339
1923	56506	15725	2971	491	63146	-	331	137832
1924	54407	6741	3015	528	77974	-	295	138183
1925	48618	4273	831	480	60091	-	280	116016
1926	41340	1833	445	458	83264	-	262	125949
1927	37208	2288	559	417	79716	-	238	117523
1928	36057	3830	630	508	62629	-	422	105139
1929	41880	8454	224	470	68574	-	345	120122
1930	37057	8409	288	527	57087	527	355	103548
1931	32185	5030	237	389	76581	697	331	114857
1932	30091	4227	132	342	51424	168	247	92270
1933	34078	4261	84	368	40092	62	332	85593
1934	33162	4823	12	419	39814	5	249	87170
1935	15502	2180	3	68	13752	3	42	36588

Note: Some receipts excluded.

Source: See table 1.

The Articles of Association of the WNERSC specified two "objects for which the Company is established." The first was "to purchase, or otherwise acquire the...several steamships registered at the Port of Hull and known respectively as *Juno, Bruno, Cito, Otto, Truro* and *Dynamo*...and take over as a going concern the trades or business in which the said steamships are now employed." According to its second objective, the firm was "to employ in the conveyance of passengers...and merchandise of all kinds between the port of Kingston-upon-Hull and the continental ports of Antwerp, Ghent, Hamburg and Dunkirk, or between such other ports as may seem expedient, the ships of the Company or under charter to the Company." In short, the "Wilson amalgamation agreement company," as one of the witnesses at the 1911 Enquiry into Railway Agreements dubbed the firm, was created to take over the vessels and goodwill deployed by TWSC in the home trades.[26]

In thirty years of independent operation, the WNERSC was to deviate little from these two founding objectives. Its initial fleet comprised six of the smaller TWSC vessels, the steamers ranging in size from *Dynamo*, of 504 gross registered tons (grt), to the 905-grt *Juno*. By the spring of 1907, the fleet had been augmented by the transfer of the 775-grt *Hero* from TWSC and the purchase of the newly-built *Hull* (1112 grt) and *York* (1133 grt). Though there were further changes in its composition, with *Bruno* and *Dynamo* being replaced by *Darlington* and *Harrogate*, the firm's shipping stock remained at nine vessels between 1907 and 1914. This was the fleet's greatest extent, as the attrition suffered during the First World War was never fully replenished. As a result, the WNERSC ran six steamers during most of the postwar years, the fleet transferred to Associated Humber Lines in 1935 extending to just four vessels.

The accounts and reports prepared by the "book-keepers engaged entirely on Home Trades accounts" offer a comprehensive view of the performance of this "purely shipping concern."[27] In line with its stipulated aim, the firm largely engaged in Hull's home trades, though it also deployed steamers in the seasonal potato trade from Jersey and St. Malo. As table 1 shows, Hamburg and Antwerp, and to a lesser extent Ghent and Dunkirk, were the foci of the WNERSC's operations, although over time

---

[26]*BPP*, Departmental Committee, q. 8107, evidence of John W. Sissons; and BJL, DEW (2) 41/1, Memorandum of Articles of Association.

[27]BJL, DEW (2) 41/52, Audit of Managerial Services, 1926.

there were variations in the scale and direction of its business. While the voyages undertaken were roughly twice as great before 1914 as between 1921 and 1934, the cessation of sailings to Hamburg and the Belgian ports between 1915 and 1918 was the most striking fluctuation evident in the WNERSC's sailing record.

Details of income and expenses from the 5976.5 voyages completed in the company's core business were collated in annual trade analyses by WNERSC staff. Voyage earnings rose unspectacularly and unevenly to £165,000 in 1913 (see table 2). After falling precipitously to under £60,000 over the next two years, a dramatic reversal in fortunes led to an increase to over £340,000 in 1920. Thereafter, the trend was downward to £137,832 in 1923, £103,548 in 1930 and £87,170 in 1934, the last full year in which the WNERSC operated as a single entity. General cargo, a category embracing such disparate items as fruit, vegetables, weapons, machinery, timber, textiles and breakfast goods, was the mainstay of the firm's business, especially in the homeward trade.[28] Outward from Hull the carriage of coal generated substantial earnings before 1917, while the carriage of people and horses provided a supplementary revenue stream in all except the 1915-1918 period.

Some twenty or so items of debit appear in the WNERSC's trade analyses. When aggregated into ten coherent groupings, the labour of seafarers (the bulk of "captains' disbursements"), port costs, and bunker coal emerge as the largest of the voyage expenses. Set against earnings (table 3), these costs flowed in broadly similar directions between 1906 and 1935. Accordingly, each category remained more or less stable as a percentage of voyage earnings down to 1915, when a sharp and substantial decline was apparent across the board. This period of falling relative costs was short-lived, however, as all three areas of cost trended upward from 1920, with captains' disbursements and port costs exceeding pre-1915 levels from the mid-1920s. Of course, voyage balances, the surplus of earnings over expenses, moved conversely, accounting for at least forty-nine percent of earnings in each year from 1915 to 1920, before declining to less than one percent in the trough year of 1930.

---

[28]BJL, DEW (2) 41/21-61, Trade Reports, 1906-1935.

Table 3
Principal Voyage Expenses, 1906-1935

	Captains' Disbursements		Port Costs		Bunkers		Voyage Balances		Total Net Earnings
	£	%	£	%	£	%	£	%	£
1906	11624	9.4	62818	50.7	14726	11.9	11702	9.4	124021
1907	14893	10.5	68256	47.9	19061	13.4	12881	9.0	142378
1908	14855	11.9	51904	41.6	16488	13.2	21500	17.2	124653
1909	14875	12.1	49946	40.7	14222	11.6	26057	21.2	122763
1910	14432	11.9	47908	39.4	14592	12.0	25636	21.1	121482
1911	14984	12.0	51476	41.1	14519	11.6	24354	19.4	125303
1912	17845	11.6	58082	37.8	19617	12.8	35802	23.3	153739
1913	20229	12.3	62811	38.1	21400	13.0	36397	22.1	164750
1914	11963	14.6	32252	39.3	11926	14.5	13576	16.5	82123
1915	7015	11.8	11467	19.3	4284	7.2	29386	49.4	59442
1916	16124	10.4	20562	13.3	7860	5.1	93144	60.2	154716
1917	-	-	-	-	-	-	101372	62.1	163153
1918	11607	8.5	18060	13.2	6491	4.8	82145	60.3	136321
1919	26666	9.8	44545	16.4	19534	7.2	147427	54.2	271841
1920	35575	10.5	58441	17.3	28752	8.5	174880	51.9	337207
1921	33014	16.8	59039	30.1	29281	14.9	47375	24.2	195946
1922	28525	19.0	50835	33.8	18434	12.3	28455	18.9	150339
1923	22414	16.3	49828	36.2	18185	13.2	26035	18.9	137832
1924	23539	17.0	59841	43.3	17977	13.0	14701	10.6	138183
1925	22526	19.4	50903	43.9	13418	11.6	10765	9.3	116016
1926	22949	18.2	54791	43.5	22613	18.0	4787	3.8	125949
1927	21597	18.4	51850	44.1	12458	10.6	11760	10.0	117523
1928	21296	20.3	48750	46.4	10474	10.0	7806	7.4	105139
1929	21500	17.9	59306	49.4	12254	10.2	8539	7.1	120122
1930	20813	20.1	53553	51.7	11907	11.5	640	0.6	103548
1931	18798	16.4	54891	47.8	10125	8.8	13830	12.0	114857
1932	16233	17.6	42915	46.5	8593	9.3	10897	11.8	92270
1933	15644	18.3	41401	48.4	7831	9.1	7839	9.2	85593
1934	15515	17.8	44033	50.5	8150	9.3	5851	6.7	87170
1935	6599	18.0	18215	49.8	3698	10.1	2719	7.4	36588

Source: See table 1.

Table 4
Voyage Earnings, Expenses and Balances, 1906-1935

	Total Voyages	Voyage Earnings £ per voyage	Voyage Expenses £ per voyage	Voyage Balance £ per voyage
1906	419.5	295.6	267.7	27.9
1907	439.5	324	294.6	29.3
1908	349.5	356.7	295.1	61.5
1909	332	369.8	291.2	78.5
1910	325	373.8	294.9	78.9
1911	317	395.3	318.5	76.8
1912	344	446.9	342.8	104.1
1913	359	458.9	357.5	101.4
1914	199	412.7	344.5	68.2
1915	64	928.89	469.6	459.2
1916	86	1799	716	1083.1
1917	70	2330.8	882.6	1448.2
1918	47	2900.4	1152.7	1747.8
1919	110	2471.3	1131	1340.2
1920	145	2325.6	1119.5	1206.1
1921	180	1088.6	825.4	263.2
1922	173	869	704.5	164.5
1923	162	850.8	690.1	160.7
1924	169.5	815.2	728.5	86.7
1925	151.5	766.1	694.7	71.1
1926	167	754.2	725.5	28.7
1927	162	725.5	652.9	72.6
1928	155	678.3	623	50.4
1929	171.5	700.4	650.6	49.8
1930	180	575.3	571.7	3.6
1931	167	687.8	605	82.8
1932	155.5	593.4	523.3	70.1
1933	153	559.4	508.2	51.2
1934	156	558.8	521.3	37.5
1935	67	562.9	521	41.9

Source: See table 1.

Relating voyage earnings, expenses and balances to the number of voyages provides a slightly different perspective on the WNERSC's performance (see table 4). Income, costs and balances per voyage all increased steadily between 1906 and 1913. A fall in earnings bucked this trend in 1914, but from 1915 to 1920 it resumed with some vigour, as voyage earnings accelerated at a faster rate than expenses to yield extraordinarily large balances. Thereafter, revenues per voyage tended to fall faster than costs, with the smallest balance recorded in 1930.

The WNERSC's trade analyses tend to paint a rosy picture of performance, with income exceeding expenditure in each year. While this would have pleased Mr. Micawber and his disciples, it only amounts to a unidimensional picture of the venture. A fuller, less flattering portrait is revealed in the WNERSC's profit-and-loss accounts. In these appraisals of the company's situation at the end of each year, the voyage balance was just one of many variables considered (see table 5). When this positive balance was enhanced by earnings from rebates, allowances and subsidies, but diminished by management fees, bad debts, apportionments for maintenance, club calls, insurance and sundries, the resulting net trading revenue might be negative, as in 1907, 1914, 1924 and annually from 1926 to 1935. The addition of non-trading revenues - chiefly interest from investments but also surpluses from the Jersey and St. Malo trades - yielded annual figures that were in the black in all years except 1929, 1930, 1933 and 1934. Bringing down the previous year's residue after capital adjustments produced the year-end balance, a figure that can be taken as an indicator of profitability. From this it can be seen in table 5 that the firm's profits rose ten-fold from a low base between 1906 and 1913; dipped dramatically in 1914; and then surged in the 1915-1920 period. A virtually inexorable contraction took place in the 1920s, with a negative balance on each New Year's Eve from 1929 to 1934.

The contours of this financial outline broadly concur with those in the trade analyses, with sharp changes in trend occurring in 1915 and 1921 according to most indicators. Using these dates as breaks in the annual data, we can provide a summary of the firm's performance during its thirty-year lifespan (see table 6). While over half of the company's voyages were undertaken before 1915, just a fifth of the voyage balances and 17.1% of the year-end balances were generated in this period. Similar returns accrued from a smaller number of voyages from 1921 to 1935. However, the most striking feature of the analysis is the fact that the 522 sailings in the six years from 1915 to 1920 yielded over sixty percent of the balances generated in the period as a whole. In each of these three phases, a different mix of factors interacted to fashion the prosperity of the WNERSC.

Table 5
Income and Capital Adjustments, 1906-1935

	Income				Capital Adjustments				
	(1) Net Trading Income	(2) Net Non-Trading Income	(3) AnnualSurplus (Deficit) (1 + 2)	(4) Year-End Balance (3 + 8)	(5) Transfer to Reserves	(6) Dividend £	(6) Dividend (%)	(7) Transfer from Reserves	(8) Balance brought down [4+7]-[5+6]
1906	2418	2036	4454	4454	0	0		0	4454
1907	(696)	4066	3370	7824	3640	0		0	4184
1908	9863	2851	12714	16898	4184	0		0	12714
1909	4503	4434	18937	31650	12714	0		0	18937
1910	14844	3214	18058	36995	10387	7786	(5)	0	18822
1911	12205	(1330)	10875	29697	9600	7769	(5)	0	12329
1912	19757	1932	21689	34018	12066	0		0	21952
1913	21051	3195	24246	46198	13985	7769	(5)	4530	24443
1914	(777)	3450	2673	2716	10695	7769	(5)	4530	13183
1915	41725	8243	49968	63151	21578	0		7560	49134
1916	69771	10760	80531	129665	71828	21450	(15)	0	36388
1917	43998	6964	50962	87350	36618	25575	(20)	0	25157
1918	63094	14073	77167	102324	53676	14850	(12)	0	33799
1919	139270	10259	149529	183328	79179	36053	(30)	0	68087
1920	153487	18010	71497	239584	184923	17325	(15)	0	37335
1921	19014	21493	40507	77842	21098	23100	(20)	0	33645
1922	10931	17470	28401	62046	17693	23100	(20)	0	21253
1923	5285	11380	16665	37918	11000	18253	(15)	0	8665
1924	(25)	9226	9201	17866	5000	0		0	12867
1925	7884	8873	16756	29624	10000	12736	(10)	0	6887
1926	(2714)	9801	7087	13974	8500	6548	(5)	7285	6211
1927	(100)	7493	7393	13604	7600	5940	(4.5)	4000	4064
1928	(3567)	6168	2601	6665	10100	3960	(3)	7500	105
1929	(8284)	5858	(2426)	(2321)	10000	0		12015	(305)
1930	(20807)	5738	(15069)	(15374)	6750	0		10000	(12125)
1931	(2024)	5011	2988	(9137)	11000	0		10000	(10158)
1932	(4169)	5148	979	(9158)	11000	0		10000	(10158)
1933	(6246)	4485	(1761)	(11919)	11000	0		22919	0
1934	(7114)	4857	(2257)	(2257)	11000	0		13257	0
1935	(3743)	5003	1260	1260	6500	0		5951	711

Source: BJL, DEW(2) 41/21-61, Profit and Loss Accounts, WNERSC.

Table 6
Voyages and Balances by Period

	No. of Voyages		Voyage Balances		Year End Balances	
	No.	%	£	%	£	%
1906-14	3084.5	51.6	207905	20	210450	17.1
1915-20	522	8.7	628354	60.5	805402	65.7
1921-35	2370	39.7	201999	19.5	210633	17.2
	59765		1038258		1226485	

Sources: See tables 1 and 5.

"Competition...and Economies in all Directions"[29]

The fortunes of shipping firms are invariably conditioned by a range of general factors outside the direct control of individual enterprises. Chief among these are the broad economic and political forces that determine the volume, character and direction of seaborne trade which explain the demand for shipping. On the supply side, the quality and availability of factors of production, in conjunction with the prevailing shipping technology, further constrain the business. But within such bounds, shipping entrepreneurs can implement policies that can have a critical bearing on the success or otherwise of their undertakings.

Such generalisations are well illustrated by the particular experience of the WNERSC during the first third of the twentieth century. This was a volatile era in which the conjunction of forces that conditioned the performance of the WNERSC, which in turn in many ways epitomised the fortunes of Britain's short-sea shipping interests, was different in each of the three phases identified above. Between 1906 and 1914, demand for the WNERSC's services was generally buoyant. Participating in trades that linked the dynamic industrial regions of France, Germany and Belgium to northern England, the WNERSC and Hull were located at the crux of one of Britain's most substantial trade flows.[30] Nevertheless, the

---

[29]Unless otherwise stated, the evidence presented in this and the following section is drawn from the trade analyses, trade reports and Minutes of Directors' Meetings in BJL, DEW (2) 41/21-61.

[30]Gordon Jackson, *The History and Archaeology of Ports* (Tadworth, 1983), 113.

demand for shipping waned from time to time. In 1908, for instance, decreased tonnages to and from Hamburg were attributed to the "existing trade depression," while the Dunkirk trade was "fairly well maintained but homeward traffic remains scarce due to the trade depression." In the opening months of 1909, poor trading conditions were exacerbated by the "severe winter and the consequent stoppage of inland navigation on the continent," a fate that had befallen the "continental rivers" two years earlier when "the receivers of coals on the continent...were unable to accept deliveries." A further natural hazard to impact on the WNERSC's business was the harvest, with reduced cargoes from Hamburg resulting from the failure of the German beet root and sugar crops in 1912.

Short-term difficulties also arose on the supply side of the WNERSC's business before the war. In 1907, the integrated service that the firm was trying to develop exhibited teething troubles. In his Chairman's Report, Oswald Sanderson referred to delays experienced by his firm's steamers due to "the difficulty of getting coals (which had been booked) placed on board the steamers," even though "our steamers are put to the hoists in preference to outside colliers." According to Sanderson, the problem was caused by "the inability of the North Eastern Railway and its connecting company to get the coal delivered to the hoists," an inefficiency the NER promised to correct. Industrial strife at Hull and the near-continental ports also impinged upon operations.[31] When the Hamburg dock strike brought sailings to a standstill the company, supported by the Shipping Federation, paid for "free labourers" from Hull to break the strike. Moreover, wage increases won by strikers were occasionally cited as increasing operational costs; the victory of Antwerp dockers the same year added an extra £15 per month to the company's costs.

Such problems tended to be passing and incidental in the context of the 1906-1914 shipping market. In contrast, the flaws that surfaced in after the onset of war were deep-seated. With ships and men lost to enemy action, requisitioned by the state, and denied access to belligerents' ports, the supply of shipping fell well short of demand, especially in the short-sea sector. This disequilibrium was reflected in reports presented to WNERSC directors. At Dunkirk, the only regular near-continental port open to the firm, "cargo has offered in larger quantities than we could

---

[31]BJL, DEW (2) 41/9, Directors' Minute Book, 1906-1921.

accommodate [while] delays have been experienced at Dunkirk owing to lack of berths, insufficiency of labour, congestion of quays etc." Even with "all available W&NER steamers (six) running...we do not anticipate any difficulty in obtaining full general cargoes outward, although the restrictions recently imposed on beer will doubtless tend to decrease exports." As WNERSC directors noted, "a large increase in freight rates as a consequence of the war" was apparent, with rates increasing from 18s 3d per ton in January 1915 to an average of 70s 6d in the first six months of 1918.[32] Such conditions persisted after hostilities ceased, the WNERSC exporting "large quantities of machinery for the devastated areas of France," and quickly re-entering the Hamburg trade in November 1919. Indeed, it was not until 1920 that the "abnormal exports to Dunkirk eased off considerably," a loss of impetus reflected in the decline of outward freight rates from 56s 2d to 24s 10d per ton between January 1920 and December 1921.

While such conditions brought short-term benefits to the WNERSC in the form of greatly increased earnings and year-end balances (see table 6), they had less desirable long-term ramifications. Between 1921 and 1935 the short-sea shipping market was generally slack due to excess tonnage and falling freight rates. This was reflected in the annual employment records of the WNERSC steamers, most of which were regularly "laid up due to slackness of trade" after 1920. To compound matters, the difficulties that had appeared incidental in the prewar era assumed almost endemic proportions in the 1920s. Such adverse factors loom large in the reports of WNERSC managers. Reflecting general economic conditions, demand remained weak. For instance, in 1921, it was decided that the construction of *Harrogate* should be postponed "in view of the depressed state of our trade," while in 1928 "conditions generally in the Home Trades continued extraordinarily difficult," a state of affairs that persisted until 1930, when the directors were informed that "owing to the widespread depression, reductions in carryings have taken place in all trades, with the exception of Dunkirk." This had a knock-on effect; as Sir John Ellerman reported to the WNERSC directors in November 1928, "as is usual in times of acute trade depression, when small tonnage is cheap and plentiful, there is more tendency for shippers to charter whenever possible, and this has the effect of depressing liner

---

[32] *Ibid.*

rates of freight." Natural factors further disrupted demand, with misfortunes such as the light growth of Jersey potatoes caused by ill-timed bursts of hot sun, hailstones and drought in 1922, and the small yield of Belgian fruit and root crops in 1925, being advanced to explain fluctuations in tonnage carried. Industrial disputes also damaged business, either by reducing cargo availability and consumer purchasing power or by retarding the supply of shipping resources. Among the many disputes that affected demand, the 1921 coal strike not only diminished exports but also indirectly depressed the carriage of potatoes from Jersey "owing to lack of wages for purchasing, and a dearth of coal for cooking purposes" in the northern mining districts served by Hull. The company was often frustrated by its suppliers. Work stoppages in near-continental ports were especially frequent in the immediate postwar years, with strikes by dockers, pilots and railway workers detaining the company's vessels at Hamburg, Antwerp and Dunkirk at various times. Strikes at home also posed problems. For instance, in 1921 and again in 1926, national coal strikes obliged the firm to purchase bunker coal overseas, while the engineering lock-out of 1920 delayed the refit of *Otto* and the 1923 boilermakers' lock-out retarded construction of *Harrogate*.

Interacting with the market forces to shape the WNERSC's destiny were policies implemented by the company. While its responses to vacillations were varied, its desire to compete and a tendency to err on the side of caution were the most significant facets of its business strategy. This was evident in the 1906-1914 period. Working in a comparatively stable market, the company concentrated on sustaining Hull's presence in the home trades in the face of stiff competition from the railway steamers of Grimsby and Goole. For instance, in 1907, after the L&Y terminated the pooling arrangement it had long maintained with the WNERSC, preferring "that each should canvass & do its best," the volume of fruit carried from Hamburg and Ghent to Hull increased from 136,000 tons in 1906 to 147,000 in 1907, while that conveyed to Goole declined from 186,000 to 112,000 tons. The decisive factor in this favourable result was identified as "the acquisition in the Hamburg trade of the steamers *Hull* and *York* which have...with one exception made faster passages than the *Mersey* and *Irwell* of the Lancashire & Yorkshire Railway Company, which have been deliberately placed against them." Bowing to this pressure, the L&Y agreed to re-establish the "Fruit & Onion Pool" in the Hamburg trade on 1 January 1911, though the net sea freights were to be divided on equally, a victory for the WNERSC, which had only received forty percent of the proceeds under the agreement that had lapsed in 1906.[33]

The judicious deployment of vessels was at the heart of the WNERSC's competitive strategy before the First World War. In 1908, the firm reduced its services from three to two sailings per week to Antwerp and Hamburg. Also trimmed was the Ghent service, which had been run at a loss for the previous two years, "in view of the importance of retaining the trade," as the company, perhaps deciding to follow a shipowning rather than a railway agenda, sought to equate supply with demand.[34] In none of the three trades did this hurt total earnings, largely because the company was deploying relatively large and efficient steamers, which gave it an edge over its Humber rivals. This was demonstrated in a statistical analysis prepared in 1913, on the insistence of Mr. Geddes, a railway director concerned about falling returns from the Antwerp trade. Comparing the home trades of the Humber ports in terms of voyages undertaken, this indicated that in 1912 the Hull steamers conveyed 843 tons of cargo per voyage in the Hamburg trade, while the Goole and Grimsby vessels respectively carried averages of just 625 and 373 tons on each passage.[35]

This is suggestive of the care and attention to detail the WNERSC afforded to its business. In a similar vein, its vessel acquisition policy was measured to the point of being cautious. While *Hull* and *York* were purchased by increasing the capital of the company from £100,000 to £165,000, the newly-built *Darlington* was bought in 1910 for £32,000, which was "practically the reinvestment of the proceeds of the sale of the *Bruno*, and the amount of the Depreciation Fund." Having accumulated reserves to cover depreciation at the rate of six percent per annum on the full cost of its original steamships and five percent per annum on the first cost of new ships, in 1910 the WNERSC felt that:

---

[33]BJL, DEW (2), 2/4, Agreement Relating To Hamburg Pool, 17 July 1911.

[34]Irving, *North Eastern Railway,* 232, implies that the Ghent trade was unprofitable and therefore maintained in the interest of railway traffic. Though the least remunerative of the WNERSC lines, the company's trade analyses indicate that the Ghent trade was profitable from 1909 until its suspension in 1915.

[35]BJL, DEW (2) 41/98. Summary of Hull, Grimsby and Goole home trades, 1909-1912.

> As opportunity offers, it will be desirable to add to the Depreciation Fund as fully as possible, in excess of the rates mentioned above, if necessary keeping the dividend low for that purpose, so that the Board may be quite prepared to replace any unit of the fleet whenever that course may appear desirable.[36]

In the very different circumstances of the 1915-1920 period, the WNERSC was not so obliged to compete with regional rivals, as cargoes were available in some abundance. Rather, the company was confronted with the problem of obtaining the resources to exploit the advantageous conditions that characterised the wartime market. In a sense, therefore, competition was constrained by both the British and German governments, the former seeking to redeploy merchant vessels and seafarers to the war service and the latter intent on damaging such strategically-valuable resources. In the course of these unequal conflicts, the WNERSC suffered losses. While *Hull* was interned in Hamburg for the duration of hostilities, *York*, *Darlington* and *Harrogate* were requisitioned by the Admiralty in the later stages of the war, and *Cito* and *Harrogate* (under naval orders) were sunk by the enemy. On the waterfront, the company faced a delay of three months in 1915 as Dunkirk was "bombarded by a large German gun which caused the population [including its port workers] to flee panic-stricken." Similar problems arose after further bombardments later in the conflict.

Notwithstanding such difficulties, the WNERSC completed 267 voyages during the war years, with another 255 in the postwar boom of 1919-1920. The large windfall profits that accrued were treated with some caution. While substantial dividends were paid, including a thirty percent distribution in 1919, the bulk of earnings were transferred to reserve accounts. As early as November 1914, a provision of £960 was made to cover a possible liability for the wages of *Hull*'s crew after its detention. In addition to the normal depreciation provision, substantial transfers were made in 1916 to the new "Reserve for Taxation, Increased Cost of Vessels, and General Contingencies" and "Investment Fluctuation Reserve." By the end of 1920, a total of £405,773 was held in reserve

---

[36]BJL, DEW (2) 41/29, General Memorandum, 1910.

accounts, with £83,871 earmarked for depreciation, £4902 for investment fluctuations, and £317,000 for taxation and vessel replacement.

With its coffers full but its fleet diminished, the WNERSC entered the changing business environment of the early 1920s. Competition once more became a strong feature of a market in which demand and freight rates were falling and were to remain chronically depressed. But now the competitors in the home trades were not only the familiar rivals from across the Humber but also a variety of new entrants. In this situation, the WNERSC adopted a defensive posture. This entailed collaborating with the railway steamship enterprises of Grimsby and Goole – a policy facilitated by the formation of railway groupings in 1922 which thrust the NER together with the GCR in the LNER – to resist the encroachments of "outside shipowners," chiefly foreign, into the Humber short-sea trades. The main weapons in this resistance were the acquisition of information about the intentions of interlopers and a drastic reduction of rates to ensure that "the opposition does not mature." At the same time, Sir John Ellerman, the chairman from 1926 to 1933, was concerned to counter "competition in all directions of the keenest description" by making "economies in all directions." Cost-cutting exercises were therefore implemented. In the coal supply department, attempts were made in 1927 to reduce fuel expenses by replacing the tried and trusted mix of Dinnington and Glapwell Hards with a combination of Large Coal and Washed Smalls, an experiment that proved highly successful. In contrast, a proposal to reduce insurance premiums by adding the WNERSC to the collective policy that covered the LNER's Grimsby steamers was rejected by the railway company.

In 1917 Ellerman had remarked to his fellow directors that "after the war there would be great changes and that it might become advisable to extend the scope of the Company." But as the 1920s wore on he clearly changed his mind and no semblance of an expansionist policy emerged. Despite the existence of large reserves, the WNERSC attempted neither to diversify into other trades nor to enhance substantially the size and quality of its fleet. In some contrast to the prewar era, when the measured improvement of its capital stock had advanced the company's competitive position in the short-sea trades, the only vessel acquisitions were the return from internment of *Hull*, the 1922 purchase of *Selby*, and the replacement of *Juno* by the second *Harrogate* in 1925. Instead, the WNERSC pursued a conservative operational policy, responding to periodic crises with *ad hoc* expedients. As trading results deteriorated in the late 1920s, the true poverty of the company's performance since the postwar boom was revealed in an internal memo which showed from an income tax point of view that it made a loss on trading, after depreciation but before adding interest earnings, in each year from 1921 to 1930, with the exception of 1922. While dividends for 1921-1927 were paid out of reserves and interest returns, "no dividends were paid for 1928 or 1929 and transfers were made during these years from the capital reserve fund to offset the excess of trading losses over and above the receipts of interest etc."[37]

This seemingly dire situation was exacerbated by two factors. First, reserves had been reduced significantly in 1927 when the directors agreed that a division of half the undivided capital surpluses, amounting to £82,500, should be made to paid-up shareholders in accordance with the 1908 Companies (Consolidation) Act. Second, due to a combination of factors – on top of the deep depression in general trade, the Belgian and German fruit crops failed, and Jersey potatoes had a disastrous season – 1930 turned out to be the worst trading year on record, with the year-end balance showing a deficit of £15,374. In these adverse circumstances, TWSC tried to persuade the LNER to take over the WNERSC, arguing that the "little company" was no longer viable on "purely a shipowner's basis," and that "the whole of the Hull/Continental services, if they are ever to hold their own with Goole and Grimsby, must be entirely railway owned." The railway company, unimpressed with the financial implications of the deal and wary of losing the managerial and administrative expertise of TWSC, politely declined the offer.[38]

Even as the LNER was rebuffing these confidential overtures, another option emerged in the guise of a pooling agreement precipitated by the entry on 1 January 1931 of Nord Deutscher Lloyd (NDL) into the Hull-Bremen and Hull-Hamburg lines. This altered the situation substantially, for the NDL was a firm of "influence and resources" that was intent on putting an end "to the ruinous rate cutting which for some years played havoc in the Humber/Hamburg and Bremen trades." Under the terms of this arrangement, the sea freights earned by the Humber Conference Lines (the WNERSC, LNER and LMS) and NDL were pooled

---

[37]BJL, DEW (2) 41/88.

[38]*Ibid.*, Holden to Wedgwood, 13 January 1931; and Report on Meeting with C.H. Newton, Chief Accountant, LNER, 10 June 1931.

and divided in agreed proportions. This principle was soon extended to a "General Pooling Arrangement" between the three Humber companies that embraced the Hamburg, Antwerp, Ghent and Dunkirk services from Hull, Goole and Grimsby. In turn, the general pool formed the basis of Associated Humber Lines, which began operations on 1 June 1935, a development that the Chairman of the WNERSC welcomed, expressing "the hope that the presentation of a united front in the Short Trades between the Humber ports and the continent would result in material economies being made and improved results being reflected in the Company's accounts." In the mid-1930s, therefore, the firms - and ports - that in an earlier era had competed so vigorously combined their resources in a regional grouping that was to compete in the short-sea market for a further forty years.

"More Tonnage...than Present Circumstances Warrant"

In some ways, this case study suggests that the WNERSC suffered from "entrepreneurial failure," the malady that many authorities believe afflicted British business after the First World War. The company had operated with some comfort in the relatively stable prewar years when demand was buoyant and competition restricted. It had enjoyed an extraordinary surge in revenue during the later years of the First World War and the immediate postwar era as unprecedented demand and restricted supply elevated freight rates to highly advantageous levels. But from 1921, as excess tonnage pervaded the market, the WNERSC was reluctant to invest, innovate or diversify, opting instead to continue operating as it had done before the war and to consume its reserves until the market improved.

But such a judgement is perhaps harsh. In establishing the WNERSC, TWSC and the NER were pursuing distinct, though mutually compatible, aims. The shipping company was not only feeling the pressure of competition in its home trades but also, as a family-based, privately-owned firm, was struggling to stay afloat in a commercial sea increasingly dominated by large-scale predators.[39] From the perspective of the Wilson brothers, and the influential managing director, Oswald Sanderson,

[39]David J. Starkey, "Ownership Structures in the British Shipping Industry: The Case of Hull, 1830-1916," *International Journal of Maritime History*, VIII (1996), 71-95.

combining with the NER was part of a multifaceted strategy to safeguard the independence of TWSC. For its part, the NER was concerned to meld shipping to its rail and port interests in Hull, thereby extending its markets across the sea. A latecomer to this specialist, increasingly competitive market, the NER acquired the ship management and agency expertise of a major, well-established shipowner in return for the capital that TWSC so urgently required. That TWSC survived for a further decade as an independent concern, while the NER added an efficient shipping dimension to its transport network, suggests that the initial objectives of both partners in this marriage of convenience were largely achieved.

The offspring of this union evidently performed satisfactorily down to 1920, maintaining Hull's interests in the short-sea trades and exploiting the profitable opportunities thrown up by the Great War. In the 1920s, the WNERSC, like British shipping in general, found it difficult to "cope with the suddenness of the changes [as] war compressed perhaps forty years of economic evolution into four."[40] Although it responded fairly passively to changing market conditions, returning losses rather than profits with disturbing regularity, the firm's strategy was perhaps appropriate to the economic context in which it now operated. Its guiding lights, after all, were Oswald Sanderson and Sir John Ellerman, two of the most experienced, skilled and successful businessmen of their generation. Having recognised that "purely from a shipowner's point of view...there was more tonnage employed in the Humber/near Continental trades than present circumstances warranted," the principals of the WNERSC were possibly acting rationally in choosing to restrict expenditure and distribute capital.

An account drawn up by the WNERSC is instructive in this respect. Adding the aggregate dividends paid to the two principal shareholders between 1906 and 1927 to the distribution of capital made in 1927, and subtracting the capital originally staked by each partner, produced a bottom line – the figure that most interests businessmen – that was black and read £78,645 11s 10d.

[40]Jackson, *History and Archaeology*, 141.

The Changing Functions of a Rural Port: Dumfries, 1700-1850

Carol Hill

The difficulty of inland communication has long encouraged the proliferation of ports along the Scottish coastline with little to choose between them *before* the expansion and reorientation of trade in the decades following the Restoration. This long period of growth created a new disparity between ports and was linked to the growing specialisation of regional economies.[1] Mineral ports, such as Alloa, Kirkcaldy, Ayr and Irvine, grew rapidly from the mid-eighteenth century, while the bulk of the nation's foreign trade was increasingly channelled through a handful of larger entrepots, notably Port Glasgow and Greenock on the Clyde, and Leith and Bo'ness on the Forth – together accounting for forty-six percent of tonnage entering and fifty-seven percent of tonnage clearing Scottish ports between 1776 and 1780.[2] Such ports benefited from deep-water sites, navigable communication with industrialising hinterlands, extensive commercial networks built from long experience of overseas trade and, in the case of the Clyde, shifts in the direction of trade occasioned by the opening of transatlantic routes. Yet they were atypical: most Scottish ports were considerably smaller and evolved to accommodate the limited requirements of their hinterlands for goods they could not produce, and the ability of local populations to identify and service external markets for the goods they could.

[1]For a detailed analysis of the changing structure and functions of British ports, see G. Jackson, *The History and Archaeology of Ports* (Tadworth, 1983).

[2]This percentage had changed slightly by 1789-1791 to forty-three and forty-seven percent, respectively, reflecting the growth of other western ports, such as Port Patrick, Ayr and Irvine, which were involved in the Irish trade.

In this respect transport, which in Scotland meant shipping - and in small ports predominately coastal shipping - was crucial.[3] It was the means of interchange within and between regions, diffusing imports from overseas and servicing the requirements of hinterlands for access to external markets and distribution centres. In a national and international context, ports and shipping provided infrastructure for an integrated transport system that facilitated and perpetuated the process of regional specialisation underpinning the industrial revolution and the subsequent exploitation of Britain's favourable factor endowment.[4] Yet with only a handful of notable exceptions Scottish ports, trade and shipping have been neglected by historians.[5] In particular, we know almost nothing of the way small ports experienced or contributed to economic change in this era. Dumfries is typical of the many places that were not major ports serving industrial regions but were nonetheless significant cogs in the development of both local and national economies.

This paper examines the role of a small, seemingly unimportant port as the fulcrum for local mercantile activity and the regional link to the wider national economy. In the process, it demonstrates the changing function of the port as agrarian reform and industrialisation got underway and the concomitant change in the nature of shipping within it.

Dumfriesshire lies in the southwest corner of Scotland. A predominantly rural, sparsely populated area, its geography was undoubt-

---

[3]Between 1760 and 1784, coasters averaged sixty-nine percent of entrances and seventy-two percent of clearances in Scottish ports. Their distribution was uneven and, compared with foreign trade, proportionately higher in small ports. See G. Jackson, "Scottish Shipping, 1775-1805," in P.L. Cottrell and D.H. Aldcroft (eds.), *Shipping Trade and Commerce: Essays in Memory of Ralph Davis* (Leicester, 1981), 117-136.

[4]The significance of coastal trade and shipping during the Industrial Revolution is well established. See, for example, J. Armstrong (ed.), *Coastal and Short Sea Shipping* (Aldershot, 1997); Armstrong, "The Significance of Coastal Shipping in British Domestic Transport, 1550-1830," *International Journal of Maritime History*, III, No. 2 (December 1991), 63-94; and Armstrong and P.S. Bagwell, "Coastal Shipping," in J. Armstrong and M. Freeman (eds.), *Transport in The Industrial Revolution* (Manchester, 1983), 142-176.

[5]G. Jackson with K. Kinnear, *The Trade and Shipping of Dundee* (Dundee, 1991); Jackson and S.G.E. Lythe (eds.), *The Port of Montrose* (Tayport, 1993); Jackson, "Scottish Shipping;" and Jackson, "Glasgow in Transition, 1660-1740" and "New Horizons in Trade, 1780-1830," both in T.M. Devine and G. Jackson (eds.), *Glasgow, Volume 1: Beginnings to 1830* (Manchester, 1995), 63-105 and 214-238.

edly a key factor in its development, with the sea to the south, hills to the west and high mountains in the north and east forming natural physical barriers and restricting inland communication. Dumfries, its principal town, lies on the banks of the River Nith, nine miles upriver from the point at which it discharges into the Solway. The town enjoyed a level of prosperity during the medieval and early modern periods largely because of its status as a royal burgh and its function as a port. As a result, it emerged during the eighteenth century as the commercial and administrative capital of southwest Scotland.[6]

For much of its history as an active port, vessels loaded and discharged not at Dumfries, but downriver at Glencaple, Kelton and Kingholm Quay, or near the mouth of the Nith at Carsethorne. This enabled shippers to avoid the difficulties of navigating a river affected by dangerous currents, shifting sandbanks and extreme tidal ranges, all of which led one early commentator to suggest that "the badness of coming into the river upon which [Dumfries] lies hinders its commerce by sea."[7] But early trade was limited even more by the paucity of the hinterland. While merchants were able to generate sufficient profits to encompass cartage rates - over which they had some control - trade was unlikely to have been affected by poor access to the town.[8] Indeed, during the port's "heyday" in the tobacco trade, it mattered little whether merchandise for the colonies was assembled in Dumfries or in the village of Carsethorne, where tobacco was unloaded and warehoused or from whence it was dispatched as long as storage facilities and landing sites were safe, legal and accessible. Only with the re-orientation of the port's function in the late eighteenth century, coterminous with developments in the rural economy and a rise in coastal traffic, might this deficiency have hindered port development or inhibited merchants wishing to bring their goods to the heart of the region's commercial centre.

---

[6]W. McDowall, *The History of Dumfries* (Dumfries, 1867); and J.A. Russell, *The Book of Dumfriesshire* (Dumfries, 1964).

[7]T. Tucker, "Report upon the Settlement of the Revenues of Excise and Customs in Scotland," Scottish Burgh Records Society *Miscellany* (Edinburgh, 1881). The same view was expressed by the authors of "Register Containing the State and Condition of Every Borough Within the Kingdom of Scotland in the Year 1692," *ibid.*

[8]Dumfries Regional Archive (DRA), RG5/5, Petition of the Carters' Residenter in Dumfries, 28 November 1795.

The first dock at Dumfries was laid out on a four-acre site in 1707, when the Burgh Treasurer's Accounts record the first serious attempts to improve navigation by blasting and clearing the river bed, introducing buoys and planting willows to strengthen the banks. Although costs were modest, maintaining the river was beyond local resources, prompting the introduction of tonnage and impost duties in 1737 of one and one half pence per ton on vessels entering from Britain and Ireland, three pence per ton on vessels from foreign parts and eight pence per ton on all goods imported or exported.[9] These charges were intended to defray the cost of future river maintenance. Forty-three pounds were raised during the first complete year, a figure that more than doubled by 1769/1770, and came increasingly from coastal shipping (see figure 1).

Figure 1
Income from Tonnage and Impost Duties, Selected Years, 1769-1801

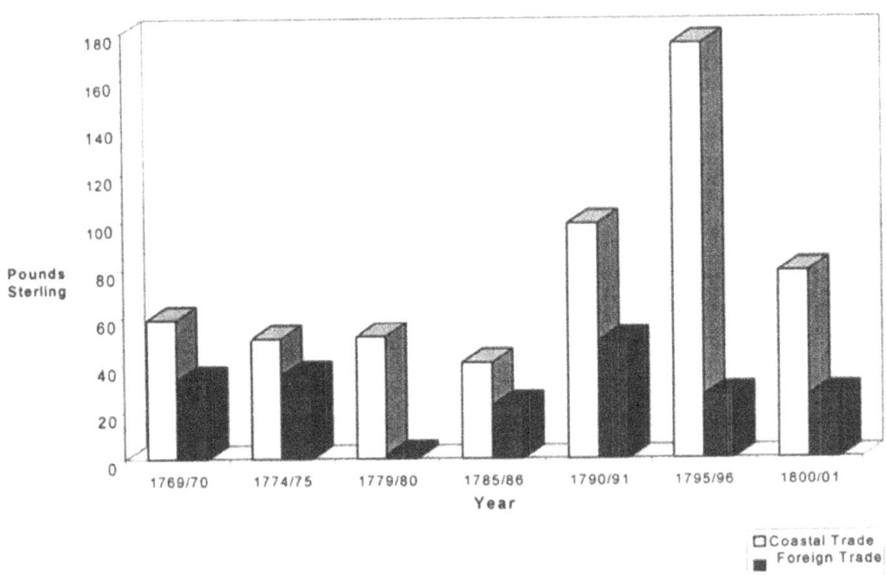

Source: Dumfries Regional Archive (DRA), Series GH1/1, 1-28, Tonnage and Impost 1769-1801.

[9]These duties were tacked onto the Parliamentary Bill renewing the duties on ale, in May 1737.

Unlike many of the "rising ports," which occupied prime positions on the principal estuaries and had good internal communications, Dumfries exemplified the isolated river port situated too far from the sea to become a major port. Throughout the eighteenth and early nineteenth centuries, the authorities fought a losing battle to maintain the channel, a struggle which owed as much to the lack of funds as to the challenge of nature, and which prompted development of the more accessible quays at Glencaple, Kelton and Kingholm. Thus, by 1810, when civil engineers were first employed to straighten and deepen the Nith, the reorganisation of ports, which was both an outcome of and integral to the industrial revolution, was virtually complete. Those that would command the bulk of trade had emerged and, where necessary, had been developed to accommodate the growing tonnage.

There is no indication that in seeking to improve Dumfries the mercantile community sought to emulate these other ports. Indeed, the level of trade did not justify major expenditure on elaborate facilities, but with the dangers of the Nith too great even for the smallest vessels; with Kingholm silted to the extent that "few tides fill the dock;" and with Glencaple and Kelton closed by shifting sands - forcing vessels to "land on the bare beach" - the port faced a stark choice: improve or fail.

Failure, however, would have upset the delicate balance of a rural economy in transition that was dependent upon coastal shipping to bring in the raw materials for fertilisation and to transport the produce of the hinterland to markets. It was this process that enabled Dumfries to function as the local link in an agricultural chain which assembled products for newly industrialising areas. As a result, it is no surprise to find the initiative for the 1812 "Act for Improving the Harbour at Dumfries and the Navigation of the Nith" coming from landed interests, represented by the Commissioners of Supply, and supported by merchants ever keen to protect their property from the "damage and embezzlement to which it has ever been subjected by land carriage."[10] The Act removed control of navigation from a borough perceived as incompetent in favour of commissioners - who were to prove no more astute - drawn largely from landed interests, *ex-officio* representatives of the borough and trades,

---

[10]"Act for Improving the Harbour at Dumfries and the Navigation of the Nith," 1812; and 51 Geo. III c. 147, Nith Navigation Bill.

and merchants and shipowners, whose goal was to secure conditions that would enable "ships, vessels, barques and lighters to come and go."[11]

Working to plans prepared by the civil engineer James Hollinsworth, and under the direction of Walter Newall (variously described as "cabinet maker" and "engineer"), a mile of river was straightened and deepened to ten feet at the town dock. Access to Kelton, Glencaple and Kingholm was improved and embankments built on both sides of the river. Although Hollinsworth estimated the work would cost £5000, the Commission minutes suggest an actual cost of about £7225, most of which was spent on land purchase and similar items (see table 1).

Table 1
Identified Costs for Improving Nith Navigation 1811/12

Cost of Obtaining the Act of Parliament	£947
Survey	£51
Land Purchase	£2349
Cuttings	£1000
Embankments	£1000
Other	£1212
Fixing Buoys etc.	£90

Source: DRA, RG/1/2/3, Minutes and Memorial of the Nith Navigation Commission.

In the following decade the Commission erected new quays, wharves and jetties; maintained embankments and navigational aids; and built a new road for carters from Kingholm to the town. But for all their efforts the river continued to "ramble from place to place to the great agitation of shipping." Moreover, a ridge of rock at Kingholm was never adequately removed, undermining the value of the improvements in bringing vessels right up to the town. As a result, Glencaple and Kingholm continued to handle the great bulk of Dumfries' traffic. It was a substantial stretch of river to maintain on limited resources and by 1824 the Commission's debts, which had been growing by an average of £500-600 per annum, had reached more than £13,000. Seven thousand pounds

[11]Merchants and shipowners alone had to satisfy a residential qualification, own shares in a Dumfries-registered vessel of twenty or more tons, and pay minimum freight charges of £10 per annum before qualifying for appointment. All appointments were subject to annual re-election.

still owed to the original subscribers was repaid, using a loan imprudently secured on an inflated assessment of revenue from tonnage dues, which no doubt satisfied creditors seeking repayment of capital proffered in 1810/1812 but breached the terms of the 1812 Act, which stipulated that subscribers were not entitled to repayment of either capital or interest until all necessary work was finished.[12] This created insurmountable difficulties when later attempts were made to reduce outgoings with a new loan that would have the benefit of a lower interest rate.[13]

The simplified tonnage and impost duties imposed by the 1812 Act (two pence per registered ton; six pence per ton of coal and lime - or nine pence per chaldron - and ten pence on all other goods) were modified in 1824 to one pence per ton on all vessels entering from Great Britain or anchoring at Carsethorne; six pence on those from foreign ports; and one-half pence per ton on goods - except coal and lime which remained the same.[14] It is possible that, had the Commission not indulged in profligate expenditure - including ten guineas on a "suitable piece of plate" for Mr. Kerr and the building of massive harbour walls and ornamentation that were of little value to shipping - the port might have become commercially viable.[15] As it was, a series of further expenditures, including a large but never finished sea dyke financed by loans from the Bank of Scotland and discontinued in 1864, and competition from the Carlisle-Glasgow rail link and other ports led ultimately to insolvency in 1875.

Little is known of the detail of Dumfries' commerce in the period between the Restoration and Union of Parliaments in 1707, although Coutts' examination of the mercantile community presents a fairly typical profile of Scottish overseas trade in the early seventeenth century based on

---

[12]DRA, RG1/1/2A. The loan was obtained from Mr. Greenshields of Lanark at five percent.

[13]DRA, RG1/1/3, "Memorial of The Commissioners of the Nith Navigation to The Honourable the Magistrates and Town Council of Dumfries," n.d. (1824?).

[14]DRA, RG/1/2, "Minutes of The Nith Navigation Trust," n.d. (1824?).

[15]This first was a "reward" to Mr. Kerr, who had secured a loan of £400 from the Convention of Royal Burghs. As to the second, by 1850 Dumfries possessed 470 linear yards of wharfage and the ground behind it had been raised and cobbled.

North Sea routes and coastal connections with England.[16] Income from exporting hides and skins enabled merchants like William Irvine, James Maxwell and George Bell to acquire cloth and grain from England and an array of luxury goods from Europe. They formed partnerships to reduce the cost and risk of owning vessels and occasionally engaged in joint ventures with like-minded merchants in Glasgow and Edinburgh. But for much of the seventeenth century, southern Scotland was blighted by religious and civil conflict, arising largely from attempts to enforce episcopacy on a region overwhelmingly committed to Presbyterianism. This impacted heavily on Dumfries which, in common with most ports, was pre-disposed to non-conformity. Repression and financial penalties brought both town and countryside close to ruin.[17] Yet the resilience of the mercantile community is evident from Christopher Smout's examination of Dumfries' trade in the closing decades of the seventeenth century, which shows established connections with Europe, Norway and the Baltic, along with England's west coast ports.[18] By the 1690s foreign trade, though limited, averaged five vessels arriving annually with provisions from Ireland; wine and luxury goods from France and Holland; and timber from Norway. Small coastal vessels brought coal, lime, tobacco and general goods to Dumfries.

From at least the early eighteenth century – in common with most ports – Dumfries' foreign trade was controlled by a mercantile elite operating in a variety of fluid partnerships: Edward and Robert Maxwell, Hugh Lawson, James Jardine, Charles Stewart, James Guthrie, and

---

[16]W. Coutts, "Provincial Merchants and Society: A Study of Dumfries Based on the Registers of Testaments 1600-1665," in M. Lynch (ed.), *The Early Modern Town in Scotland* (London, 1987).

[17]In 1662, fines for non-conformity totalled £16,683 sterling. In 1663-1666 they exceeded £51,575, with individual fines ranging from £240 to £3600. As the inheritors along with farmers and merchants had already been forcibly taxed by the Covenanting War Committee, these fresh imposts brought near ruin to many families. See McDowall, *History*; and Russell, *Book of Dumfriesshire*, 51.

[18]C. Smout, "The Foreign Trade of Dumfries and Kirkcudbright, 1672-1696," Dumfries and Galloway Natural History and Antiquarian Society *Transactions*, XXXVII (1958-1959), 36-47. Local merchants were quick to exploit new opportunities, entering the Baltic trade in 1682 when the *Adventure* was sent on a pioneering voyage to Danzig, returning with lint, hemp, iron and glass. A further fourteen voyages were made to Baltic ports between 1682 and 1707.

William and George Bell. These were men with capital, connections and the ability to take advantage of the commercial clauses of the Act of Union that allowed the Scots to trade openly with the colonies. For these merchants, based in a port whose hinterland lacked both exports and a substantial population demanding imports, the particular attractions of tobacco are self-evident. As a high-earning re-export it offered an opportunity to expand international trade unfettered by the poverty of the hinterland. While it was generally regarded as a high-risk trade before the mid-eighteenth century, there was steady growth in Dumfries, whose share of the trade rose from around eight percent of the Scottish total in 1731 to fifteen percent in 1743 (see table 2).[19]

Table 2
Schedule of Tonnage from Foreign Parts and Imports of Timber, Wine and Tobacco, 1731-1743

Year	Vessel Tons	Timber Tons	Wine Tons	Tobacco Lbs.
1731	495	1470	145	627,200
1732	893	2306	20	1,081,920
1733	684	987	30	454,720
1734	963	1068	21	954,240
1735	805	803	15	2,322,800
1736	1770	1398	340	5,241,600
1737	1530	1002	203	3,543,680
1738	650	990	60	2,571,520
1739	762	879	20	2,381,120
1740	804	736	30	2,020,480
1741	1004	450	12	1,115,520
1742	633	650	11	1,193,920
1743	860	400	13	1,348,840

Source: DRA, GH1/1, Abstract of Tonnage and Impost, 1731-1743.

Customs' records for the period 1750-1753, peak years for Dumfries' foreign trade, reveal nothing exceptional about the goods brought to the port but apart from a single cargo of oak bark, bear and finished clothing for Dublin, the export trade seems to have revolved

---

[19]Jackson, "Glasgow in Transition."

exclusively around tobacco.[20] An average of seventeen vessels entered the port each year bringing tobacco from Virginia; iron, timber and flax from Scandinavia and the Baltic; fruit and wine from Southern Europe and the Channel Islands; dyestuffs and luxury goods from Rotterdam; and a small quantity of Spanish wine and Swedish iron transhipped from Ireland (see table 3). With the exception of Ireland, where the occasional export cargo offers some indication of the developing nature of the hinterland, the export trade revolved exclusively around tobacco. Dumfries merchants re-exported their tobacco to all these destinations on their own account or on behalf of William Alexander and Sons, Edinburgh agents for the Farmers General of the French Customs. Indeed, all outward-bound vessels carried either tobacco or supplies for Virginia. While the cargoes were apparently owned by local merchants, the goods were almost certainly produced outside the region "the industry of [the] town being employed for the accommodation of its own inhabitants and those of the adjacent country rather than any considerable manufacture or article for distant markets."[21] Indeed, between June 1750 and June 1751, 383 tons of merchant goods were brought into the port compared with only 205 tons during 1778/1779. Whilst the American War of Independence undoubtedly impacted on the level of trade, it is probably fair to say that during its peak in the tobacco trade Dumfries functioned as a collection port for goods transhipped coastwise and a distribution port for those brought in from abroad. Furthermore, since few vessels bothered with the treacherous journey to the town dock - preferring to use the facilities down river at Carsethorne - the indications are that during this period the port functioned as an entity quite separate from the economy of its hinterland.

Although local merchants were quite capable of filling a vessel alone, and frequently did, they were not averse to sharing freight, risk and expertise. In May 1751 four partnerships - Hugh Lawson and Co., James Guthrie and Co., William Bell and Co. and George Gordon and Robert Maxwell - dispatched their cargoes on *St. Andrew* for Virginia. The vessel returned in February 1752 with each partnership's consignments of

---

[20]The data used in this paper are taken from Scottish Record Office, E504/9/2, "Customs Quarterly Accounts and Tonnage and Impost Accounts belonging to the Port of Dumfries."

[21]Sir John Sinclair (ed.), *The Statistical Account of Scotland*, Vol. IV, Dumfriesshire.

tobacco and timber. In the same year, James and Thomas Corbett and Co. and Edward and Robert Maxwell and George Gordon shared space on *Lilly*. These were men with wide-ranging mercantile interests who re-exported tobacco to Europe in return for dyestuffs, linseed and flax from Rotterdam; timber and hemp from Riga; deals from Norway; and wine and fruit from southern Europe, much of which they transhipped in smaller vessels to other ports in Britain and Ireland.

Table 3
Ships Entering and Leaving by Port of Origin and Destination, 1750-1753

	July 1750/51		July 1751/52		July 1752/53	
	In	Out	In	Out	In	Out
Belfast			1			
Bergen	3	1	2	1	1	
Cadiz	1					
Dieppe				4		
Drogheda						
Drunton			4	2	1	1
Dublin	1	1	3		1	
Gothenburg	3		1		1	2
Guernsey			1		1	
Hamburg		1				
Harve-Le-Grace		2		1		
Longsound	3		1	1		
Leghorn						1
Leghorn &					1	
Malaga	1		1			
Morlaix				1		
Norway		1				
Riga			2		1	
Rotterdam	3	3	2			1
Virginia	3	3	3	4	4	

Source: DRA, GH1/1/4/5/6, Port of Dumfries Tonnage and Impost Accounts.

As Gordon Jackson has shown, there is no such thing as permanence in trading relationships.[22] The disadvantage of over-specialisation in a single commodity is evident from the 1760s, when the Dumfries tobacco trade declined rapidly, coterminous with the growing monopoly of Greenock and Port Glasgow, where wet dock operations facilitated the larger hulls and speedy turnaround that shipowners increasingly demanded. Tobacco had been the lynch-pin of the region's foreign trade and the principal determinant of vessel deployment. With its collapse in the 1760s, the rationale for sending vessels on long and dangerous voyages for goods that might just as easily be procured from other British ports ceased to exist. By the 1770s, the port was receiving an annual average of only three vessels from foreign ports and rarely dispatched more than one.[23]

During the nineteenth century the pattern of overseas trade remained broadly similar, with the notable exception of the emigrant and timber trades, and in particular the development of a triangular trade between Dumfries, Canada and Liverpool. Canadian timber was dispatched via Liverpool in vessels such as the 182-ton *Frances*, built at Bridgetown, NS in 1843, and the 212-ton *John Wilson*, built at Roseway in 1846 by Solway shipwrights taken out by the Thomson Company - one brother in Dumfries, one in Liverpool and one in New Brunswick. On arrival at Liverpool, manufactured goods for Prince Edward Island and New Brunswick were loaded before the vessels sailed up the coast to Dumfries, where emigrants were embarked at Glencaple and Carsethorne for Richibucto, Miramichi and the Baie de Chaleur. The emigrant trade appears to have developed quite rapidly in the second quarter of the nineteenth century, when local newspaper advertisements show emigrant ships sailing regularly to the Maritimes and Québec in spring and early summer, and to Australia and New Zealand by way of South Africa. In 1851 around 10,000 departed Carsethorne for North America, with an additional 7000 bound for Australia and 4000 for New Zealand. But by the end of the nineteenth century this trade had also declined, as most emigrants preferred to depart from Glasgow or Liverpool, where the ports could accommodate larger vessels with better facilities.

---

[22]Jackson, *History and Archaeology of Ports*, 10.

[23]While there was a slight upturn from the 1780s, and again early in the nineteenth century (linked to the import of North American timber), foreign trade never again approached the levels of the first half of the century.

From the 1740s Dumfries increasingly engaged in the exploitation of its rural economy. "Improving landlords," such as William Craik of Arbigland, the "father of improved husbandry in Dumfries;" Millar of Dalswinton; Monteith of Closeburn; and Major-General Dirom of Mount Annan, bore the cost of enclosure, drainage and fertilisation before offering new leases to forward-thinking tenants. The Marquis of Queensberry actively sought out and accommodated several eminent farmers from Roxburgh and Midlothian with 500-600 acre farms, while others offered incentives in the form of longer leases or lower rents to farmers willing to undertake improvements.[24] New crops and rotations were established; output, yield and acreage under cultivation increased; and new strains of livestock were introduced. By 1812 a professional agricultural sector was well advanced and farmers in both Berwickshire and Northumberland, themselves eminent in agriculture, had publicly acknowledged Dumfries as their role model.[25]

Because of these developments, Dumfries was well placed to respond to the growing demands of emerging urban centres for food and raw materials. Yet any potential for sustained economic advance was challenged by the region's geographic isolation and dependence on external markets. In this respect shipping and port facilities were critical, and from the mid-eighteenth century Dumfries's staple industries and its shipping became mutually self-supporting.

From the beginnings of compulsory registration in 1786/1787 until 1800, at least twenty-four vessels, averaging thirty-seven tons burthen, were registered as belonging to Dumfries.[26] Prior to 1786, it cannot be said with certainty which, if any, of the vessels using the port belonged to it, although work by Eric Graham suggests a fleet of 166 tons in 1759, and the Port Tonnage and Impost Ledgers provide a remarkably clear

---

[24]Singer, *General View of the Agriculture, State of Property and Improvements in the County of Dumfries* (Edinburgh, 1812); Sinclair (ed.), *Statistical Account of Scotland*, IV, Dumfriesshire; and *The New Statistical Account of Dumfriesshire, 1841*.

[25]Singer, *General View*, note 24.

[26]Cumbria Archive, TSR4/1, Carlisle Register of Shipping. This volume contains a separate listing of vessels registered as belonging to the Port of Dumfries, 1786-1818. It is the only official record of Dumfries-registered vessels known to have survived for this period and may not be complete.

picture of the nature and direction of the port's growing coastal trade.[27] Between 1750 and 1762, a fleet averaging only twenty tons shuttled back and forth, with those importing goods exceeding those taking produce away by a ratio of three to two. Whitehaven was the favoured destination and port of departure followed by Liverpool, but there were a whole raft of other ports, ranging from London, Bristol and Preston in England; Cardigan and Caernarvon in Wales; and Aberdeen and Leith in Scotland, although Scottish entries were a rarity. Dumfries merchants increasingly looked to England and the Solway acted as the linkage between the two economies.

Details recorded in the Tonnage and Impost Accounts vary, making identification of merchants directly engaged in the coasting trade possible only for the period 1750-1762, when many of the same mercantile partnerships that featured prominently in foreign trade reappeared. Most vessels brought in lime and coal and carried out agricultural produce, but in line with what we know of the port's foreign trade, a small number specialised in the movement of goods around the coast. This trend continued long after the collapse of the tobacco trade which, in the continued absence of local manufactures, suggests an ongoing role for the port in a chain moving imported goods and domestic manufactures around the coast. Uniquely, the accounts for the fiscal year 1779/1780 identify cargoes beyond the simple classification required for local revenue purposes. During that year, sixty-two percent of vessels entering carried coal or lime; twenty-six percent were laden with merchant goods; and the remainder brought a mixed bag of earthenware, herrings, iron, kelp, porter, salt, slates and spades. Of the vessels departing with cargo, fifty-three percent carried agricultural produce - including three with live sheep - twenty-seven percent carried merchant goods and the rest carried timber, empty casks and barrel staves, charcoal, kelp, oak bark, spirits and wagon rails. Vessels such as *Providence* and *Seahorse* specialised in

---

[27]E.J. Graham, "The Impact of Mercantilism and War on the Scottish Marine 1661-1791" (Unpublished PhD thesis, University of Strathclyde, 1998), appendix C. There are no known port books for Scottish coastal trade. Dumfries, in common with other ports, secured the right to impose local taxes on vessels using the port. The income from this source was recorded in the Port Tonnage and Impost Ledgers, a number of which survive from 1750. At a minimum, these record all entrances and clearances and indicate if the vessel is in ballast. Additionally, for some years they detail vessel size, destination and port of departure, along with itemised cargoes and names of owners. They are invaluable for many aspects of Dumfries coastal trade.

trade with Whitehaven, bringing in coals and lime and taking out potatoes, corn, oats, barley, flour and lambs. Others, such as *Dumfries*, traded with a variety of ports in merchant goods.

With growth so heavily reliant on external markets, the success of local entrepreneurs and shipowners in creating and servicing new opportunities rested on the capacity of individuals to anticipate demand and ensure a plentiful supply of appropriate vessels. These were men and women who made investment decisions from the perspective of the community in which they lived. They did not invest to see their vessels lie idle; while registered tonnage is not a surrogate for the volume of trade, it is reasonable to assume that growth in local shipping capital reflected growth in the level of actual or anticipated commerce through the port.

Only a small amount of registry information for the port survives for the late eighteenth and early nineteenth century, although I.F. MacLeod has detailed the status of the port's shipping in 1820, when seventy-five vessels totalling 4781 tons were registered.[28] Forty percent of the vessels were less than five years-old and a further thirty-three percent under ten, indicating real growth in port activity from 1810, when the first significant efforts were made to develop its physical structure and ease navigation. More substantially, the Registers of Transactions Relating to Ships Registered at Dumfries have survived intact from the general re-registration of shipping in 1824/1825 until 1850. These provide a continuous flow of information. Registered tonnage grew to nearly 26,000 tons in 1850 (see figure 2). While this was dwarfed by larger ports such as Dundee, where registered tonnage had risen to 58,000 tons by 1850, it does serve to demonstrate the growth of the local economy and concomitant demand on port facilities.[29]

It is self-evident that trade requires ships and that ships require builders. Shipbuilders had been active on the Nith since at least the 1730s, concentrated initially at Kelton, although by the early 1800s Glencaple was also producing a considerable number of vessels. The shipping registers show just how important local shipbuilding had become to the function of the port, with over sixty-four percent of vessels registered for the first

---

[28]I.F. MacLeod, *Shipping in Dumfries and Galloway in 1820* (Dumfries, 1973) 4. This work is based on Underwriters' records.

[29]DRA, CE51/11/4/75-77, Registers of Transactions Relating to Ships Registered at Dumfries, 1824-1850; and Jackson with Kinnear, *Trade and Shipping of Dundee*, 47.

time between 1824 and 1850 built within its jurisdiction: 19.6% at Kelton and 12.3% at Glencaple. Of those built at Glencaple, all but two were constructed in the year of registration. Shipwrights in the port built a variety of vessels: eleven brigs; seventeen sloops; eighteen schooners; and six smacks. Similarly, all but twelve of the fifty-nine Kelton-built vessels were built in the year of registration; the builders in this town specialised in small sloops of around thirty-nine tons. Indeed, the "newness" of vessels at first registration is noteworthy. Shareholders were clearly not investing in "old tubs" as might be expected in a port of this nature. Most of the remaining vessels came from ports around Britain, although some 5000 tons originated in North America. Many of these vessels were built by men originating from the Solway ports and were used in the emigrant/timber trade.

Figure 2
Newly Registered Tonnage, Dumfries, 1824-1850

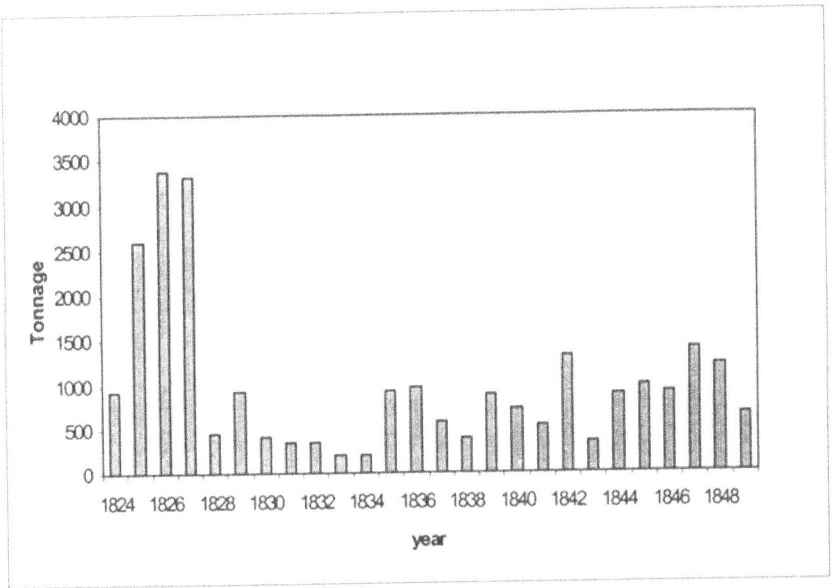

Source: DRA, CE51/11/4/75-77, Registers of Transactions Relating to Ships Registered at the Port of Dumfries, 1824-1850.

Figure 3 demonstrates the changing structure of the fleet in terms of tonnage and rig. Year-on-year, brigs used largely in the Canadian trade accounted for a substantial proportion of tonnage, although only seventeen percent of vessels registering for the first time. In contrast sloops, which accounted for thirty-nine percent of all vessels registering, comprised only fifty-nine percent of the tonnage of the brigs. Their simple rig, small crew and low operating costs guaranteed a role in coastal waters, where manoeuvrability took preference over size. Small schooners, averaging just forty tons, accounted for a further twenty-three percent of first registries: they offered versatility and greater efficiency than the standard foreign-going brig. Clearly, it was important to have the appropriate vessels for a particular trade and economy of scale was not the dominant factor.

Figure 3
Composition of Dumfries Fleet, 1825-1850

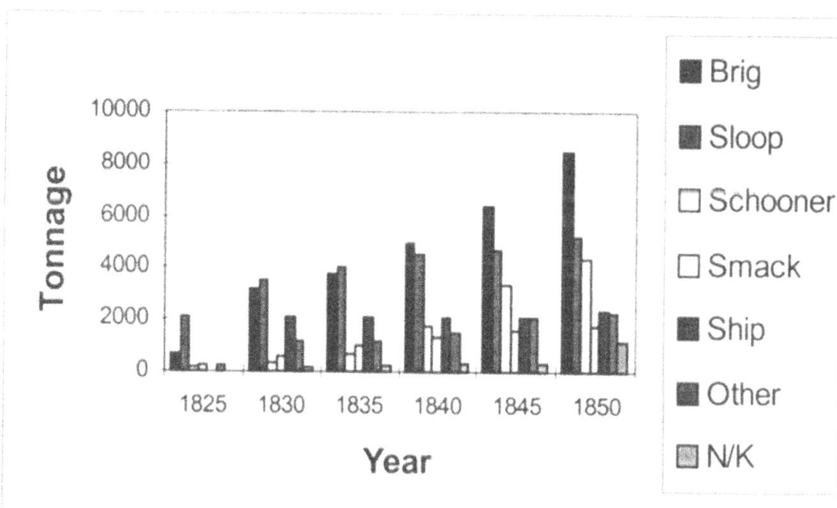

Source: See figure 2.

Shipping was an industry that encouraged investors through a system of share ownership and was one of the few early examples of capital investment with "limited liability" that enabled local savings to be directed to a central requirement of the developing economy. In small ports like Dumfries, local fleets were among the principal fixed assets. As figure 4 demonstrates, the increasing demand for shipping capital was financed largely from within Dumfriesshire. Indeed, much of it came from within the industry, although a large share also came from a broad socio-economic spectrum of the community (see appendix 1).

Unlike the early modern period, when there was little non-mercantile investment in shipping, examination of shareholders' occupations for the period 1824-1850 shows a wide cross-section of society concerned in the ownership of vessels. Although sixty-eight occupations have been identified, ninety-two percent of these contributed less than five percent of total shareholdings, while the top seven percent held sixty-one percent.[30] Merchants and mariners - those most directly concerned with shipping - held the highest proportions (20.52% and 23.86% of shares, respectively) followed by shipowners and shipbuilders with 14.52%. This contrasts with John Armstrong and Philip Bagwell's analysis of 315 ships registered in nine ports, which showed that only ten percent of shares were in the hands of mariners and that around one-third belonged to merchants and manufacturers.[31] Somewhat surprisingly given the rural nature of the region, farmers held only 6.04% of shares, little more than half the percentage found in a comparable study of the adjoining port of Kirkcudbright.[32] Multiple shareholdings were common, with men like Sam Blaind, John Thomson and James Scott, draper, merchant and banker, respectively, holding shares in eight vessels; William Thomson, shipbuilder, in sixteen; and John Nicholson, merchant in twenty. Still, shares in two or three vessels were more common.

During much of the period the fleet was largely owned and controlled by the mercantile sector, but there was a continuous movement

---

[30]Data on shareholding have been extracted from the shipping registers. It was impossible to identify occupations for thirteen percent of shareholders.

[31]Armstrong and Bagwell, "Coastal Shipping," 166.

[32]C. Hill, "Galloway Shipping and Regional Development, 1750-1850," *Scottish Economic and Social History*, XIX, No. 2 (1999), forthcoming.

of funds from townsfolk, whose level of investment increased during the 1840s as mercantile investment began to decline. The reason for this is unclear, but it is probably no coincidence that mercantile withdrawal from coastal shipping began against a background of continuous difficulties with port navigation, the construction of new rail links and the opening of a wet dock at Silloth on the Cumbrian side of the Solway. Although the port remained functional until well into the twentieth century – its outports still attract pleasure craft and small fishing vessels today – it peaked commercially in 1844, when tonnage dues reached £1212. Even then, the Commission was still heavily in debt and unable to meet its annual repayment of £1356 to the Bank of Scotland. In an obvious attempt to meet the shortfall, tonnage rates were increased to two pence per ton on coastal vessels and to one shilling and two pence on goods, but the port was becoming too expensive and shipowners increasingly sought cheaper alternatives.[33] The port's trade began to decline as goods were landed at Granton or Glasgow and brought to Dumfries by rail, or at Silloth where freights were lower and it was more profitable to discharge timber onto rafts and float it to Dumfries than to sail into the port.

Figure 4
Residential Analysis of Shareholders in Dumfries Vessels at Initial Registration, 1824-1850

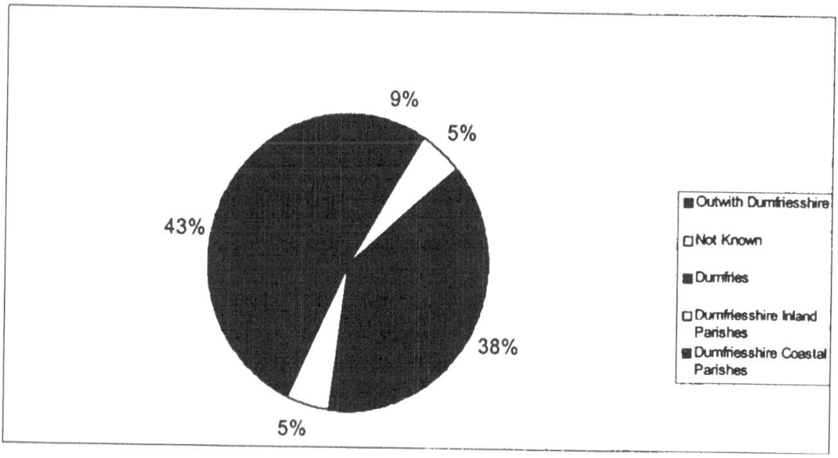

Source: See figure 2.

[33]The rates remained the same for foreign vessels, coal and lime.

Most ports began life as little more than convenient landing sites which were improved and modified in response to demand or in occasional futile attempts to compete with other ports. During the eighteenth century, industrialisation and changes in the nature and direction of trade led to a new diversity among ports, with the successful ones generally being those blessed with river links to rapidly developing hinterlands and engaging in extensive foreign trade. But as Gordon Jackson has argued, ports should be judged by the way they respond to change; provide commerical expertise facilities for shipping; and develop new initiatives within the constraints of their location.[34] By these measures Dumfries, which adapted and survived for nearly 300 years, was indeed successful despite its limited facilities, rural hinterland and predisposition for coastal trade. Indeed, the economic progress of Dumfries and its immediate hinterland is, in part, mirrored in its function as a port and to a lesser extent in the efforts of its mercantile community to improve navigation on the Nith.

In 1707, the Act of Union offered Scotland the same advantages that the transatlantic trades had bestowed on the western outports in England. It brought the Scottish west coast economy within the sphere of the Navigation Acts and gave legitimate access to British colonial markets. Dumfries was well located to take advantage of this and was quick to exploit the opportunity to develop wider markets and to seek new imports, notably tobacco. This highly successful trade was conducted over several decades by a mercantile elite using vessels that landed and departed from an outport at Carsethorne. But it was a business wholly detached from the port's hinterland. Unlike Glasgow, which was able to compensate for the collapse of its tobacco commerce with sugar and rum, and to benefit from the demands of growing industrial areas in the central belt, Dumfries had nothing to offer before the emigration/timber trade took off in the second quarter of the nineteenth century.

But from mid-eighteenth century the agricultural hinterland began to develop rapidly and it became the new dynamic of trade, as evinced in the rapid growth of coastal shipping and the development of important centres of shipbuilding in the outports. Because of the difficulty of navigation on the Nith, these outports handled most of trade before 1810, when vested interests achieved enough improvement to allow the port's growing tonnage to reach the town dock in relative safety. Unfortunately,

---

[34]Jackson and Lythe (eds.), *Port of Montrose*, xxix.

the level of trade was never sufficient to finance the expensive physical improvements for the port to remain attractive to shippers after the development of alternatives. Yet it cannot be argued that Dumfries was just another port spending for no return. Given the rural nature and relative isolation of its hinterland and the nature of its imports and exports, neither the economy of Dumfries and its hinterland nor the ability of its merchants to provision urban centres would have developed without proximity to the sea and shipping. Thus, what is at face value an unimportant port spending to achieve little was in fact a port spending to ensure the survival of itself and its hinterland.

In the restructuring linked to the economic changes of the eighteenth and nineteenth century, the majority of Scottish ports like Dumfries remained small, offering fairly primitive facilities to merchants and shippers engaged primarily in coasting. While these ports never approached the size of the complex structures at Port Glasgow, Greenock, Leith or Dundee, in the days of difficult overland transport they were of inestimable value to the social and economic development of local economies and the process of regional specialisation by which the economies of diverse hinterlands were integrated into the wider national economy. This was a significant role for any "unimportant port."

Appendix 1
Port of Dumfries, Occupational Analysis of Shareholders in Dumfries Shipping at Initial Registration, 1824-1850

Occupation	Percentage of Total Shares in Fleet	Occupation	Percentage of Total Shares in Fleet
Stamper	0.01%	Slater	0.2%
Tallow-Chandler	0.02%	Surgeon	0.2%
Book Seller	0.03%	Brewer	0.2%
Clerk	0.03%	Flesher	0.3%
Clerk & Merchant	0.03%	Hat Manufacturer	0.3%
Coach Builder	0.03%	Wine/Spirit Merchant	0.3%
Iron Merchant	0.03%	Spouse	0.3%
Leather Cutter	0.03%	Fisherman	0.5%
Tinsmith	0.03%	Grain Dealer	0.4%
Dry Salter	0.04%	Manufacturer	0.4%
Millwright	0.04%	Tea Dealer	0.5%
Seedsman	0.06%	Residenter	0.5%
Tobacconist	0.06%	Grocer	0.6%
Yeoman	0.06%	Widow	0.7%
Rope Manufacturer	0.07%	Cooper	0.7%
Iron Founder	0.07%	Mason	0.7%
Chairmaker	0.08%	Baker	0.7%
Tacksman	0.08%	Draper	0.8%
Minister	0.09%	Ship Carpenter	0.8%
Builder	0.1%	Joiner	0.8%
Chaise Driver	0.1%	Corn Merchant	0.9%
Hosier	0.1%	Coal Dealer	1.06%
Ship Broker	0.1%	Writer	1.06%
Carrier	0.2%	Gentleman	1.11%
Sail Maker	0.2%	Painter/Glazer	1.11%
Watch Maker	0.2%	Banker	1.34%
Engineer	0.2%	Ship Master	1.46%
Druggist	0.2%	Timber Merchant	2.04%
Town Clerk	0.2%	Unknown	12.12%
Ironmonger	0.2%	Farmer	6.04%
Cabinet Maker	0.2%	Shipbuilder	6.75%
Carter	0.2%	Shipowner	7.77%
Merchant/Shipowner	0.2%	Merchant	18.28%
Shipowner/Grain Dealer	0.2%	Mariner	22.4%

Source: See figure 2.

Australian Ports Since 1945

Malcolm Tull

Introduction

Since the arrival of the First Fleet in 1788, ports have provided vital gateways for Australian shipping and trade. The vast size of the country, with its widely-separated centres of population concentrated along the coast, has meant that both coastal and overseas shipping have been important consumers of port services. In the late 1990s Australia had about eighty ports, ranging from minor ones designed primarily to serve the needs of local communities, the fishing industry or recreational boating, to specialised bulk-handling and major commercial hubs. Together, such ports handled ninety-nine percent of Australia's international cargo by volume and seventy-four percent by value. In 1995/1996 international trade at Australian ports totalled 420 million tonnes worth AUS $115,770 million. To remain efficient interfaces between land and sea transport, after 1945 the ports were forced to adjust to major changes in trade, shipping and cargo-handling technology. The technological changes were part of a worldwide revolution, the major features of which were the exploitation of the economies of scale from increased ship size and the extension of mechanisation to the handling of general cargo.

In many respects, the movement of cargo fifty metres across a wharf is as important as its carriage 1000 kilometres by sea. While goods must be kept flowing at a steady rate if cargo handling is not to become a costly and tortuous process, Australia's ports over the years have achieved a relatively poor reputation for speed of turnround, industrial disputes and restrictive work practices. Since the Second World War, governments have been involved in numerous attempts to restructure the industry, a task made more difficult by the diverse elements involved and the sometimes dismal climate of labour relations on the waterfront. Since the late 1980s the ports have been the targets of on-going and sometimes controversial reforms which have had a major impact on efficiency. The early months of 1998 were dominated by a struggle between government, employers and the Maritime Union of Australia (MUA) over the use of non-union labour on the wharves.

Gordon Jackson, in whose honour this chapter is written, has observed that "ports are living organisms" that must adapt if they are to prosper and grow.[1] The aim of this essay is to survey the spectacular shifts that have occurred in Australian ports since 1945 and to evaluate their success in adapting to changes in the scale and nature of port activity. Alan Jamieson has characterised the postwar history of British ports as a story of "not more ports, but better ports."[2] In the case of Australia, it remains to be seen whether "more ports, not better ports" is more apposite. The changes to the ports were the outcome of a complex process of decision-making and adjustment in which a large number of actors played a part, among whom the most important were the port authorities, governments, stevedores, shipowners and waterfront unions. Due to space limitations this piece focuses on four topics: changes in port activity, technological change, port and city interaction and microeconomic reform. Each will be considered in turn.

The Growth of Port Activity, 1945 to 1995-1996[3]

Port activity, measured by cargo, ship or passenger flows, is derived from the demand for the transfer of goods and people between different geographic locales.[4] Thus, its growth is influenced by a wide variety of factors, including economic (the growth of population, incomes, trade and industry) and political considerations (such as tariffs, commercial policies

---

[1]Cited by D. Williams, "History of Ports and Harbours - Adaptations to Change. Conference Summary," in P. Holm and J. Edwards (eds.) *North Sea Ports and Harbours-Adaptations to Change* (Esbjerg, 1991), 226.

[2]A.G. Jamieson, "'Not More Ports, but Better Ports:' The Development of British Ports Since 1945," *The Northern Mariner/Le Marin du nord*, VI, No. 1 (January 1996), 29-34.

[3]This section draws on M. Tull, *A Community Enterprise: The History of the Port of Fremantle, 1897 to 1997* (St. John's, 1997).

[4]Since passenger flows are only a minor component of port activity, the focus will be on cargoes and ships. Most of the discussion will examine volumes due to the greater availability of such data and the impact of cargo and ship tonnages on the scale of facilities provided in ports. But because the willingness to invest in ports depends upon revenues relative to costs, values of trade are also important. Unfortunately, this information is often lacking at the port level.

and industrial militancy). The volume of international cargo grew from about 22.3 million tonnes in 1954-1955 to 420 million tonnes in 1995/1996; over the same period, the value of trade increased from AUS $3236 to AUS $115,770 million (in current dollars).[5] It is not possible in this chapter to go into detail about the circumstances behind all of the changes in postwar port activity.[6] Instead, a detailed case study of the 1950s import boom will be used to illustrate the way in which ports are enmeshed in the general economic situation.

During the late 1940s the Australian economy was going through the transition from war to peace. Although there were shortages of goods and services, there was high employment and fairly rapid economic growth. In 1948-1949, the government expanded immigration, which helped alleviate labour shortages. At the same time, overseas suppliers were also recovering, which led to a rise in imports. In June 1950 the Korean War broke out and the fear that it might spread led to a rapid rise in world demand for raw materials. For example, because wool, one of Australia's major exports, was in especially high demand for military purposes, its price soared. In 1950-1951 Australia's overseas exports grew by sixty percent in value, even though they fell six percent in volume. The record export earnings were used to finance increased imports. But pent-up domestic demand once released was not easy to check, and the country was flooded with a variety of finished goods, raw materials and equipment. Indeed, imports regained their pre-war level of about seven million tons in 1947-1948 and peaked at 14.7 million tonnes in 1951-1952, when they were checked by the introduction of import controls.

The import boom led to serious congestion and long turnround times at Sydney, Melbourne, Fremantle and most other capital city ports. Fortunately, domestic export tonnages were down that year, although the effect was doubtless reciprocal, as the movement of exports was hindered

---

[5]All tonnage data has been converted to tonnes on the basis that one ton = 1.02 tonnes.

[6]There is an extensive literature on postwar Australian economic history and economic policy. See, for example, R. Maddock and I. McLean (eds.), *The Australian Economy in the Long Run* (New York, 1986); B. Dyster and D. Meridith, *Australia in the International Economy* (Cambridge, 1990); C White, *Mastering Risk. Environment, Markets and Politics in Australian Economic History* (Oxford, 1992); E.A. Boehm, *20th Century Economic Development in Australia* (3rd ed., Melbourne, 1993); and G. Whitwell, *The Treasury Line* (Sydney, 1986).

by the imports. Turnround times at Sydney and Melbourne, the country's major ports, were extraordinarily slow in the early 1950s (see table 1).

Table 1
Turnround Times of Ships at Sydney and Melbourne
(Days)

Year	Sydney	Melbourne
1951	11.3	15.7
Mid-1952	7.7	9.1
Early 1953	7.6	6.1

Source: Australian Stevedoring Industry Board, *Annual Report*, 1952-1953.

The congestion was exacerbated by a number of factors, including the inefficiency of conventional stevedoring, labour disputes, restrictive labour practices and antiquated and dilapidated wharves and equipment.[7] Conventional stevedoring was labour-intensive and involved lifting cargo in units of two to five tons, with extensive manhandling in the ship's hold, on the wharf and in the transit sheds.[8] The main requirement for wharf labour was "a mighty arm, a hard muscle, and a large strong back."[9] During World War II, US forces had introduced forklifts and pallets, which greatly sped up cargo handling and which after the war rapidly found widespread use beyond the waterfront in warehouses, factories and other parts of the transport chain. But the efficiency of fork-lifts was reduced by restrictive labour practices and limitations on manoeuvrability imposed by the forests of support pillars in most wharf sheds.[10] The efficient use of new technology required related changes in shed design, an interdependency that is a fundamental characteristic of port operations.

---

[7]J.M. Hewitt, "Some Problems Associated with Sea Transport," *Journal of the Institute of Transport*, VIII, No. 10 (1952), 13-19.

[8]S. Gillman, "An Investigation into Some Effects of New Handling Technologies on the Structure of Maritime Transport Systems," *Maritime Studies and Management*, II (1975), 166.

[9]H. Jerome, *Mechanisation in Industry* (New York, 1934), 154. For a detailed discussion, see M. Tull, "Blood on the Cargo: Cargo-Handling and Working Conditions on the Waterfront at Fremantle, 1900-1930," *Labour History*, No. 52 (May 1987), 15-29.

[10]M. Tull, "American Technology and the Mechanisation of Australian Ports 1942 to 1958," *Journal of Transport History*, VI (1985), 79-90.

Blue Funnel vessels engaged in the Australian trade, for example, spent up to sixty percent of their time in port. Moreover, only fifteen percent or so of that time was actually spent working cargoes; the remainder was taken up with waiting for clearances, delays caused by weekends and nights, industrial action and other factors.[11]

The case of the *Imperial Star*, which arrived at Sydney on 16 April 1949 and left on 5 May, illustrates well the state of ports in the late 1940s and early 1950s.[12] The vessel carried a cargo of 10,480 tons, which took three weeks to discharge using conventional methods. By the end of the third week, sixty percent of the cargo was still in the wharf sheds awaiting delivery; five weeks after arrival, about 100 tons of cargo still remained undelivered. In the early 1950s it was rare for a ship to berth at a wharf that was not cluttered with earlier cargo, which led to confusion and inefficiency. With turnaround taking as long as three weeks and cargo clearance as long as five, radical changes were clearly required.

In an attempt to ensure more rapid clearance, port authorities introduced penalty rates on cargo left on the wharves beyond three days. An indication of the pressure on the Port of Fremantle is provided by the fact that between 1949-1950 and 1951-1952 revenue from storage charges increased by eighty-five percent to a record £48,600. On the other hand, charges were no panacea, as Sydney's port authority found.

> The increased wharf storage charges only achieve their purpose up to a point. There is no doubt that, in their absence, delivery rates would be considerably slower, but the fact that the rates are not improving beyond a certain degree shows that some other cause must be behind the failure of consignees to take delivery of cargo prior to the storage charges commencing.[13]

---

[11]M. Falkus, *The Blue Funnel Legend. A History of the Ocean Steam Ship Company, 1865-1973* (Houndsmill, 1990), 358; and R.O. Goss, *Studies in Maritime Economics* (Cambridge, 1970), 153.

[12]The example is taken from Steward Howard and Associates, *Results of a Preliminary Inquiry into the Slow Turnround of Ships in the Port of Sydney* (Sydney, 1950).

[13]Maritime Services Board, *Annual Report* (1950-1951), 12.

When congestion drew public attention to the state of the ports, the federal government in July 1951 commissioned Mr. H. Basten to inquire into the causes. Basten found that Australian ports were unable to cope with the level and nature of postwar cargoes because they were suffering from a lack of investment during the interwar years and overuse during the Second World War.[14]

In May 1952, due to delays and the high cost of chartering extra vessels to cope with peak cargoes, British shipowners imposed a surcharge of twenty-five percent on UK/Australia rates for general cargo. Although the surcharge was removed on 1 September, freight rates were increased by ten percent to cover higher operating costs. The boom thus provides a good example of the way ports are enmeshed in the general economic situation. In this case, there was a line of causation running from the government's management of the economy to trade, port congestion, freight rates, and ultimately to the price paid by the Australian consumer for imports. Furthermore, high transport costs reduced the competitiveness of Australian exports in overseas markets.

The import controls introduced in 1952, coupled with other measures taken to check the boom, led to a short recession in 1952-1953. Improvements in the balance of payments allowed the government to increase import quotas by ten percent in April 1953 and again in July by the same amount. There was a time lag of about six months between the granting of export licenses and the arrival of goods, so port traffic did not increase immediately. In 1953-1954 general cargo imports into Sydney, for example, soared by twenty-two percent as the relaxation of controls took effect. Another deterioration in the balance of payments led to the reimposition of controls in 1955. From 1957 import controls were progressively relaxed until their virtual abolition in 1960. Henceforth, monetary and fiscal policy rather than direct controls were used to manage balance-of-payments problems. The use of such measures led to a severe recession in 1961-1962 from which the economy was slow to recover. But from 1967 it rebounded strongly, leading to steady growth in trade.

On the export side, government policy was probably less important than the state of harvests and the level of world commodity prices. Climatic conditions always varied across the country, but in 1957-1958 a

[14]H. Basten, *Report on the Turn-round of Ships in Australian Ports* (Canberra, 1952).

widespread drought led to the failure of the wheat crop: Sydney's grain exports fell to about 1000 tons and Australia was forced to import wheat for only the third time since 1900. By contrast, in 1959-1960, a good season for primary produce, wheat exports at Sydney increased almost five-fold to 478,000 tons. These fluctuations meant that demand for port facilities could vary widely from year to year; in addition, the strong seasonality of much primary production affected the intensity of port use during the year. In 1960 the government lifted the export embargo on iron ore it had introduced in 1938; this led to rapid development of known reserves, especially in the Pilbara region of northwestern Australia. By the mid-1960s Japan was the main customer for Australia's mineral exports and had replaced the UK as Australia's major trading partner.

The "oil shocks" of the 1970s helped plunge the world economy into an era of uncertainty. As a trading nation, Australia was not immune from these problems. Because of its reliance on primary exports and inadequacies in government policy, the nation experienced a prolonged bout of "stagflation." By 1974 the postwar boom was well and truly over. To combat inflation, the Whitlam Labor government (1972-1975) reduced tariffs by twenty-five percent in July 1973. As a consequence, the following year all of Australia's capital city ports experienced an upsurge in imports. In 1973-1974, the value of total imports jumped twenty-seven percent, again putting pressure on port facilities. By contrast, the Fraser Liberal National Party government (1975-1983) attempted to control inflation by cutting government expenditures and reducing the rate of growth of the money supply. While there was a short-lived resource boom in 1979, this quickly collapsed and inflation continued to be a problem. The Hawke Labor government (1983-1991) introduced significant changes, including a consensus approach to policy-making; the establishment of a prices and incomes policy (the "Accord"); floating the Australian dollar; deregulation of the financial sector; and microeconomic reform.[15] Inflation was slowly brought under control and the economy began to recover. The Stock Market Crash of October 1987, while traumatic for financial markets, left cargo tonnages unaffected. In the early 1990s the tight monetary policy pursued by the Keating Labor government (1991-1996) caused a slowing of growth and a fall in imports. The economy enjoyed relatively strong growth, a trend that has continued

---

[15]For an overview see Indecs, *State of Play 8* (St. Leonards, NSW, 1995).

under the Howard Liberal National Party government elected in March 1996. As we will see later, the Howard government also has embarked on a controversial programme of waterfront reform.

Table 2
International Trade at Australian Ports, 1954-1955 and 1995-1996

	1954-1955				**1995-1996**			
Port	tonnes million	Per cent	A$ million	Per cent	tonnes million	Per cent	A$ million	Per cent
Brisbane	1.4	6.4	317.8	9.8	14.6	3.5	9,898	8.5
Dampier					69.4	16.5	4,399	3.8
Fremantle/ Kwinana	2.5	11.4	210.6	6.5	15.5	3.7	10,139	8.8
Gladstone	0.1	0.5	10.1	0.3	26.7	6.4	2,667	2.3
Hay Point	-	-	-	-	45.5	10.8	2,769	2.4
Hobart	0.3	1.4	42.0	1.3	0.2	*	241	0.2
Melbourne	4.7	21.5	930.4	28.8	12.0	2.9	29,706	25.7
Newcastle	0.9	4.1	62.2	1.9	54.5	13.0	4,277	3.7
Port Adelaide	1.6	7.3	254.0	7.8	2.9	0.7	3,151	2.7
Port Hedland	-	-	-	-	57.6	13.7	1,511	1.3
Port Kembla	0.4	1.8	26.4	0.8	15.9	3.8	1,644	1.4
Port Walcott	-	-	-	-	25.1	6.0	349	0.3
Sydney/ Kurnell	4.8	21.9	1,044	32.3	14.2	3.4	28,972	25.0
Others	5.2	23.7	338.5	10.5	65.9	15.7		
Total	21.9	100.0	3,236	100.0	420	100.0	115,770	100.0

Note: * = less than 0.1 percent. Percentages may not add to 100 due to rounding.

Sources: Commonwealth of Australia, *Yearbook*, 1956; and Australian Bureau of Statistics (ABS), *International Cargo Statistics* (Canberra, 1995-1996).

In the 1980s Australian trade became increasingly oriented towards Asia. The progress of Asian industrialisation created a prosperous middle class and expanding markets for raw materials and foodstuffs in such countries as Indonesia, Malaysia, Singapore, South Korea and Taiwan. By 1992-1993 fifty-eight percent of Australia's exports were going to East and Southeast Asia and thirty-eight percent of imports were coming from this region.[16] Meanwhile, the UK now received less than four percent of exports and supplied only six percent of imports. Although the Asian economic crisis, which erupted in 1997, threatens to reduce commodity prices and exports, at the time of writing there is still a great deal of uncertainty about its impact on the Australian economy.[17]

As table 2 shows, these changes in the level and pattern of port activity clearly affected the market shares of the various ports. The mineral boom of the 1960s, for example, altered the spatial pattern of foreign trade and led to the rise of specialised bulk-handling ports, such as Dampier, Gladstone, Hay Point, Port Hedland and Port Walcott. Port Hedland, situated in Western Australia, enjoyed a meteoric rise to the status of Australia's major port if trade is measured by volume. By the late 1970s it was handling about forty million tonnes of cargo per annum, about forty times the level of the mid-1960s.

To a great degree geography has insulated Australia's capital city ports from competition and enabled them to enjoy a natural monopoly over much of their state's general trade. Since the nineteenth century, rail and road networks have been mostly designed to radiate from the capital cities to ensure that regional centres cannot challenge their dominance. To achieve the utilisation levels to cover their large capital cost, container terminals have been located in the capital city ports rather than elsewhere. Thus, while the capital city ports have lost market share in tonnage terms, they have retained their dominance of high-value general cargoes.

Melbourne and Sydney have always been Australia's major ports when trade is measured by value: in 1995-1996 they accounted for about half of total international trade. While they also account for almost three-quarters of container cargo, the development of "landbridging," in which feeder services carry containers from a gateway to other ports, has the potential to increase the market share of the smaller centres. For example, the Fremantle Port Authority (FPA) has attempted to promote a landbridging service in which a feeder service carries containers from Singapore to Fremantle for distribution to Adelaide by rail. But this move

---

[16]S. Tweedie, *Trading Partners. Australia and Asia 1790-1993* (Sydney, 1994), 233.

[17]See I.J. Macfarlane, "Some Thoughts on Australia's Position in Light of Recent Events in Asia," Speech given to Australian Stock Exchange, Brisbane, 26 March 1998.

to make Fremantle a "Gateway to Australia" has yet to threaten seriously the market shares of Melbourne and Sydney.

In short, periods of feast and famine in port use were induced by a large variety of factors, including the level of primary production, world prices, shifts in economic structure and government policy. Changes in cargo flows were thus mainly dictated by factors outside the control of the ports. In the next section we will see that this was also true of the technological nature of the ships in which the cargo was carried. In a very real sense, the ports had become pawns in a global game of commerce.[18]

Technological Change in Shipping and Cargo Handling

After the Second World War ship size increased rapidly, especially in bulk carriers. The closure of the Suez Canal during the 1956 crisis accelerated the trend toward larger bulk carriers because shipowners needed to offset the higher cost of steaming around the Cape of Good Hope. By the early 1970s bulk carriers and oil tankers in excess of 200,000 deadweight tons (dwt) traversed the world's oceans. Bulk carriers over 40,000 dwt accounted for twenty-three percent of the world fleet, compared to only four percent a decade earlier.[19] The ports had to cope with the vastly increased length, beam and draught of these ships. Draught in particular posed problems because berth deepening is costly and adequate depths could not always be achieved in existing ports.

Gains from increased efficiency in shipping were, however, partially dissipated by the inefficiency of handling general cargoes. The escalating cost eventually forced shipowners to introduce radical innovations, including roll-on/roll-off ships and containerisation, which have made port operations much more capital intensive. The first innovations occurred in the coastal trade, where shipowners were battling to regain market share from land transport and civil aviation. Interstate cargoes carried by sea around Australia fell from eighteen million tons in 1938-1939 to 15.9 million tonnes in 1949-1950; by the late 1950s Australia's six capital city ports together only handled 2.4 million tonnes of interstate

---

[18]See B. Slack, "Pawns in the Game: Ports in a Global Transportation System," *Growth and Change*, XXIV (Fall 1993), 579-588.

[19]Battye Library (BL), Fremantle Port Authority (FPA), 88/1/6/9, "Port Development in Australia."

general cargo. Shipowners were using obsolete vessels and were plagued by waterfront disputes and excess capacity, which in turn led to pressure to raise freight rates, further driving away trade.[20]

According to Frank Broeze, "containers were introduced as a radical measure to turn the tide."[21] In 1964 Associated Steamships introduced *Kooringah*, the world's first purpose-built cellular container vessel, on the route between Fremantle and Melbourne. In 1969 it put two more vessels into service between Brisbane and Fremantle. Container vessels were, however, slower to appear in the international trades because, unlike the coastal sector, they were not protected and the risks of innovation were far greater. In March 1966 the world's first fully integrated container service was introduced on the North Atlantic by Sea-Land Service Inc., which enjoyed the security of a long-term contract to supply US troops in West Germany. It was not until three years later that two British consortia, Overseas Containers Ltd. (OCL) and Associated Container Transportation Ltd. (ACT), introduced a container service on the UK/Australia route.[22] By the early 1970s about fourteen container vessels were regularly engaged in the Australia/UK/Europe trade.

Shipowners scheduled a turnround time of 100 hours in Australian ports compared to three-four weeks for conventional vessels.[23] But teething problems with the ships and containers, as well as delays caused by industrial disputes, meant that the full potential of containerisation was not immediately realised. The first frozen cargo of meat, which landed at Fremantle in March 1969, was tainted by styrene used in the insulation of the containers and all refrigerated containers had to be replaced.[24]

---

[20] J. Bach, *A Maritime History of Australia* (Melbourne, 1976), chapter 17.

[21] F. Broeze, "Containerization: The Globalization of Liner Shipping," in David J. Starkey and Gelina Harlaftis (eds.), *Global Markets: The Internationalization of the Sea Transport Industries since 1850* (St. John's, 1998), 386.

[22] OCL was formed by Alfred Holt and Co., British and Commonwealth Shipping, Furness Withy and Oriental Steamship Navigation Company. ACT was formed by the Port Line, Cunard, Blue Star, Ellerman, Ben Lines and the Harrison Line.

[23] P.E. Stoneham, "Conferences and Competition in Australia's Overseas Liner Trades," *Economic Record*, XLVI (1970), 203.

[24] Falkus, *Blue Funnel*, 366-367.

Containerisation, however, advanced faster than many had predicted. In the mid-1990s about sixty-five percent of the value of Australia's imports and forty percent of its exports were transported in containers. Yet by international standards the volumes handled in Australian ports are not large. In 1994 Hong Kong, the world's major container port, handled over eleven million Twenty-foot Equivalent Units (TEUs), while Sydney handled only 540,000 TEUs.[25] In 1997 Felixstowe handled 2.25 million TEUs, a record quantity for a British port; on 24 March 1998 Singapore handled its 100-millionth container.[26] As Frank Broeze put it, "containerization, offering the highest quality form of maritime transport, both reflects and confirms the distribution of economic power throughout the world."[27]

One of the most striking characteristics of container ships is that they are usually "gearless" - that is, they depend on shore terminals with gantry cranes, rather than ships' gear, to handle the containers. By eliminating on-board handling gear, considerable economies in ship construction are possible. Thus, the implications of containerisation were as momentous for the ports as for the shipowners. At a simple physical level, port skylines were altered by the presence of giant skyscraper container cranes, while the luffing cranes used to handle general cargo gradually fell into disuse and sat idle and unsaleable. By the late 1990s the stevedoring workforce had shrunk to about 3000, less than one-tenth of its size in the 1960s. It is clear that the ports and the workforce were forced to adapt to enormous changes imposed externally.

Port and City Interactions

In the twentieth century, industries such as oil and steel have increasingly migrated to the seaboard to minimise transport costs. In 1915, for example, Broken Hill Proprietary Company (BHP) built its blast furnace at Newcastle, NSW. The port location meant that raw materials could be imported cheaply by sea, and steel acted as a magnet for other industries,

---

[25]Containers are usually counted in TEUs, which refer to the International Standards Organisation's twenty-foot by eight-foot containers.

[26]*World Maritime News*, 3 and 24 April 1998.

[27]Broeze, "Containerization," 416.

triggering the rise of one of Australia's major "seaport industrial machines."[28] BHP's decision in 1997 to phase out production at Newcastle was a severe blow for both the city and its port. While the main function of a port is to provide a link in the transport chain, "a modern seaport node within a multimodal transport system frequently develops also as a major urban centre, an industrial focus, an important source of employment and an influential factor in national and regional development."[29]

After the Second World War, port-based industrialisation and metropolitan expansion meant that the capital city ports were gradually swamped by industrial, commercial and residential development, making it increasingly difficult to provide adequate space for the largest bulk carriers and tankers. The new cargo-handling technologies exacerbated the situation: container terminals, for example, required extensive land areas, a requirement not easily met in a cramped metropolitan port. In Sydney the terrain limited the availability of suitable land for port development. The steep foreshores and limited flat land at the water's edge meant that expensive rock blasting and/or reclamation was required to create sufficient space for terminal facilities. Even if reclamation were undertaken, it was restricted by the need to retain an adequate area of water for the safe manoeuvring of ships. The port was "precociously supplied with deep water, yet now hemmed in on all sides not only by a great city but also by its beautiful and unyielding sandstone."[30]

Thus, some of the original port sites, which were adequate in the nineteenth century, suffered from excessive costs in the late twentieth due to poor location. A generation ago, one writer observed that:

> The principal historical lesson appears to be that wherever a port is established there will grow a town. The town will eventually surround the port, thus confining its growth and causing congestion on the land transport side which will prove damaging both to the amenity of the

---

[28]The phrase is from J. Bird, *Seaport Gateways of Australia* (London, 1968), 139.

[29]B.S. Hoyle and D.A. Pinder, *Seaports, Cities and Transport Systems. Cityport Industrialisation and Regional Development* (Oxford, 1981), 1.

[30]Bird, *Seaport Gateways*, 67.

> town and to the port's reputation as a convenient place for the transaction of its business.[31]

"Competition" between ports and cities for land use represented a highly complicated interaction of economics and politics. The large number of metropolitan agencies whose interests, powers and responsibilities did not easily mesh with those of the port authorities retarded adaptation to this "competition." The powers of the port authorities were usually limited to the immediate port areas and they had no control over metropolitan development. The provision of vital land transport links, for example, depended on the joint efforts of various public and private agencies, each with differing and possibly conflicting interests and responsibilities. Thus, the provision of road and rail access involved a large number of trade-offs between public and private, port and city, and rich and poor interests. Such compromises greatly complicated the solutions to problems of port development.

Suffering from excessive costs as a result of poor location, the ports were eventually forced to break out of their metropolitan straitjackets, but the relocation of facilities proceeded slowly because alterations to established patterns of port investment entailed significant costs. The financial cost for the port authority was often considerable, as container ships made fewer calls, thus reducing revenues. Another important factor was the longevity of most port assets. Once their capital cost was amortised, they could be maintained in operational condition for a relative pittance. Unless the benefits of the new technology were compelling, it was often more economic to use the obsolete capacity rather than invest in new facilities. Container terminals, for example, required special wharves which rendering existing ones, otherwise useable for many years, obsolete. Port authorities were forced to either demolish or find alternative uses for existing cargo sheds. Some imaginative uses included boat museums, art galleries, restaurants and shopping arcades.[32]

---

[31]S. Wilson, "The Effect on the Land Transport System of Ports and Water Transport," *Dock and Harbour Authority*, XLVI (1965), 89.

[32]For a general discussion of waterfront redevelopment, see P.R. Proudfoot, "A Model for Government Control in Urban Waterfront Renewal," *International Journal of Maritime History*, VIII, No. 1 (June 1996), 183-198.

In Fremantle, a new harbour was created in the 1950s at Kwinana, physically separate from the existing urban area, as part of an overall programme of economic expansion by the state government. The Outer Harbour offered natural anchorages with up to sixty-foot depths, but extensive dredging was necessary to provide access to the Sound. Careful planning ensured that port growth did not outstrip the capacity of the transport network. The establishment of an oil refinery in 1954 set off an "industrial chain reaction," and it was followed by an iron and steel works, alumina refinery, fertiliser plant and nickel refinery.[33]

In the 1960s, the Maritime Services Board began to develop Botany Bay as the site for Sydney's second port.[34] The problem was that Botany Bay was not in open country but virtually in the heart of the metropolitan area. A detailed study by Noel Butlin concluded that on at least three grounds Botany Bay was a planning failure: first, no systematic attempt was made to gauge whether the social benefits exceeded social costs; second, the wider environmental impacts of port development on the city were neglected; and finally, port planning was carried out in isolation and not integrated with overall city development.[35]

The continued expansion of both port and city land use also led to increased pressure on the environment. There have, of course, always been environmental risks associated with operating ports in close proximity to metropolitan areas: dredging and land reclamation can destroy the habitats of marine species; pollution, noise and congestion often accompany port operations. The development of specialised container and bulk-handling facilities, with their intensive high-speed operations, has also affected the environment.

Two incidents in the history of the Port of Fremantle show that operations can be especially hazardous during wartime.[36] In 1918 SS *Polgowan*, which reputedly was carrying sufficient TNT to blow up the city, caught fire in the Inner Harbour. Luckily, the ship's crew and the

---

[33]Tull, *Community Enterprise*, 180-183.

[34]N.G Butlin (ed.), *The Impact of Port Botany* (Canberra, 1976), 93-94.

[35]*Ibid.* See also P.R. Proudfoot, *Seaport Sydney. The Making of the City Landscape* (Sydney, 1996).

[36]This paragraph draws on Tull, *Community Enterprise*, 144 and 192.

local fire brigade brought the fire under control. On 17 January 1944, a day the harbour was crowded with shipping, *Panamian* was loading when a discarded cigarette butt set a piece of hessian sacking alight. The sacking was thrown overboard but the surface of the water was covered with oil, probably from refuelling submarines, and instead of being extinguished the flaming sack started a major conflagration. *Panamian* was engulfed in flames and the blaze threatened to spread to HMS *Maidstone*, a tender moored nearby loaded with explosives and fuel. *Maidstone* had no steam up and had to be dragged out of harm's way by tugs. The ship was moved just in the nick of time because its paintwork had caught fire. It took six days to extinguish the blaze.

A horrific accident at the Canadian port of Halifax on 6 December 1917 provides an indication of the catastrophe that could have occurred. *Mont Blanc*, a French munitions ship with a full cargo of explosives, collided with another vessel and blew up. The massive explosion instantly killed 1600, injured more than 9000 and left 25,000 homeless. The shattered city took many years to recover.[37] Clearly, the environmental costs and other risks of port operations have to be weighed against the considerable economic benefits.[38]

By the 1990s there were signs that technological change had weakened the links between ports and cities and even altered the traditional culture of the waterfront. According to Frank Broeze, "the port city as a social phenomenon has largely ceased to exist: despite the huge space taken up by harbours and ancillary installations, Australia's port cities have in fact become general cities that also happen to contain ports."[39] Ships are more sparsely crewed and spend less time in port, leading to the decline of taverns and other service industries catering for itinerant sailors. Container crane operators are isolated in their cabs thirty metres in the air, and with fewer workers around there is less opportunity for the development of the union solidarity for which the waterfront is well

---

[37]J.F. Kitz, *Shattered City. The Halifax Explosion and the Road to Recovery* (Halifax, 1989).

[38]A.C. Burdall and H.J. Williamson, "A Green Port: An Engineer's View," in C.R. Ford (ed.), *Ports into the Next Century* (London, 1991), 247-248.

[39]F. Broeze, *Island Nation. A History of Australians and the Sea* (St. Leonards NSW, 1998), 174.

known. Even the male-dominated culture has changed: in 1975 the Waterside Workers' Federation altered its rules to allow women to join.[40] Microeconomic reform has also had major implications for working conditions and labour relations in the port industry.

Microeconomic Reform and the Ports

In 1975, following continued complaints about the adequacy of Australian ports, the federal government appointed a Commission of Inquiry into the Maritime Industry. It found that, on the whole, the bulk ports performed well and that the major problems were in container handling. Shipowners complained that container-handling rates were well below the twenty-five per hour achieved in ports like Rotterdam, Tilbury, Oakland and New York. The low productivity was attributed to a series of factors, including the state of the physical infrastructure and problems with the workforce.[41] A report by the Inter-State Commission (ISC) in 1989 found that the Australian waterfront industry was characterised by "high costs, endemic unreliability, a high level of industrial disputation, inappropriate manning levels and work practices, poor discipline, poor motivation throughout the industry, and a pervasive lack of competition."[42]

It was agreed that the Australian waterfront was close to the bottom in international comparisons of efficiency and that radical reforms were needed. At that time the federal government was pursuing a programme of microeconomic reform to improve the efficiency of the economy and the waterfront was an obvious target.[43] In order to clarify the

---

[40]M. Beasley, *Wharfies. A History of the Waterside Workers' Federation of Australia* (Rushcutters Bay, NSW, 1996), 229.

[41]Australia, Commission of Inquiry into the Maritime Industry, *Report on the Adequacy of Australia's Ports* (Canberra, 1976), 5-6 and 21-22.

[42]Australia, Inter-State Commission (ISC), *Waterfront Investigation: Conclusions and Recommendations* (Canberra, 1989), I, xv.

[43]Microeconomic reform refers to measures taken at the firm or industry level to increase the efficiency of inputs and so improve economic performance and incomes. For a more detailed discussion see P. Forsyth, *Microeconomic Reform in Australia* (St. Leonards, NSW, 1992).

reform process it is, however, necessary to examine briefly some key features of the waterfront labour market and industry structure.

The demand for waterfront labour is derived from the level of trade. While technological change has improved communications and reduced the historical unpredictability of trade flows, labour requirements still vary widely due to fluctuations in the type of cargoes, level of investment in port facilities and availability of mechanical equipment. Demand fluctuations give rise to a dual problem: it can be just as undesirable from an efficiency viewpoint to have too large a reserve of labour which is often unemployed as a persistent shortage which delays ships. Under the system of casual employment which prevailed in Australia until the 1940s, workers were hired only when there was work and the employers avoided as far as possible the costs of maintaining an idle labour force. The introduction of attendance money and other benefits in the 1940s meant that the workforce was only nominally casual. Finally, in 1967 permanent employment was introduced.

There were two major reasons for the introduction of permanent employment. First, and most important, containerisation required fewer but more highly skilled workers, and the introduction of the necessary training programs was difficult to implement with casual employees. Second, the casual nature of waterfront employment meant that a worker's employer could change from day to day; under these circumstances the worker tended to owe allegiance to his union rather than his employer. Employers generally recognised that casuals were less productive and more unreliable.[44] It was hoped, somewhat naively given the long history of icy industrial relations, that permanent employment would lead to the development of greater employee loyalty. A number of industry-wide levies were used to fund idle-time payments and other benefits. These became increasingly costly and were abolished in the 1990s.

The main target of reform was the MUA's monopoly of waterfront employment and its use of restrictive practices.[45] A restrictive practice may be defined as "an institutional arrangement requiring the

---

[44]R. Saundry and P. Turnbull, "Melee on the Mersey: Contracts, Competition and Labour Relations on the Docks," *Industrial Relations Journal*, XXVII, No. 4 (1996), 284.

[45]The powerful MUA was created in 1989 when the Waterside Workers' Federation merged with the Seamen's Union.

employer to hire more labor than he would have hired in the absence of compulsion, at a given wage rate."[46] Such practices have a long history throughout the world.[47] In 1989 the ISC identified a number, including overmanning of tasks, rostering restrictions, refusal to transfer between tasks or locations within a shift, and equalisation of earnings and idle time.[48]

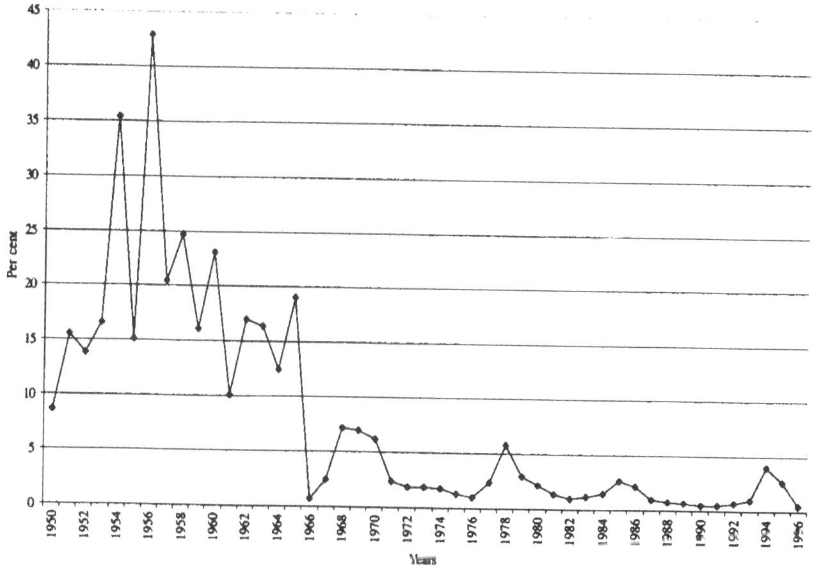

Figure 1: Working Days Lost.

Source: Commonwealth of Australia, Labour Reports and Australian Bureau of Statistics, Industrial Disputes, Cat 6322, various issues.

---

[46]P.T. Hartman, *Collective Bargaining and Productivity; The Longshore Mechanization Agreement* (Berkeley, 1969), 42.

[47]A. Green, "Spelling, Go-slows, Gliding Away and Theft: Informal Control over Work on the New Zealand Waterfront 1915-1951," *Labour History*, LXIII (1992), 100-114.

[48]ISC, *Waterfront Investigation*, 54.

It is important to note, however, that the ability of unions to impose restrictive practices depends on two main factors: first, the extent of union control over the workforce and productive process; and second, the willingness of employers to resist strikes and stoppages.[49] The MUA's effective monopoly of waterfront employment was originally limited to general cargoes because the Stevedoring Industry Act of 1956 prescribed that bulk handling be done by non-MUA workers. But in the 1980s the union succeeded in winning coverage of some workers employed in bulk-handling operations. Clearly the MUA exerts significant job control. Since the first priority of shipowners is rapid turnround, they have often been willing to grant concessions to maritime unions, particularly as the increased costs can be passed on in the form of higher freight rates. As a result of industry restructuring by the 1990s two firms, P&O Ports and Patrick Stevedores, dominated the supply of container stevedoring services in Australia. The lack of competition weakened the incentives for management to minimise labour costs. It can thus be argued that it was this lack of competition that allowed restrictive practices to survive. Stevedoring and shipping companies tolerate them because they can readily pass higher costs onto shippers and exporters.

Stevedoring, together with coal mining, has traditionally been one of Australia's most strike-prone industries. Between 1955 and 1966 time lost through industrial disputes totalled fifty-five days per worker in coal mining, fifty-seven days in stevedoring, and about one and one-half days per worker in all other industries.[50] Figure 1 illustrates working days lost through stevedoring disputes as a percentage of the Australian total of days lost between 1950 and 1996. The industry's poor strike record persisted until the late 1960s, when there was a brief pause for negotiations over permanent employment. Industrial trouble soon resumed, however, and in 1970 there was a national waterfront strike, the largest since 1956.[51] Between 1950 and 1965 stevedoring averaged 19.2% of total working days lost due to strikes; subsequently, it accounted for only 2.2%. But this decline was also partly due to the shrinkage of the stevedoring workforce:

---

[49]E. Mansfield, *The Economics of Technological Change* (London, 1969), 153-154.

[50]F.T. Nankervis, *Descriptive Economics* (8th ed., Croydon, VIC, 1968), 87.

[51]Beasley, *Wharfies*, 231.

between 1983-1995 working days lost per thousand employees were about eleven times higher than the Australian average.[52] Waterside workers remained relatively prone to strike.

But change was on the way. The ISC recommended a reform programme with two main elements: labour market reforms, which included a shift from industry to company employment, a reduction in the number of unions and a cut in restrictive practices; and reforms to make port authorities more commercially oriented, to force them to withdraw from most direct service provision and to compel them to take a more strategic role in port management, planning and development. The ISC estimated that savings from reforms could amount to nineteen percent of all waterfront costs.[53] The federal government created the Waterfront Industry Reform Authority (WIRA) in July 1989 to oversee changes to the labour market. As we shall see, the WIRA reform process achieved important gains but by 1995 had cost about $420 million.[54] According to Peter Turnbull, the cooperative approach adopted in Australia offered more potential for long-term productivity improvement than the re-casualisation and cost-cutting reforms introduced in the UK.[55]

Figure 2 illustrates a partial measure of productivity, the average crane rate, for Australia's five container ports between June 1990 and June 1997. The crane rate is the number of TEUs moved per crane per hour. The rate has risen from about fourteen per hour in 1990 to about twenty-one per hour in 1996, an increase of fifty percent. Obviously, an average conceals variations among ports. For example, in 1996 Brisbane moved 20.3 TEUs per net crane hour; Sydney, 19.8; Melbourne, 22.4; Adelaide, 22.4; and Fremantle, 21.7. Melbourne, Adelaide and Fremantle were performing slightly above average and Brisbane and Sydney slightly below. It is important to stress, however, that port performance is a multi-

---

[52]P. Reith, "Waterfront Reform: Seven Benchmark Objectives," Speech given in Canberra, 8 April 1998, table 1-B.

[53]ISC, *Waterfront Investigation*, 164.

[54]Australia, Bureau of Industry Economics, *International Benchmarking. Overview 1995* (Canberra, 1995), 51.

[55]P.J. Turnbull, "Waterfront Reform in Britain and Australia - In Practice and in Principle," *Journal of Industrial Relations*, XXXIV (June 1992), 229-246.

dimensional concept and cannot be assessed on the basis of a single indicator.

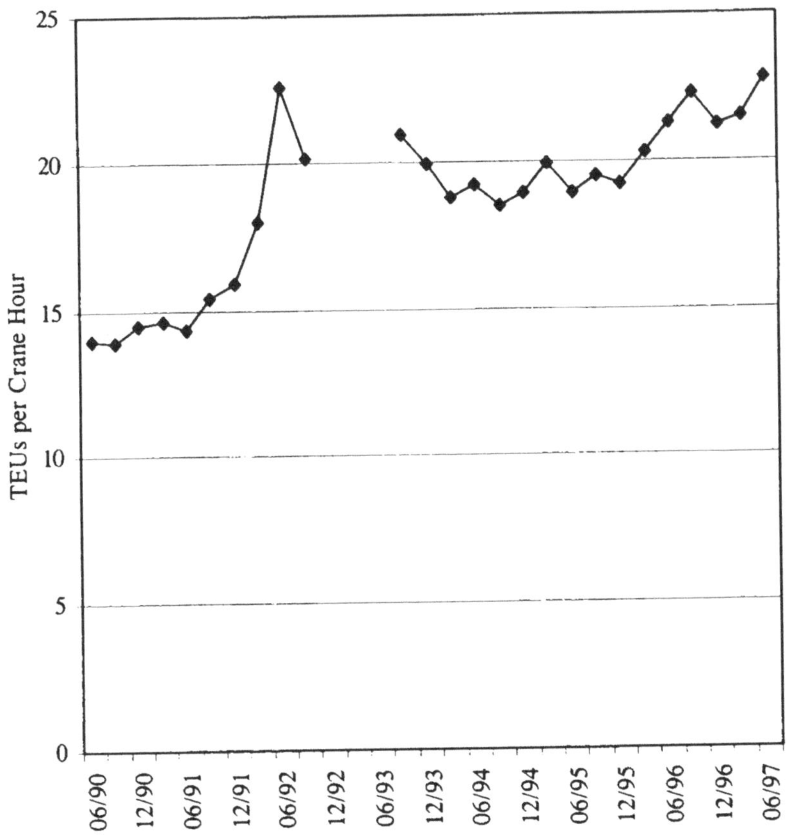

Figure 2: National Container Crane Rates.

Source: Bureau of Transport and Communications Economics, Waterline, various issues.

Figure 3 illustrates the national port interface cost index (1989-1990 = 100), which measures shore-based shipping charges for containers moving through the capital city ports. The index declined by about fourteen percent to $558 per TEU for imports and by about eleven percent to $511 per TEU for exports. This suggests that some progress had been made in reducing stevedoring and other port charges.

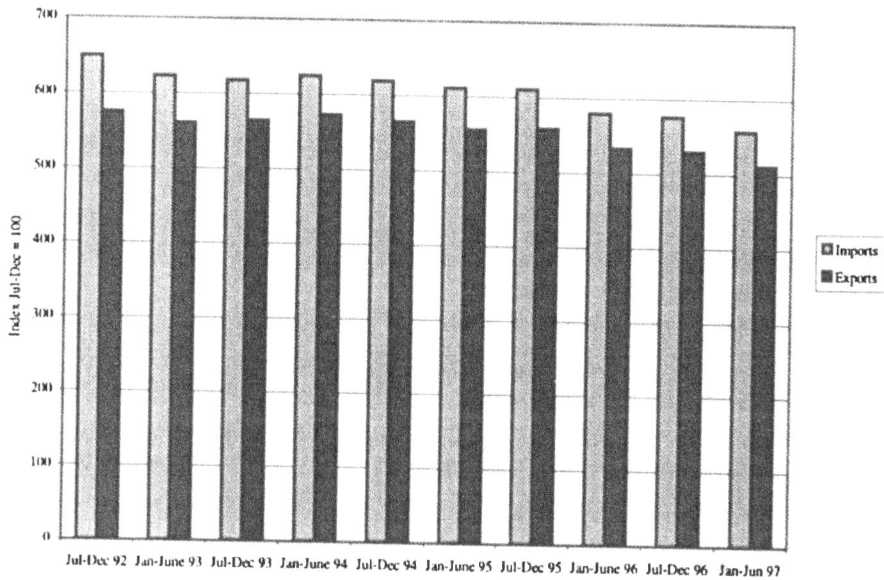

Figure 3: The National Port Interface Index

Source: See figure 2.

While there have been gains in performance at Australian ports, a comparison of indicators covering waterfront charges, timeliness and productivity shows they still fall short of international standards. Comparisons are often made with Asian ports such as Singapore, Hong Kong and Kaohsiung. In the 1960s the efficiency of such ports was generally low but by the 1990s had increased dramatically; Singapore, for example, was the world's leading container port.[56] But comparing port productivity is complex, since performance measures are affected by a

---

[56]See K. Trace, "Asean Ports since 1945. Maritime Change and Port Rivalry," in F. Broeze (ed.), *Gateways of Asia. Port Cities of Asia in the 13th-20th Centuries* (London, 1997), 318-338.

variety of factors, including port geography and differences in the volumes and composition of shipping and cargoes. For example, ports where ships unload or load part cargoes will always find it difficult to achieve the productivity levels of those where vessels routinely load or discharge their entire cargo. A study by London-based Drewy Shipping Consultants has suggested that this is the major reason why there are differences in productivity between container terminals.[57] At Fremantle, for instance, in the mid-1990s the average number of container moves per hour on ships of the Maersk Line, which discharged full cargoes from Singapore, was about twelve percent higher than for other vessels.[58] Ports that handle less-than-container-load traffic, where cargoes have to be packed and unpacked from containers within or near the port, are handicapped compared to those that handle full containers.[59]

The second element of the ISC's programme, the reform of the port authorities, involved state governments because, with the exception of the Northern Territory, port operation and development is a state responsibility. The reform process at this level was designed to improve the efficiency of port management and has involved commercialisation, privatisation, and contracting out. Commercialisation involves restructuring to introduce accountability and efficiency into government activities. A key element has been the establishment of "competitive neutrality," that is, a situation where the port authority faces exactly the same conditions as competing organisations in the private sector.

In the 1990s Australia has had one of the largest privatisation programmes among OECD countries, second by value to the UK and second relative to GDP to New Zealand.[60] Despite this, only the government of Victoria has privatised ports. In 1995/1996 the sale of the

---

[57]Cited by C. Hamilton, "Productivity in Australian Container Terminals" (Unpublished paper for the Australia Institute Ltd., 25 April 1998). The original report is Drewy Shipping consultants, *World Container Terminals: Global Growth and Private Profit* (London, 1998).

[58]M. Tull, "The Fremantle Port Authority: A Case Study in Microeconomic Reform," *Economic Papers*, XVI, No. 4 (1997), 47-48.

[59]Trace, "Asean Ports since 1945," 326-327.

[60]"Privatisation in Australia," *Reserve Bank of Australia Bulletin* (December 1997), 7-16.

regional ports of Portland and Geelong raised $51 million and $30 million, respectively. The general reluctance to privatise all Australian public utilities has been attributed to a variety of factors, including conservatism, the influence of unions and "a lingering historical belief in the efficacy of public provision."[61]

In most ports enterprise bargaining agreements have been successfully introduced; the number of unions has been reduced; and workforce flexibility has been enhanced with the removal of many restrictive work practices and the introduction of multi-skilling. As a result of contracting out and other reforms, between 1993 and 1997 total employment at Australian port authorities fell by about fifty-two percent.

The experience of the Port of Fremantle can be used to illustrate the reform process.[62] In November 1995, for the first time in the history of the port, government spelled out the FPA's role: "to facilitate trade in an efficient and commercial manner." Government "commercialised" the FPA in July 1996 and the relationship between the port and government is now primarily strategic, with the former having greater autonomy to work within an annual performance plan. Immediate benefits included the removal, in the interests of competitive neutrality, of a three-percent statutory levy on turnover and the establishment of a dividend policy that allows the port to reduce debt and provide for future investment before paying dividends. The number of divisions within the FPA was reduced from five to three: Strategic and Commercial Development, Marine and Technical Services and Commercial Operations. As a result of the reforms, the FPA's rate of return on assets increased substantially to about fifteen percent per annum between 1993-1994 and 1995-1996, almost twice the average for Australian ports. A new cost-based tariff system was introduced in 1990-1991, and by 1995-1996 charges had fallen by 18.5% in real terms. In the early 1990s turnround times for container ships improved by about twenty-two percent and for bulk ships by about thirteen percent, suggesting that there were substantial gains in efficiency. As a result of the contracting out of non-core functions, in the six years between 1990 and 1996 staff numbers fell from 753 to 208. The loss of about three-quarters of the staff was obviously fairly traumatic but there

---

[61]S. King and R. Maddock, *Unlocking the Infrastructure. The Reform of Public Utilities in Australia* (St. Leonards, NSW, 1996), 17.

[62]This paragraph draws on Tull, "The Fremantle Port Authority," 33-53.

was a widespread acceptance of the need for change. Many staff took early retirement or found employment elsewhere in the port, often with the private contractors providing services previously supplied by the FPA.

Nevertheless, while the cooperative approach of the early 1990s was "a great leap forward" for the industry, the reform process, in terms of increases in container stevedoring productivity, seems to have stalled.[63] Container stevedoring productivity is still lower, and charges higher, than in many Asian and European ports. A key reason is the absence of effective competition in stevedoring. In recent years there have been some attempts to increase competition in this area. In Fremantle, for example, since 1996 Western Stevedores has competed with Patricks and P&O Ports for non-containerised cargoes. The American company Sea-Land took over the Adelaide container terminal in January 1992 and management successfully negotiated an aggregate wage that includes overtime and penalties with the MUA.[64] This has removed the incentive for workers to spin out work so that they can earn penalty rates. Sea-Land appears to be happy to continue working with the MUA.[65] But about ninety-five percent of container handling remains firmly in the hands of the duopoly.

Since 1997 the Howard government, spearheaded by Peter Reith, the Workplace Relations Minister, has supported a series of controversial attempts to reform the waterfront. The government set a number of targets, including ending restrictive work practices, increasing container crane movements from the existing level of eighteen per hour to twenty-five per hour, reducing injuries, and improving training.[66] The main aim, however, was to break the power of the MUA. If the Howard government had succeeded, it would have struck the most serious blow to waterfront labour since 1928, when the federal government introduced a system of labour licensing that became known as the "Dog Collar Act" because the

---

[63]See *Australian Financial Review*, 28 February and 5 June 1997.

[64]Sea-Land Service Inc. is a worldwide operator in container-shipping, operating a fleet of 105 container ships and approximately 200,000 containers in US and foreign trade and serving 120 ports in eighty countries and territories. A division, Sea-Land (Australia) Terminals Pty. Ltd., operates the Adelaide Container Terminal.

[65]*The Australian Magazine*, 11-12 April 1998.

[66]Reith, "Waterfront Reform."

cost of a licence was the same as the cost of a dog license.[67] The Act was, in effect, a political move against the Waterside Workers' Federation (the forerunner of the MUA) and resulted in the loss of its effective monopoly over waterfront employment. The union had to tolerate a rival until its members were absorbed into the Waterside Workers' Federation in 1950.

The Chamber of Commerce and Industry of Western Australia (CCI) has argued that in focussing policy on the MUA alone government is attacking the symptoms rather than the problem.[68] The CCI has suggested that the federal government use the Australian Competition and Consumer Commission to set price caps for stevedoring charges at a level significantly below current prices. The idea is to force stevedores to manage their operations efficiently because their profitability will depend on it. Clearly, reducing the MUA's power is a necessary but not a sufficient condition to improve waterfront efficiency.

The most dramatic development occurred in April 1998, when Patricks sacked its entire union workforce of 1400, leading to major industrial and legal warfare.[69] The MUA challenged the legality of the sackings in court, and on 21 April Justice North found that there was an arguable case that Patricks had breached the Workplace Relations Act 1996 and was engaged in an unlawful conspiracy to replace the workforce with non-union labour. The company and government unsuccessfully appealed the decision. The key reason for the MUA's victory was that the Workplace Relations Act's freedom of association provisions, designed to stop employees from being forced to join unions, also guaranteed them the right to belong to a union of their choice. It was thus illegal to dismiss workers simply because they were members of a particular union. The

---

[67]See R. Morris, "Australian Stevedoring and Shipping Labour under the Transport Workers Act 1928-47," *The Great Circle*, XI (1989), 17-31.

[68]Chamber of Commerce and Industry of Western Australia, *Policy Paper on Waterfront Reform* (Perth, 1998), 3.

[69]For a detailed account of the strike, see G. Griffin and S. Svensen, "Industrial Relations Implications of the Australian Waterside Dispute," *Australian Bulletin of Labour*, XXIV (September 1998), 194-206. See also the MUA's and Patrick Stevedores' respective web sites: http://mua.tcp.net.au/welcome.ssi and http://www.patrick.com.au.

government and employers had been caught in their own trap.[70] On 27 May Patricks capitulated and began talks with the union. On 25 June an agreement was announced in which the MUA agreed to 626 voluntary redundancies and the contracting out of security, cleaning and line-marking. The MUA's General Secretary, John Coombs, declared that the union had "probably finished up just in front," but there were no clear winners in the dispute.[71]

Conclusions

This essay has demonstrated that since 1945 Australian ports have had to adapt to enormous changes, including growth in the volume and alterations in the composition of shipping and trade flows; revolutionary technological change in shipping and cargo handling; and microeconomic reform of stevedoring and port administration. In some cases, competition between ports and cities for land use, and the need to provide deep-water berths, forced ports to develop new areas. While it is an oversimplification to see ports merely as "passive agents," there is no doubt that to a large extent they were forced to adjust to changes imposed externally.

The fact that Australian ports have generally had poor reputations for efficiency and reliability suggests that adaptation to changing circumstances has not been very successful. Despite major reforms in the early 1990s, container-handling rates at Australian ports still lagged and there were claims that inertia was setting in on the wharves. In 1998 the federal government, in conjunction with employers, launched a major assault on the high wages and restrictive practices of waterside workers. It can be argued, however, that the "war on the wharves" has focussed unduly on the faults of the MUA and that a more balanced approach would recognise that some degree of blame must be attributed to management. All parties agree that seaports are vital interfaces and must function efficiently if Australia is to survive as a trading nation in an increasingly globalised and competitive world economy.

---

[70]R.C. McCallum, "A Priority of Rights: Freedom of Association and the Waterfront Dispute," *Australian Bulletin of Labour*, XXIV (September 1998), 207-221.

[71]Griffin and Svensen, "Industrial Relations Implications," 203.

Aspinall, Cornes and Company and the Early Development of the Port of Yokohama

Peter N. Davies

Any attempt to provide an overview of the emergence of Japanese deep-sea ports needs to take account of a number of factors. These include the special topography of the archipelago, its unique history and the difficulties encountered when it was decided that its era of seclusion had to end. This essay will therefore survey these aspects to provide some perspective on the establishment and initial growth of what was to become the port of Yokohama. It will rely to a great extent on a case study of Aspinall, Cornes and Company, a pioneer expatriate mercantile firm in the city.[1]

I

Japan consists of four main islands – Hokkaido, Honshu, Shikoku and Kyushu – which extend for over 2000 kilometres. This variation in latitude results in considerable climatic differences, so that while northern Hokkaido is sub-arctic, southern Kyushu is nearly tropical. The total land mass is approximately fifty percent more than the UK, although only about one-fifth of the land can be farmed, with wet-rice being the most important crop by far. The limited amount of flat area has also had the effect of concentrating the population into a coastal strip which runs from the Kantō Plain, around Tokyo, through to the Kansai Plain, which includes the cities of Osaka, Kobe and Kyoto.[2] As a result of these factors, it was predictable that when deep-water harbours were required they would be situated mainly in this region.

---

[1]The author wishes to thank the Leverhulme Trust and the Cornes Group for the financial assistance which has supported the basic research on which this paper is based. He also acknowledges the assistance of his collaborator on this project, Professor Yoshinori Suzuki of Kanagawa University.

[2]Janet E. Hunter, *The Emergence of Modern Japan: An Introductory History Since 1853* (London, 1989).

Although some claim that the first emperor of Japan was a descendent of the Sun Goddess and ruled in 600 BC, it was not until the seventh century that the head of the Yamato clan adopted the title. Subsequent emperors exercised both political and religious authority in the central regions of Japan, but as their military powers declined, others found it convenient to rule in their name. This process came to a head in 1185 and thereafter Japan had a dual system, with the reigning emperor based in Kyoto and a *shogun*, who exercised real power, located elsewhere.[3]

The ensuing four centuries were marked by a series of power struggles and civil wars between conflicting *hans*, or extended families, and it was not until late in the sixteenth century that the country was finally pacified. By then power had fallen into the hands of Tokugawa Ieysu, who with his son Hidetada developed a system which kept authority in the family for the next 250 years. As they originated from the Kantō area, their military administration (*bakufu*) was established at Edo (later Tokyo), which served as the capital. At the same time, successive emperors continued to reside in Kyoto, where they enjoyed great respect but played no role in running what was now a unified country.

Japan was in contact with Europe for a brief period in the sixteenth and seventeenth centuries, and a tiny trade began to grow with Dutch, English, Spanish and, especially, Portuguese merchants. One aspect of these links was the introduction of firearms, which were quickly taken up by the various *hans*. Another was the arrival of Jesuit missionaries, who at first were well received, particularly in Kyushu. Although the Jesuits were opposed by many Buddhist groups, they gained much favour with the local *daimyo* (lords), for Portuguese merchants tended to bring their vessels to places where they felt welcome. This development was further strengthened when one of these minor *daimyo*, with the aid of the Portuguese, was able to transform the fishing village of Nagasaki into what was to become the major port for foreign trade. By 1578, when one of the most important of the Kyushu *daimyo* was converted, more than

---

[3]For an excellent concise account of Japanese geography and history, see Richard Bowring and Peter Kornicki (eds.), *The Cambridge Encyclopedia of Japan* (Cambridge, 1993). This volume also includes a comprehensive bibliography of recent studies.

150,000 Japanese had become Christians, a figure that was to double by 1610.[4]

The Tokugawas had no objection to the new religion but became increasingly distrustful of a sect which appeared to owe political allegiance elsewhere. They were also mindful that the growth of Christianity was coinciding with a rising European interest in the area; indeed, some feared that the missionaries might be the precursors of attempts to control or colonize the islands. Accordingly, they decided to ban all missionaries from Japan, but no action was taken until 1597, when arguments between the Portuguese Jesuits and the recently-arrived Spanish Franciscans led to a number of executions. This policy was then reversed for a while because the Tokugawas came to value trade with Europe. But the subsequent settlement of Dutch and English merchants, who showed no concern for proselytizing, demonstrated that trade could be pursued without religious constraints. The policy of persecution was later renewed with considerable vigour. This eventually led to a revolt by the Christian peasantry of Kyushu, which was put down with great slaughter in 1638. The *bakufu* then took a series of measures which effectively isolated Japan from the outside world.

The decrees from Edo prohibited Japanese nationals from travelling overseas and stopped those already living abroad from returning. As large Japanese communities had developed in many parts of Southeast Asia, this was a severe blow, especially since it was enforced by the threat of the death penalty. The decrees of 1638 also included provision for the expulsion of the Portuguese (the English had already left and the Spanish had been expelled in 1624). Moreover, the construction of sea-going vessels was totally forbidden. In spite of these draconian regulations the "era of seclusion" was never characterized by complete isolation. The *bakufu* authorized the retention of a single station on the island of Deshima in Nagasaki harbour, which was to be visited by a carefully controlled number of Dutch vessels each year. In addition, small groups of Chinese merchants were allowed to trade in Nagasaki from time to time. While these contacts were limited and very much at the pleasure of the state, the situation was ameliorated somewhat by large-scale smuggling from both China and Korea for much of this long period.

---

[4]Edwin O. Reischauer, *Japan: The Story of a Nation* (4th ed., New York, 1989), 92.

II

These decisions had a major impact on Japanese shipping. Prior to 1600 Japanese merchants were actively engaged in trade throughout Southeast Asia using wooden vessels of up to 700 tons that incorporated features of both the galley and the junk. Ocean voyages required quite sophisticated navigation techniques, but it is not certain if these were developed by the Japanese or borrowed from foreigners. In any event, the decision to end the building of large ships had serious consequences. The expansion southward, which had already resulted in small communities in Luzon, Siam and elsewhere, was reversed. According to one authority:

> A Japanese conquest of the Philippines would have been well within their capacity during the 17th Century and in the eighteenth they might well have anticipated Great Britain in the navigation of Australian waters...Certainly the story of European colonization would have been very different if the Tokugawa Government had not forced the Japanese to turn inwards upon themselves.[5]

Throughout the era of seclusion, Japan's "window on the world" at Nagasaki provided the authorities with some idea of events in Europe and America. Most Japanese, however, had little knowledge of external affairs and even those in positions of power were only vaguely aware of the internal forces which were gradually weakening the *bakufu*. These included the emergence of a merchant class; moves toward a monetary economy; and the growth of the population. As the latter increased, reaching thirty million by 1870, it placed enormous pressure on the available land and led to an even greater dependence on rice, which steadily became the desired food for virtually all Japanese. While these trends presaged the future and caused much resentment in some quarters, there was no real opposition to the *status quo* and the *bakufu* continued to exercise their customary level of control. It was not, in fact, until the early nineteenth century that these internal changes, plus a series of external events, led to a reappraisal of Japanese society.

---

[5]Richard Storry, *A History of Japan* (Harmondsworth, 1985), 65.

III

The spread of European influence to India and East Asia, the development of colonialism and the growth of trade were important factors in the changing international environment. The growing number of American whaling vessels and advances in steam technology were other aspects which led to the decisions by several countries to attempt to re-establish contact with Japan. But the rising commerce with the region was the principal motivation. This had already led to the establishment of trading centres at Singapore (1819), Hong Kong (1841) and at four ports in China, including Shanghai in 1842. This development brought into focus the need for convenient and secure supplies of water, food, repair facilities and (potentially) coal. Better provision for the care and return of shipwrecked seamen was a further consideration, while the possibility of a valuable trade with Japan also prompted action.

At first the most active nation was Russia, which was interested in securing supplies to aid its expansion in Alaska and Eastern Siberia. This began in 1805 but all overtures were rejected by Japan. Britain also sought unsuccessfully to establish diplomatic relations. While greater efforts would doubtless have followed, they were forestalled by the United States, which mounted a large-scale expedition under Commodore Perry. His so-called "black ships" arrived in what is now Tokyo Bay in July 1853 and a few days later he landed at Uraga, where he presented the governor with a list of demands to be sent to the *shogun*. Perry then sailed away without waiting for an answer, merely stating that he would be returning the following spring for a formal reply. When he was permitted to land in February 1854, he agreed as a gesture of goodwill to come ashore at the fishing village of Yokohama rather than at Edo.

The negotiations that followed resulted in the Treaty of Kanagawa, which established diplomatic relations, but not trade, and arranged for the opening of ports at Hakodate in Hokkaido and Shimoda, an isolated place at the extreme edge of Tokyo Bay. It was further agreed that an American consul could reside at Shimoda and that additional talks would take place at an unspecified date. In the interim, a Russian fleet under Admiral Putyatin arrived in Nagasaki during August 1853. Although Japanese procrastination meant that he left without making any progress, he made it clear that he would return. These manoeuvres undoubtedly helped to convince the *bakufu* that some form of agreement with foreign nations was mandatory. The key factor in convincing the Japanese to come to terms with Perry was the clear knowledge that his fleet was in a strong position to blockade all seaborne supplies entering Edo. This city of over one million was almost entirely dependent upon food brought in from northern and western Japan by coastal vessels. As a result, some within government were persuaded that effective resistance was impractical.[6] But this view was not universally accepted throughout the *hans* and the following years - known as the *bakumatsu*, or end of the shogunate - were marked by a massive difference of opinion between conflicting forces.

Nevertheless, the immediate view of the shogunate was confirmed after the outbreak of the Crimean War when a British fleet under Admiral Sterling came to Japan to search for Russian ships. In October 1854 permission was given to call at Nagasaki and Hakodate for supplies, a further indication of the end of Japanese isolation. This was finally completed in 1858 when the first American consul, Townsend Harris, concluded a treaty which covered most aspects of commerce and navigation. This was quickly followed by similar arrangements with the major European powers, which provided in particular for certain designated ports to be opened for foreign trade. These *ansei* (unequal) treaties also provided foreigners with extra-territoriality within the trading settlements set up to cater for the more important population centres.[7]

One such area was in the Osaka region. Osaka was already a major port for coasting vessels and catered not only for its own locality but also for Kyoto, twenty-seven miles away. The *bakufu* felt it would be dangerous to have Western merchants and seafarers within the confines of a massive conurbation and decided to site a new, separate enclave at the more distant village of Hyogo, which was to be developed as a modern port to serve the entire Kansai area. This was then re-named Kobe and for a while was quite successful in isolating foreigners from locals.

The other great centre of population was at Edo. Although this was already a major port dealing with the large coastal trade, and while it could have been developed to some extent, the *bakufu* claimed that this was impossible. In practice the government was anxious to keep foreigners away from the city but it conceded that some provision had to be made for this region. As a compromise it was finally agreed that Yokohama, the

---

[6]Storry, *History*, 87.

[7]Hugh Cortazzi, *Victorians in Japan. In and Around the Treaty Ports* (London, 1987), xi-xii, provides a useful guide to these treaties.

fishing village situated eighteen miles from the capital where the negotiation with Perry had taken place, would be transformed into a modern port and a centre for overseas trade.

Construction at Yokohama began in the summer of 1858, soon after the *ansei* treaties had been approved. Early work included the building of a stone pier and a number of jetties. This was followed by the erection of many flimsy buildings which were to serve as warehouses (known as "godowns"), houses and shops. There was also a stone Customs House. The area on which they were built was separated from the mainland by a swamp and a river. A bridge was built over the latter and a causeway and bridge over the former; both were then closely guarded by the *shogun*'s troops, who closed both entrances to the enclave at sunset, by which time all foreigners without special permission were obliged to be back in residence.

While the site was regarded by British officials as totally inadequate, as soon as the port was opened near the end of 1859 foreign merchants and adventurers streamed in. This meant that the available land, which was divided into small sections and sold to the early arrivals, was quickly exhausted. Further sections were created by draining the adjoining swamp and settlement quickly expanded. Yet it was kept within these original boundaries for a number of years, and the lack of space gave rise to many problems.[8]

IV

Among the first group of traders to arrive at Yokohama was the Liverpudlian William Gregson Aspinall, who set up as a "Tea Inspector and General Commission Agent" on 1 May 1860.[9] That he quickly became a respected member of the community can be seen from his signature on a letter of protest in December of that year. The protest was against an instruction from the local authorities that residents should not carry revolvers on their persons, an order that had been issued after Michael Moss, one of Yokohama's pioneer traders, had shot and maimed a Japanese policeman who sought to arrest him after he had killed a wild

---

[8]*Ibid.*, 54-92, provides a vivid description of life for expatriates in early Yokohama.

[9]*North-China Herald*, 12 May 1860.

goose on the Kanagawa marshes. Further evidence for the idea that it was necessary to keep a pistol handy was the murder of Henry Heusken, an assistant to the US consul, in January 1861. This event was followed by representatives from Britain, France, Holland and Prussia moving their legations to Yokohama. But when Townsend Harris decided to stay in the capital, the protest ended and the diplomats returned to Edo.[10]

In spite of these difficulties Yokohama's trade continued to expand. In its second year exports were valued at over £1,000,000, with 3000 bales of silk and 1.25 million pounds of tea being shipped.[11] This was in spite of the fact that the initial export of gold had ended once the Japanese realised the consequences of valuing their silver currency at too high a rate.[12] The result of this rising level of activity was that many more merchants and entrepreneurs were attracted. These included John Black, an itinerant printer who later published the *Japan Herald*, and Frederick Cornes, who arrived in Yokohama early in 1861. After careful examination of the available possibilities, Cornes decided to join his knowledge of the silk trade with W.G. Aspinall's expertise with tea; on 1 April they entered business under the title of Aspinall, Cornes and Company.[13]

Frederick Cornes had been born in 1837 in Macclesfield, one of the main centres of the British silk trade, the younger son of the owner of a small silk mill where the young man secured a sound grasp of the business. It appears that the family firm offered insufficient scope for his talents, so in 1858 he was sent by Holliday, Wise and Company of Manchester to Shanghai as a silk buyer. There he established a reputation as a shrewd and knowledgeable agent. As part of his duties he came into contact with many other expatriate buyers and learned of the fresh sources of silk becoming available in the new Japanese treaty ports.[14] At the end of 1860 he resigned from Holliday, Wise and sailed for Yokohama.

---

[10]Pat Barr, *The Coming of the Barbarians* (London, 1967), 100.

[11]*Ibid.*

[12]*Ibid.*, 87.

[13]*North-China Herald*, 18 May 1861.

[14]Giovanni Federico, *An Economic History of the Silk Trade, 1830-1930* (Cambridge, 1997), 38.

At first the principal function of Aspinall, Cornes was to export silk (in various forms) and green tea. It also shipped large quantities of cotton during the American Civil War, when total quantities from all firms rose from only 4616 *piculs* in 1862 to 46,697 *piculs* the following year.[15] In addition, it was quickly engaged in the import of many profitable items, of which the most important were Lancashire cottons, metal and consumer goods, coals and other raw materials, including kerosene. These, of course, were in response to local demand and it was necessary to keep a sharp eye on rapidly changing conditions. The firm was also anxious to secure as many agencies as practicable and in 1863 was appointed to represent P&O. This seal of approval then led to further agencies, including Universal Marine Insurance Company, London and Oriental Steam Transit Insurance Company, Commercial Union and Queen Insurance Companies and, eventually, Lloyds.[16]

These agencies were obtained after fierce competition from other expatriate firms. The most important at first were Jardine, Matheson, W.R. Adamson and Dent and Company, who were all present when William Aspinall arrived in 1860. At that time it was estimated that thirty foreign traders, mainly British, had rented land and that 200 Japanese had already opened shops and other facilities. By the beginning of 1862 Yokohama had about 140 foreign residents and approximately fifty-five houses occupied by expatriates. By then most goods and services were available even though there was little formal structure until a municipal council was set up in 1862.[17] This initially had little authority but since trading conditions were good, most residents were at least moderately content. All were aware of the ever-present danger of fire but at least the risk to life from dissident groups appeared to have diminished.

---

[15]Grace Fox, *Britain and Japan, 1858-1883* (Oxford, 1969), 322.

[16]This discussion is based upon the Cornes Mss. in the possession of the author. This material consists of the business correspondence of Frederick Cornes, who lived in Yokohama from 1861 to 1865 and again after 1871 for various periods until 1911, when he returned permanently to England. During the times he was away from Japan and resident in London, Cornes conducted his business via a weekly exchange of letters with a partner or senior manager in Yokohama. This has survived in the form of 119 fifty-page copy books and two volumes of private letter books, which cover the period 1865-1889 in approximately 1300 pages.

[17]Barr, *Coming of the Barbarians*, 144 and 156.

This illusion was shattered on 14 September 1862 when Charles Lennox Richardson was attacked. Richardson and three companions had been riding their horses along the main street of Kanagawa when they met a Lord of Satsuma with his retinue. By not waiting for him to pass they gave such offence that Richardson was killed and the others barely escaped. Richardson's body was subsequently buried in the Foreigners' Cemetery on a site provided when one of Perry's seamen died in 1854 and where, by law, all foreigners who died in Japan had to be interred. The inquest took place on 15 September in Aspinall's house - a clear indication of the status of his firm. Although the *shogun* paid £100,000 in compensation, a British naval squadron subsequently bombarded Kagoshima in Satsuma in an abortive attempt to force further payment from the local *daimyo*.[18] Yet despite such difficulties, trade continued to grow. Other firms arrived while existing companies increased their scale of operations. By April 1863 close to $3,000,000 worth of property was owned in the port by the principal British merchants (see table 1).

Table 1
List of British Property at Yokohama-Kanagawa in 1863

Owners Names	Value $	%
Jardine, Matheson & Co.	763,719	26.5
Fletcher & Co.	478,423	16.6
Macpherson & Marshall	224,065	7.8
W. Kemptner	161,200	5.6
Ross, Barber & Co.	152,079	5.3
G. Barnet & Co.	140,662	4.9
D. Sassoon & Co.	120,580	4.2
Dent & Co.	100,793	3.5
Adamson & Co.	100,697	3.5
H.J. Hooper	82,164	2.9
Aspinall, Cornes & Co.	77,289	2.7
Hughes, Willgoss & Co.	53,835	1.9
Other	419,930	14.6
Total	2,879,796	100.0

Source: Tamakusu, "The West in Yokohama," *Yokohama Archives of History*, No. 5 (March 1987), table 4.

[18] *Ibid.*, 158-166.

Table 2
Export of Raw Silk, 1867-1869

Company Name		**Bales**	**%**
Aspinall, Cornes & Co.	(Br)	1,892	7.0
Textor & Co.	(Dut)	1,879	6.9
Gilman & Co.	(Br)	1,839	6.8
Valmale, Schoene & Milsom	(Br)	1,727	6.4
Bavier & Co.	(Swiss)	1,664	6.1
Aymonin & Co.	(Fr)	1,496	5.5
Hecht, Lilienthal & Co.	(Fr)	1,478	5.4
Strachan & Thomas	(Br)	1,382	5.1
Vincent Comi	(Fr)	1,296	4.8
Wilkin & Robison	(Br)	1,188	4.4
Ravel, Blanc & Co.	(Fr)	1,010	3.7
Bernard, Eccard & Raud	(Fr)	943	3.5
Sibel & Brenwald	(Swiss)	710	2.6
W.M. Van der Tak (Netherlands Trading Co.)	(Dut)	683	2.5
Jardine, Matheson & Co.	(Br)	637	2.3
Reiss & Co.	(Br)	572	2.1
Macpherson & Marshall	(Br)	549	2.0
Kniffler & Co.	(Pr)	542	2.0
A. Heard & Co.	(Am)	425	1.6
Petrocochino & Co.	(Br)	404	1.5
Other		4,822	17.8
Total		**27,138**	**100.0**

Source: Tamakusu, "The West in Yokohama, table 6.

Many small fires occurred from time to time. These were accepted as inevitable by the Japanese and led to the expatiates constructing fireproof godowns and a growing demand for insurance cover. A combination of circumstances led to both of these strategies being severely tested. A long dry spell was followed by a strong northerly wind, so when a minor spillage took place on the morning of 26 November 1866 it produced a conflagration which threatened all of Yokohama. Considerable damage was inflicted before the wind dropped and most of the Japanese quarter was destroyed. The Western sector also suffered significantly, with Jardine, Matheson and the Netherlands Trading Company, among many others, being completely destroyed. Even the Customs House and a number of "fireproof" warehouses suffered extensive damage.[19]

The port quickly recovered. Although some attempt was made to widen the main streets, the Japanese stoically rebuilt the same flimsy buildings on their previous sites. Expatriate rebuilding took longer, with business conducted in temporary premises until better arrangements could be made. Encouraged by the rising level of trade, many firms erected much stronger and more commodious properties. This was also the case for the foreign consulates, all of which had been destroyed. These developments put further pressure on space and led to the filling of the remainder of the swamp. In retrospect, the Great Fire played a useful role in modernizing the port and preparing it for further expansion, which was organized mainly by the pre-existing firms, although others were also attracted. By 1868 forty-six British concerns, including Butterfield and Swire, were operating in Yokohama.[20] Proof that commercial success was not guaranteed, however, was the failure of the venerable Dent and Company in 1868. Still, many enjoyed success, including Aspinall, Cornes, which between 1867 and 1869 was responsible for seven percent of the raw silk exported (see table 2).

V

Aspinall, Cornes' success was, of course, part of the general expansion of Japanese trade, which was reflected in the export of raw silk through the port of Yokohama (see table 3). In many respects Yokohama was well placed to take advantage of the demand encouraged by the blight of the European silk crop in the early 1860s. The port lay close to the main silk-producing areas and was the obvious outlet for these districts. It was also convenient for many of the principal tea-growing regions. Its growth was further ensured by its position near Japan's two main conurbations.

At first, cargoes were carried mainly by traditional *wasen* (small, wooden sailing vessels), although some less weighty items for the immediate hinterland could also utilize the Tōkaido highway, which connected with both Kyoto and Edo. But the supreme importance of water transport quickly ensured that Western-style sailing vessels and small

---

[19]Barr, *Coming of the Barbarians*, 186.

[20]Fox, *Britain and Japan*, 313-314.

steamships were acquired at an early date (although regular steam services did not begin until 1869). The extent of these acquisitions can be judged from statistics which show that when the new Meiji government came to power it took over 138 ships, totalling 17,000 tons, of which only one steamer and twenty sailing vessels had been constructed in Japan.[21] The need for similar improvements in land transport were met by constructing a rail network - significantly, the first nineteen miles of track were laid between Yokohama and Tokyo and became operational in 1872.

Table 3
Export and Value of Silk and Export of Cards

Seasons	Bales of 80 Catties	Piculs	Average Value in $	Amount in $	Average Sterling Rate	In £ Sterling	Card of Silkworms' Eggs
1860-61	11,318	9,055	372	3,369,864	5/2	870,548	
1861-62	11,915	9,532	403	3,844,023	5/1	977,022	
1862-63	25,891	20,712	459	9,493,400	5/1	2,412,905	
1863-64	15,931	12,744	500	6,374,685	5/0½	1,613,072	
1864-65	16,523	13,218	617	8,153,031	4/10	1,948,321	
1865-66	11,619	9,296	744	6,916,559	4/7¾	1,605,908	2,000,000
1866-67	13,564	10,852	765	8,304,969	4/7	1,904,468	950,000
1867-68	12,306	9,845	741	7,295,044	4/5¾	1,630,591	850,000
1868-69	15,500	12,400	800	9,920,000	4/6½	2,252,666	2,500,000

Source: Yokohama Chamber of Commerce, F.O.Adams, *et al.*, "Report upon the Central Silk Districts of Japan, June and July, 1869."

VI

The movement of ever-larger quantities of imports and exports was at first undertaken by individual sailing vessels, each of which had a separate owner. A list of these vessels, which covers the period from mid-1859 to 1868, suggests that in the early days the only steamships were naval vessels. While the first sailing ship, the 500-ton *Carthage*, arrived from Nagasaki on 2 July 1859, the first merchant steamer, the 759-ton *Scotland*, did not arrive from Shanghai until 7 March 1862. Later that same year Aspinall, Cornes was the agent for its first vessel, the 403-ton

---

[21]Tomohei Chida and Peter N. Davies, *The Japanese Shipping and Shipbuilding Industries* (London, 1990), 3 and notes 1 and 4.

Romeo, which was scheduled to sail direct to London loaded entirely with silk.[22] Aspinall, Cornes was subsequently to act for many independent sailing vessels and handled its first steamship, *Sarah*, in September 1863. This event, however, was completely overshadowed by the firm's appointment as agents for P&O. The first sailing of the new service was undertaken by the 812-ton *Aden*, which was scheduled to leave just one week after *Sarah*.

The importance of what became P&O's twice-monthly service to Shanghai was that it linked Yokohama with its main steamships lines which operated to Australia, India and Europe. At this time the route from the UK had three separate stages. The first was from Southampton (or Marseilles) to Alexandria; then came a rail journey across Egypt to Suez; while the third section was onward via P&O's "second" fleet to Ceylon, Singapore, Hong Kong and Shanghai. By this means passengers and mail could reach China in approximately fifty-four days. By 1866 the French Messageries Imperiales was operating a similar service to Shanghai with a connecting link to Yokohama. This originated in Marseilles and, like the separate P&O route, enabled passengers and mail from Britain to save six or seven days by crossing France via special trains. These rapid transits were not suitable for normal cargoes, which continued to be carried by sailing vessels. The fastest outward passage from London to Hong Kong was achieved by *Ariel* in eighty days, while the quickest recorded passage of eighty-nine days from Foochow to London was completed by *Sir Lancelot* in 1869. These vessels, like *Nightingale*, which took ninety-one days from Shanghai, sailed round the Cape of Good Hope. But despite these records the average voyage time was between 120 and 150 days.[23]

A serious challenge to these sailing vessels came in 1866 with the early voyages arranged by Alfred Holt and Company. By developing steamers with economical compound engines, Blue Funnel extended their range to over 8500 miles. These advanced craft were then able to undertake the long route around the Cape of Good Hope with only a single stop for coal at Mauritius. Although their scheduled outward passage was seventy-seven days and the homeward leg (after loading tea at Foochow) was eighty-two days, this was only marginally quicker than the fastest "clippers." As a result, apart from luxury items for which speed and

---

[22]Tomio Hora, *Ships Entered at Yokohama* (Yokohama, 1996).

[23]F.E. Hyde and J.R. Harris, *Blue Funnel* (Liverpool, 1957), 24.

certainty were essential, most cargo continued to be carried by sail via the Cape. This situation was dramatically transformed by the opening in 1869 of the Suez Canal, which reduced voyages to East Asia by about 3300 miles each way.[24] This development had little value for sailing vessels, which found it difficult to navigate the Red Sea, but it cut passages for steamers by ten or twelve days. Further improvements meant that voyage times soon averaged only fifty days outward and sixty days return, and by the 1880s these had been progressively reduced to round trips of approximately 102 days. The result of these events was that sailing vessels could not compete and were finally squeezed out of the trade.

The reduction in passage times by Blue Funnel was parallelled by Messageries Imperiales and P&O. The latter found that trade with Yokohama had grown so much that in 1866 it opened its own office in the port.[25] This was soon followed by other major lines, the most important of which was the Pacific Mail Steam Ship Company. While this line was primarily concerned with connecting San Francisco with Japan and China, prior to the opening of the Suez Canal it also provided a slightly quicker alternative route for passengers from England to Yokohama.[26]

The net effect of the growth of trade and the development of direct steam communications between Yokohama and the rest of the world was that the number of independent vessels began to decline while the average size of ship steadily increased. At the same time, Japanese vessels began to take an increasing share of the trade after 1870.

VII

The expansion of trade gradually transformed the scale and extent of Yokohama's port facilities. The harbour stretched from Treaty Point to the mouth of the Tsurumi River, a distance of approximately five miles.[27] The

---

[24]D.A. Farnie, *East and West of Suez* (Oxford, 1969), 22 and 174-183.

[25]D. Howarth and S. Howarth, *The Story of P&O* (London, 1986), 103.

[26]W.F. Mayers, N.B. Dennys and C. King, *The Treaty Ports of China and Japan* (London, 1867). The passage from the UK to New York took about eleven days; it was then about seven days to Panama; a day transiting the isthmus; twelve days to San Francisco; and another seventeen days from California to Yokohama.

[27]Encyclopaedia Britannica (9th ed., London, 1888), XXIV, 744-745.

average depth was forty-six feet at high water, with a tidal range of only eight feet; this was sufficient for even the largest vessels. While it was somewhat exposed, the construction of two granite breakwaters provided adequate protection. Two landing places - the English and French *hatoba* - were completed before the port was officially opened in 1859, but no quays were to be constructed for many years. It was thus necessary for all overseas cargo to be transshipped and carried to or from shore by junk or barge. Although this situation was later partly rectified by the building of a 2000-foot pier, it was not until 1897 and 1898, when two large docks were opened, that it was completely resolved. The extent to which these projects were arranged or assisted by foreign firms is not fully known. [28]

These improvements were greatly aided by the arrival of the international cable in 1871 and the subsequent development of the regional infrastructure. They were also helped considerably by Meiji policies that provided stability and promoted every opportunity to westernize to enable Japan to be competitive. Yokohama thus emerged as a major commercial centre with almost every facility and service. This did not include any provision for ship repair, but this was readily available at Yokusuka, about twelve miles to the south. The most striking development, of course, was the growth in trade. While the values of exports and imports in 1880 were £3,792,991 and £5,378,385, respectively, by 1905 comparable figures were over £14 million and £19 million. The town grew in parallel, so that its population of 111,176 in 1886 (including 3904 foreigners) rose to 316,333 (including 2447 expatriates) in 1903.[29]

The world's silk trade grew from approximately 8075 tonnes annually in 1873-1875 to 48,904 tonnes in 1927-1929. This growth was accompanied by an increase in Japan's share from 8.7% around 1880 to 60.8% by the end of the 1920s. Since seventy percent of Japanese silk exports up to 1923 were moved via Yokohama, this was an important factor in the port's expansion.[30] This process was greatly facilitated by the breakwaters completed in the period up to 1898, which provided an

---

[28] *Encyclopaedia Britannica* (11th ed., Cambridge, 1910-1911) XXVIII, 921.

[29] *Ibid.*

[30] Federico, *Economic History*, 32 and 35; and G. Alexandersson and G. Norström, *World Shipping: An Economic Geography of Ports and Seaborne Trade* (New York, 1963), 444.

enclosed area of 1200 acres. Further improvements were undertaken between 1906 and 1917 to enable the port to continue to deal with the largest vessels then in service. As a result, Yokohama continued to handle the largest share of Japan's foreign trade until the catastrophic earthquake of 1923. Although repairs were made rapidly, the ensuing disruption allowed Kobe to surpass Yokohama; by 1929, Kobe accounted for thirty-six percent of overseas cargoes compared to Yokohama and Osaka, which handled thirty-one and seventeen percent, respectively.[31]

In 1930 Yokohama's position was further enhanced by the dredging of a channel to Tokyo. This allowed vessels with drafts up to twenty-three feet to proceed to the capital, which had previously been accessible only to small coasters and lighters. Yokohama subsequently recovered its position as Japan's premier foreign-trade port, so that by 1939 it was responsible for twenty-nine percent of a much larger total while Kobe and Osaka each handled twenty-five percent. In addition to raw silk and silk piece-goods, Yokohama's principal exports in the 1930s included clothing, tinned salmon and crab, cotton piece-goods and manufactured articles. At the same time, its major imports were cotton, wheat, wool, oil, beans, fertilizers, timber and machinery. These cargoes, together with a large volume of passenger traffic, were carried by many of the world's most important shipping lines, including Nippon Yusen Kaisha (Japan); P&O and Blue Funnel Lines (Britain); Hamburg-Amerika and North German Lloyd (Germany); Lloyd Triestino (Italy); and the Dollar Line and Canadian Pacific Steamships (North America).[32]

VIII

Both Frederick Cornes and William Aspinall remained in the port until 1865, when Cornes returned to the UK to establish an office in London. As a result, he was away when Aspinall, Cornes lost its P&O agency in 1866. But perhaps it was due to his lobbying in the City of London that the company was appointed the first Lloyds agent in Japan in 1868. This more than offset the loss of the earnings from P&O and gave the

---

[31]Clarence Winchester (ed.), *Shipping Wonders of the World* (London, 1936), 118; and Alexandersson and Norström, *World Shipping*, 446.

[32]Alexandersson and Norström, *World Shipping*, 444 and 446; and Winchester (ed.), *Sipping Wonders*, 120-122.

partnership considerable status. An indication of Aspinall, Cornes' position can be seen from the visit of the Duke of Edinburgh in September 1869. After landing, he was received with great ceremony by a deputation of twelve members of the British community at which Aspinall presented the loyal address signed by over 250 British residents.[33] Aspinall was also a principal guest at other functions during Prince Alfred's stay and was at the head table at the farewell banquet for Admiral Sir Henry Keppel on his departure from Yokohama.[34] A further indication of the scale of Aspinall, Cornes' business can be judged from the amount of land it owned in the town's commercial quarter and in the Bluff residential area (see table 4).

After his return to Britain Frederick Cornes met Henrietta Alice, the sixth daughter of John Pannett Bull, of Hyde Park Street, London. They were married in April 1870 and the couple eventually had four sons and two daughters. Cornes returned to Yokohama in October 1871 but arrived back home in March 1872. During this visit it was agreed that Aspinall would leave the partnership and Frederick then established Cornes and Company, which was registered in Tokyo on 1 April 1873.[35] Although other minority partners, including William Henry Taylor, were to come and go in succeeding years, Frederick controlled the business from his office in Great Winchester Street in London until his retirement in 1911. It was, therefore, under his guidance that the firm prospered and opened branches in Kobe and New York. This progress was based on its activities as major exporters of raw silk and green tea – most of the latter to the US. But it should be noted that Cornes' interest in raw silk steadily declined, so that in the 1882-1883 season his company's 244 bales represented only 2.5% of the total, and it did not appear in the top twenty firms for 1884-1885.[36]

---

[33]Great Britain, Foreign Office, Mss. 165, Sir Harry Parkes, to Earl of Clarendon, 2 September 1869 (copy in author's possession). This includes an account of both Aspinall's speech and a copy of the address.

[34]*The Japan Times Overland Mail*, 18 September 1869.

[35]W.G. Aspinall returned to Britain but financial problems encouraged him to go back to Yokohama, where he opened a small business. He died in 1879 at the age of fifty-seven and was buried in the Foreigners' Cemetery on the Bluff overlooking the port.

[36]Takio Saito, untitled article, *Yokohama Archives of History Review*, No. 6 (March 1988), tables 24 and 25.

Table 4
Land Held by Foreign Merchants, 1869

Names of Owners	Country of Origin	Total	Town	Bluff
Eduard S. Benson	Am	5,129	1,103	8,053
Aspinall, Cornes & Co.	Br	5,000	3,464	3,072
Jardine, Matheson & Co.	Br	4,130	2,997	2,266
Strachan & Thomas	Br	3,278	1,442	3,672
A. Gerard	Fr	3,244	578	5,333
H & A Marks	Am	3,225	1,056	4,339
Beato	Br	3,101	968	4,266
M.J.B.N. Hegt	Dut	2,802	692	4,222
Augustine Heard & Co.	Am	2,485	2,485	0
W. MacDonald	Br	2,466	432	4,068
Walsh, Hall & Co.	Am	2,342	2,342	0
Pacific Mail Co.	Am	2,260	520	3,480
Ross, Barber & Co.	Br	1,998	1,988	0
Robert Goddard	Br	1,951	220	3,462
Texter & Co.	Dut	1,935	1,480	909
G. Hurlbut	Am	1,893	0	3,785
Schoyer (Estate)	Am	1,861	1,861	0
A. Marks & Co.	Am	1,854	1,854	0
W.R. Adamson & Co.	Br	1,678	1,678	0
William Patow	Pr	1,660	1,381	558
R. Lindau	Pr	1,638	1,182	912
Smith, Archer & Co.	Am	1,622	1,622	0
J.B. Macaulay	Br	1,523	925	1,197
Macpherson & Marshall	Br	1,522	1,522	0
Hughes, Willgoss & Co.	Br	1,508	1,508	0

Note: The measurement used is the *tsubo* which equals 3.3 square metres. The figure for the Bluff is divided by two to add to that of the Town to obtain the total.

Source: Tamakusu, "The West in Yokohama," table 7.

On the other hand, Cornes took an increasing role as an importer of textiles and metal goods and continued to be active in the handling of individual ships. This aspect of the firm's work was to expand further and be placed on a more permanent footing when it was chosen to represent the Ben Line in 1888. Its agencies for Lloyds, as well as for several bunkering firms and a number of insurance companies, also helped to provide a solid base for the enterprise in Yokohama. These activities were later to be strengthened by appointments to act for the Mannheim Insurance Company, Lancashire (Fire) Insurance Company, Underwriting Agency of Lloyds (Marine), Royal Exchange Assurance Corporation and Norwich Union Fire Insurance Society. In addition, the firm became agents for the Chartered Bank of India.

Frederick Cornes died in 1927 at the age of ninety and was buried in Teddington Cemetery near his former home in Hampton Wick. His second son, Archibald John Cornes, who had become a partner in 1900, ran the business until the outbreak of the Second World War. The firm then lay dormant but was reactivated before being sold to Wheelcok, Marden and Company in 1946. It was acquired by the Hong Kong and Kowloon Wharf Company in 1985 and the Chairman of this vast enterprise, Sir Y.K. Pao, subsequently arranged for the Cornes Group to hold all of his Japanese interests, a situation that continued until his death in 1991.

Dubai: From Creek to Global Port City

Frank Broeze

"[Dubai is] a cosmopolitan metropolis with excellent financial facilities."[1]
"In the final analysis a port is not a place, but a community of merchants."[2]

Introduction

Since 1969, when Rhoads Murphey published his seminal article "Traditionalism and Colonialism," maritime and urban historians of ports and port cities have far transcended the temporal and locational boundaries of his nineteenth-century South and East Asian colonial ports.[3] They have developed their subject in many directions and genres, including urban "biographies," regional and comparative studies, and individual aspects of the functioning of ports. The study of specific economic and social groups within port cities is matched by that of external port systems, in which the fluctuating fortunes of places can be analysed in terms of inter-port rivalry and/or the interaction between maritime and terrestrial dynamics. From an international perspective, the most stimulating facet has been the realisation that there is nothing intrinsically European, western or even "modern" about ports and port cities, as the rapidly-

[1]Dilip Hiro, *Dictionary of the Middle East* (London, 1996), 76.

[2]Gordon Jackson, *Grimsby and the Haven Company, 1796-1846* (Grimsby, 1971), 54.

[3]Rhoads Murphey, "Traditionalism and Colonialism: Changing Urban Roles in Asia," *Journal of Asian Studies*, XXIX (1969), 67-84; Frank Broeze (ed.), *Brides of the Sea. Port Cities of Asia from the 16th-20th Centuries* (Sydney, 1989); J. Kathirithamby and John Villiers (eds.), *The Southeast Asian Port and Polity* (Singapore, 1990); Franklin W. Knight and Peggy K. Liss (eds.), *Atlantic Port Cities. Economy, Culture, and Society in the Atlantic World, 1650-1850* (Knoxville, 1991); B.S. Hoyle and D.R. Pinder (eds.), *European Port Cities in Transition* (London, 1992); Indu Banga (ed.), *Ports and Their Hinterlands in India 1700-1950* (New Delhi, 1992); and Frank Broeze (ed.), *Gateways of Asia. Port Cities of Asia in the 13th-20th Centuries* (London, 1997).

growing historiography of maritime Asia demonstrates.[4] Economic and technological conditions vary greatly by time and place but "brides of the sea," as both Venice and Jiddah identified themselves, can be found in all places where sufficient trade and shipping exists to form a community with a critical economic and social mass.

The purpose of this essay is to contribute to this literature through a sketch of Dubai from its origins in the early nineteenth century as a tiny settlement at a creek on the northeastern coast of Arabia (the "pirate coast," as previous European generations called it) to its current position as a prosperous (GNP per capita well over US$20,000) global port, port city and commercial centre.[5] The analysis of Dubai's growth and development is based on the four dynamic and historically interactive factors that determine the fortunes of all port cities: site, situation, entrepreneurship (economic as well as political), and sense of identity. Site and situation are the bread and butter of transport geography, relating to local topography and the location of the port in relation to hinterland, foreland and strategic commercial and naval routes. Site and situation are always relative, depending on factors such as technology, production, consumption and local, regional or global political configurations. Situation also includes consideration of the port's location in relation to the regional system to which it belongs. Entrepreneurship must be interpreted broadly as the combination of all policies and initiatives designed to protect and promote the interests of the port. In the first instance, these will include the full range of relevant economic activities, such as shipping, seafaring, trade and ancillary industries and occupations. But the concept also embraces strategic, economic and social policies aimed at, for example, maintaining the independence or at least autonomy of the port city, the construction of infrastructure, and the upholding of a suitable cultural and religious climate to attract merchants from abroad. Identity, finally, relates to the self-image of the rulers, elites and leading groups of

---

[4]For an excellent study of Asian port continuity, see Linda Cooke Johnson, *Shanghai. From Market Town to Treaty Port, 1074-1858* (Stanford, 1995). It must be recognised, however, that the Middle East and Arabia have not yet benefited from the decline of eurocentrism and the rise of non-European studies.

[5]Muhammad Al-Qasimi, *The Myth of Arab Piracy in the Gulf* (London, 1986); Charles E. Davies, *The Blood-Red Arab Flag. An Investigation into Qasimi Piracy 1797-1820* (Exeter, 1997); and *Middle East Review 1997* (Saffron Waldon, 1997), 160.

the port city, their ideas about its position and their vision about its future. It is this outlook which determines the will with which policies are formulated and implemented. In an essay written as a tribute to Gordon Jackson, it is particularly inviting to compare the fortunes of Grimsby, the Humber port where commercially inexperienced leaders unsuccessfully aimed at greatness by building the biggest dock then in existence, with Dubai, where astute shaikhs and merchants forged their future through the construction of Port Rashid and Mina Jebel Ali, the world's largest man-made harbour (see figure 1). Although, as the failure of Grimsby's dock demonstrated, a port does not create trade, the dictum of its first engineer that "[a]ll men know that good accommodation is the main spring of trade," remains true in all places and at all times.[6]

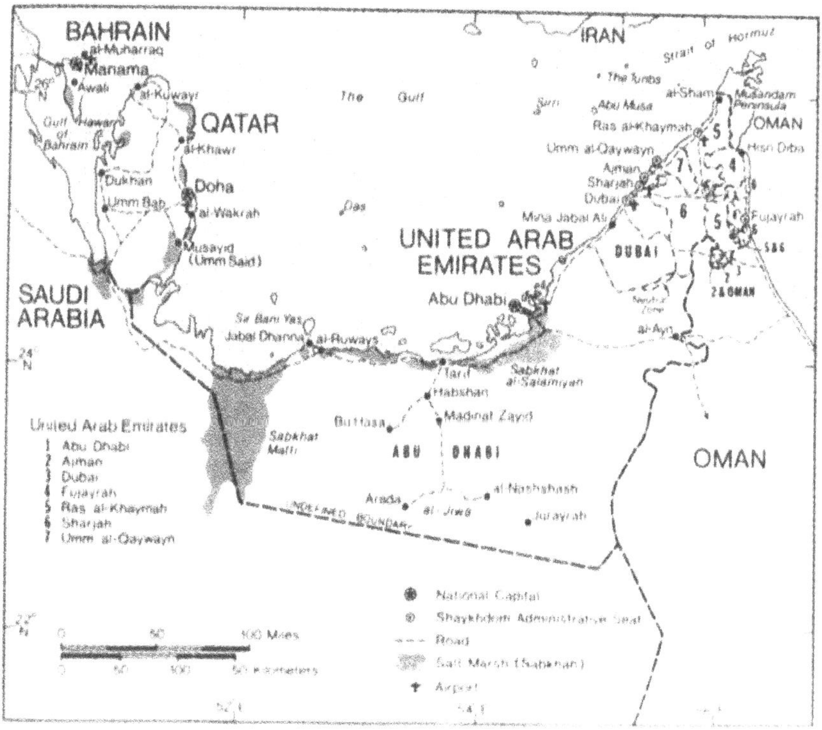

Figure 1: United Arab Emirates.

Source: C.C. Held, *Middle East Patterns* (Boulder, CO, 1994), 323.

[6]Jonathan Pickernell, 23 September 1795, quoted in Jackson, *Grimsby and the Haven Company*, 10.

Until recently, Dubai's life revolved totally around trade, shipping and seafaring; until its collapse in the 1930s, pearling had also been an important mainstay of the local economy. The essence of its existence was – and still is – its site astride Dubai Creek, an S-shaped inlet that determined both the destiny and the morphology of the city. Over the years it became the entrepot of the eastern Gulf, a position it retained after the region became the largest oil-producing area in the world. While Dubai was never a major producer, it managed to share fully in the economic growth and diversification that resulted from oil. And despite tremendous physical changes Dubai, like commercial-maritime Kuwait, slipped seamlessly into its new economic and social identity as its businessmen adapted to the new global economy. Moreover, no change of ruler – as happened in Sa'udi Arabia, Qatar, Abu Dhabi and Oman – was required to provide political leadership.[7] Port Rashid and Jebel Ali were built in the 1970s and 1980s to ensure that Dubai could handle all traffic and undertake large-scale port industrialisation projects. By the mid-1990s Dubai was the dominant port in the Gulf and a hub in the global network of container services. Ranking not far from the top ten, it was the largest port outside the three industrialised poles of the world economy, East Asia, Western Europe and the USA. More than Kuwait, Dubai after the Gulf War was able to maintain its relatively relaxed and cosmopolitan lifestyle, in recent years aiming to become a global as well as a regional city, with the promotion of sport and tourism regarded as priorities second only to its traditional trinity, commerce, shipping and finance.

Dubai before Oil: The Maritime-Commercial Foundations

Dubai in the nineteenth century developed as a small maritime centre in the shadow of its neighbours, Abu Dhabi and Sharjah. It was no more than a tiny fishing village under the control of Abu Dhabi when the Qawasim were defeated by the British and "Maritime Peace" was established in the

[7]Robert Lacey, *The Kingdom. Arabia and The House of Sa'ud* (New York, 1981), chap. 37; and Rosemary Said Zahlan, *The Making of the Modern Gulf States* (London, 1989).

eastern Gulf.[8] In 1833, however, a group of the Al Bu Falasah subsection of the dominant Bani Yas left Abu Dhabi and settled at Dubai Creek, which previously served as the boundary between Abu Dhabi and Sharjah. Indeed, at many times during the next century or so Dubai was involved in what J.G. Lorimer condescendingly called the "endless succession of petty wars" that swept the region.[9] Occasionally its survival was at stake when Abu Dhabi and Sharjah joined forces, but in each instance the two were separated at the last moment by shrewd Dubai tactics. The last of these mini-wars occurred as recently as 1940.

The exodus from Abu Dhabi had been led by Ubaid bin Sa'id and Maktoum al-Buti, but after the former's death in 1836, the latter established the dynasty that has ruled Dubai to the present.[10] Dubai's first few years as a separate political entity were extremely turbulent, as Abu Dhabi and Sharjah fought a bitter struggle and its Bani Yas took to the sea as allies of Abu Dhabi with, as Lorimer described it quaintly, the "intention of trying conclusions with the slender naval force maintained by the East India Company in the Persian Gulf."[11] When the East India Company sent reinforcements from India, the Arab fleets were annihilated. It was these hostilities that led to the first Maritime Truce between the British and the rulers of the towns along the coast that now became known as "Trucial Oman." In 1853 the regime of successive truces was transformed into the Perpetual Treaty of Peace. The relationship with Britain was advanced by an 1892 treaty that prevented any contact with representatives of foreign powers. This non-intercourse clause was both

---

[8]It was not mentioned in the comprehensive taxation lists drawn up by the Ottoman authorities between 1550 and 1650 (M. Çizakça, "An Introduction to the Economic and Social History of the Gulf of Basra," in H.G. Majers [ed.], *Proceedings of the Fourth International Congress for the Social and Economic History of Turkey* [Munich, 1988], 118-121) and figured only in minor roles during the British-Qasimi conflict (Al-Qasimi, *Myth of Arab Piracy*; and Davies, *Blood-Red Arab Flag, passim*).

[9]J.G. Lorimer, *Gazetteer of the Persian Gulf, Oman, and Central Arabia. Vol. 1: Historical* (Calcutta, 1915), 731.

[10]For a genealogical table of the Al-Maktoum family, see Muhammad Morsy Abdullah, *The United Arab Emirates. A Modern History* (London, 1978), 382. For an excellent sketch of early Dubai, see Frauke Heard-Bey, *From Trucial States to United Arab Emirates. A Society in Transition* (London, 1982), chap. 7.

[11]Lorimer, *Gazetteer, Historical*, pt 1, 205.

political and economic, as Political Resident Cox made clear when he refused to tolerate pearling contracts with foreign interests who might introduce modern equipment and destroy the traditional Arab industry.[12]

Dubai stagnated for some time after its foundation although the Al-Maktoums firmly aligned themselves with the British and their main local ally, Oman. Muscat served as an entrepot, mediating between the Gulf and the outside world, notably India and East Africa. Within the Gulf several local entrepots and gateways determined the lay-out of its port system and shipping connections. Basrah was the commercial centre for Iraq, as was Bushire for Persia. But much of Gulf trade, and especially pearling, was focussed on Bahrain. In the eastern Gulf, the Omani dependency Lingah, on the southeastern coast of Persia, served as a sub-regional distribution centre. By the early 1870s Dubai counted merely 1000-1200 inhabitants, only a slight increase over the 800 people who comprised the original settlement, and considerably less than the population of Sharjah (8000-10,000), Abu Dhabi (c. 20,000), or Lingah.[13] The mainstay of its economy was pearling but it only had access to the least valuable banks. About ninety boats were involved but their catch was sold mainly in Abu Dhabi where, like Bahrain, Indian merchants bought the pearls for export. Less important was the shark fishery and the export of fresh water to Abu Dhabi. Dates were imported from Bahrain and rice from Muscat. Dubai was on the lowest step of the port hierarchy of the Gulf, a fact also reflected in its physical appearance: "mud hovels, inside a low mud wall, having several breaches, and defended by three round towers and a square castellated building with a tower at one angle, much delapidated, in which are three or four rusty guns."[14]

During the latter part of the century, however, two major developments - one political, the other technological - pulled the foundations from underneath the established port system and created new

---

[12]Abdullah, *United Arab Emirates*, 103-104.

[13]James Horsburgh, *The India Directory. Part 1: The East Indies* (London, 1874), 244-245. No total is known for Lingah, but W.G. Palgrave, *Narrative of a Year's Journey through Central and Eastern Arabia (1862-63)* (London, 1865), II, 288, estimated the population of its old town alone to be c. 4000, with many more residents living in the extensive newer sections.

[14]R. Bowen, "The Pearl Fisheries of the Persian Gulf," *Middle East Journal*, V, No. 2 (1951), 161-180; and Horsburgh, *India Directory*, 244.

opportunities for Dubai. Fundamental changes came in 1856 after the death of Oman's sultan, Sayyid Said, and the division of his maritime empire between Muscat and Zanzibar. The loss of its African territories and trade was a tremendous blow to Oman's economic strength and power. Its interior became the site of a long civil war at the same time that Persia began to assert sovereignty over Muscat's dependencies (and, subsequently, also other Arab shaikhdoms) across the Gulf. Muscat's commercial and maritime strength was severely weakened. What remained of its position as entrepot was further reduced by the introduction of steam navigation in the Gulf. In 1862 the British India Steam Navigation Company (BISN), which had already established a strong position in the coastal trade of British India, opened a subsidised fortnightly steamer service from Bombay to Basrah via Karachi, Muscat, Bandar Abbas and Bushire, with additional calls at Lingah and Bahrain. These ports were now sub-regional centres where trade was collected and distributed. Passengers, pearls and the more valuable trade goods soon travelled by steamer. The main route betrayed the profound strategic motive: to counter Russian influence in Persia. But BISN was for its managers, agents and shareholders above all a vehicle to make money as, for example, the seasonal call at Bahrain to accommodate pearling demonstrated. For any ambitious ruler and port in the Gulf, it was imperative to be included in the steamers' schedule.

Dubai's moment came in 1903. Under the "liberal and enlightened" policies of Shaikh Maktoum bin-Hashar it had been able to achieve significant growth not only as a result of a general boom in pearling but also because it could benefit from disturbances in Oman which allowed it to tap into the Buraimi trade. It had steadily built up its participation in the pearl fishery and by the 1890s its fleet of 335 boats approximated those of Abu Dhabi (410) and Sharjah (360). Its prosperity had increased so much that it became the destination of the first wave of merchants from Lingah, which under Omani rule had enjoyed free trade but was now heavily taxed by Persia. Among those who left were Lingah's Indian merchants, Arabs and Persians, all of whom maintained their former connections with both Persia and India. Then BISN included Dubai on its fortnightly (weekly from June 1904) Bombay-Basrah service. Shaikh Maktoum abolished all duties and within a short time Dubai had replaced Lingah as the entrepot of the lower Gulf. Imports from India now came directly, with significant re-exports being made to Persia. A few years later the Bombay and Persian Steam Navigation Company included Dubai in its sailings, though mainly on inducement. After the politically-motivated Hamburg-America Line (HAL) in 1906 bypassed it on its new Gulf service, its agent, Robert Wönckhaus, was forced to abandon an exclusive agreement signed with the holders of a Sharjah mining lease.[15]

It was a greatly enlarged and multi-cultural Dubai that was portrayed in Lorimer's *Gazetteer*.[16] By 1915 the town had 10,000 "or rather more" inhabitants, spread over three sections. The original Bani Yas lived mainly in the area called Shindaghah, the triangle between the left bank of Dubai Creek and the beach front; as foreigners were not allowed to reside here, its 250 houses were all owned and occupied by Arabs. Dubai proper, further inland on the left bank of the creek, was the centre of the town, with the fort, the main mosque, and the residences of the Indian merchants; it counted about fifty shops and 100 houses. The third section, Dairah, on the other side of the creek, was the largest of all, with 1600 houses and the largest *suq* in the region, offering some 350 shops. The composition of Dubai's population reflected its prosperity and its entrepot status. It had 6936 men employed in the pearl fishery, more than any town on the coast, and also fitted out fifty fishing boats and twenty trading vessels. By 1901 Dubai had fifty-two Indian residents compared to thirty-nine in Abu Dhabi and seventy-six in Sharjah, but within a few years that number had increased to ninety (of whom thirty were merchants), with another twenty visiting during the pearling season. The town's Arab population was much more diverse, with 440 houses belonging to the Bani Yas, 400 to the Al Bu Mahair, and 490 to other groups, including Arabs from Kuwait and Bahrain. There were also 250

---

[15]Lorimer, *Gazetteer, Historical*, 774; Abdullah, *United Arab Emirates*, 30-31 and 103; and Olaf Brodacki, "Hamburg und der Persische Golf. Ein Kapitel wilhelminisch-deutscher Wirtschaftsgeschichte," *Zeitschrift des Vereins für Hamburgische Geschichte*, LXVII (1991), 54-56. The emir of Kuwait refused to allow the HAL to visit his port in order to avoid the risk of political complications (Frank Broeze, "Kuwait before Oil: The Dynamics and Morphology of an Arab Port City," in Broeze [ed.], *Gateways of Asia*, 161). After World War I several new steamship companies entered the Gulf trade, including the German DDG Hansa, which did include Dubai in its schedule.

[16]G.J. Lorimer, *Gazetteer of the Persian Gulf. Vol. 2: Geographical and Statistical* (Calcutta, 1908), 454-456.

houses each for Persians and people from the Sudan (who may well have been freed black slaves), and 200 for Baluchis.[17]

The maritime and commercial wealth of Dubai flowed to many of its merchants and traders. Taxes were relatively low and many of the original Bani Yas were exempt. They formed the town's social elite and participated mainly in pearling and maritime trade; the Persians, by contrast, were artisans and engaged in retail trading, while the Hindu and Khoja Indian banians were long-distance traders and bankers - Muslims being prevented from engaging in direct money lending operations. Dubai's liberal climate included hospitality to members of ruling families elsewhere who had fallen out with their relatives and were keen to use local commercial opportunities or to participate in the regional arms traffic. With recent immigrants from Persia playing active roles, Dubai became the centre of a trade in which re-exports of Indian rice to Oman were exchanged for rifles and other weapons for re-sale in the region and Persia. Its traditional dhows were a major asset in the trade, which to its businessmen was alluringly profitable, perfectly legal and even ideologically patriotic. As the BISN steamers, via Bombay, brought Arab nationalist newspapers from Egypt, fears were spread that Arabia was to follow the example of India or Persia. The conflicting interests exploded in December 1910 in the so-called "Dubai incident," a massive battle in which no fewer than thirty-seven residents of Dubai were killed and numerous buildings damaged. Both the RN area commander and the government of India disavowed the action and refused to accept the recommendation that a British agent be stationed at Dubai, but for quite some time the trust between Dubai and the British was severely shaken. Only the contested succession after Shaikh Buti bin-Suhail's death in 1912 allowed the British Political Resident to restore good relations; the arms trade died a natural death with the outbreak of war in 1914, in contrast to Kuwait, where the smuggling of weapons to the Ottoman army became so prevalent that the British blockaded the town.[18]

The interwar period in Dubai was characterised by three major developments that immediately related to its position as the leading port city in the region: heavy immigration from Persia; the rapid decline of the pearl fisheries as a result of the introduction of cultivated pearls from

---

[17]Abdullah, *United Arab Emirates*, 105.

[18]*Ibid.*, 34-38; and Broeze, "Kuwait," 157.

Japan; and political disturbances that, although partly of a dynastic nature, redefined the relationship between the Al-Maktoums and Dubai's commercial elite. World War I and the civil war in Persia severely affected the position of many Arabs. The shaikhdom of Mohammerah was abolished and a second wave of Arab merchants and others migrated from Persia's southern districts. Dubai attracted its fair share and allowed them to settle permanently between Dubai proper and the creek. Having direct access to the creek enabled them to maintain their links with their former customers in Persia, thus strengthening Dubai's position as the region's leading entrepot. The contrast between Dubai's positive outlook and the retrograde policies of Sharjah, whose rulers also had to cope with the silting up of their creek, was sharp and induced several Sharjah merchants to move to Dubai. These included the Owais family, prominent pearl merchants who in 1946 were estimated to be worth US $600,000.[19]

The first sign of imminent disaster in the pearling industry was the inability of a fleet of Dubai boats to leave for the grounds in 1929 because no advance payment was available. Muhammad bin Bayat was the first leading merchant to be declared bankrupt and worse was to follow. Many Indians left Dubai and other towns in the 1930s. Many shaikhs experienced acute financial and political discomfort when the British held them responsible for claims by Indian financiers, and they had to suspend their usual payments to the Bedu tribes under their authority; on several occasions these tribes raided towns to gain compensation. Dubai was fortunate that, with only one minor oasis under its control, it remained free of such disturbances.

Dubai, however, became involved in an incident on its maritime frontier with Persia which not only rocked its relationship with the British but also ignited latent tensions within the shaikhdom into open conflict which ultimately reshaped the relationship between ruler and merchants. Significantly, the domestic crisis culminated in 1938 at virtually the same time as in Kuwait and Bahrain with the establishment of a *majlis*, a formal body in which leading businessmen were prominently represented. Following from the emigration of many Arabs from Persia, considerable tension arose over Persia's treatment of Arabs who remained behind and, in particular, the shaikh of Hanjam (a relative of the Al-Maktoums) and

---

[19]Michael Field, *The Big Merchants. The Big Business Families of Saudi Arabia and the Gulf States* (Woodstock, NY, 1985), 60-61.

Persian threats to confiscate Arab dhows allegedly engaged in smuggling. The crisis was sparked off in July 1928 when a Dubai dhow was seized near Tanb island and taken to Lingah, where its cargo was confiscated and the crew and passengers, including eight women, detained. Opinion in Dubai was on the side of the husbands of the kidnapped women and called for an armed expedition against Lingah. Shaikh Sa'id bin Maktoum counselled caution and the British were able to have the dhow freed. But Persia refused to pay compensation and instead laid claim to Tanb and other islands in the Gulf. As Britain became involved in complex diplomatic negotiations, opposition within Dubai against the British connection and the shaikh grew, led by two cousins of Shaikh Sa'id and the leading pearl merchant, Muhammad bin Ahmad bin Dalmuk.[20] Sa'id was willing to resign and a public meeting of about sixty notables declared Mani bin Rashid, a son-in-law of Muhammad bin Ahmad, his successor. British intervention restored the status quo but did not lead to reconciliation. In a classic tactic, Sa'id mobilised the support of the few Beduins under his authority, a move that so alarmed his opponents that in 1934 they attempted to assassinate him. Again the British intervened, forcing his rivals to declare their complete loyalty, but the result again was only a truce, not a permanent peace.

The decline of pearling bit deeply into the Dubai economy and a first oil exploration contract was viewed with distrust by Sa'id's opponents, who feared he might monopolise all revenue and royalties. Conflicts over the manumission of slaves and the shaikh's son Rashid's operations in Dubai's taxi and freight services brought matters to a head. The apparent success of the political movements in Kuwait and Bahrain inspired the opposition. The British counselled Sa'id to make concessions but instead he brought his Beduin to the city. The two parties occupied sections of Dubai and refused to accept mediation from the shaikhs of Abu Dhabi and Sharjah, who were anxious that their own citizens not become infected. As always, British intervention brought a solution. Shifting their position to less than full support for their faithful ally, they insisted that Sa'id accept the establishment of an advisory council of fifteen notables to be vested with considerable powers. From October 1938 until its violent overthrow by Rashid bin Sa'id in late March 1939, the *majlis* embarked

---

[20]Said Zahlan, *Modern Gulf States*, 27-30, 51-53, and 68-69; and Abdullah, *United Arab Emirates*, 126-133 and 257-262.

on an impressive campaign of reform that touched almost all areas of government. The highest priority was given to improvements to Dubai Creek and reform of the customs service, but education, social welfare and urban redevelopment also received attention. Even more important was the assertion by the *majlis* that it and not the shaikh held supreme power in what it termed the state rather than the city of Dubai. A treasury was established to handle the state's finances and a municipal council to oversee all urban projects. In short, Sa'id was faced with a revolutionary situation bred by economic decline and negligent government, a situation his dynamic son could not tolerate. Although the reform movement was crushed and its leaders exiled, Rashid bin Sa'id was to adopt much of its program after 1945, when Dubai was faced with the challenges and opportunities of the new oil-based order in the Gulf.

Building up the Infrastructure

The British Naval Intelligence handbook of 1944 on the Gulf carried a brief entry on Dubai which succinctly summarised the main elements of its port city identity:

> Dibai [sic] is a distributing centre for goods for the interior and along the coast. It has large bazaars and a boat-building industry. There are two camel-routes southeast and south-south-east to the Baraimi [sic] oasis, and another south-east to Shinas on the Gulf of Oman.[21]

As pearling had been abandoned, Dubai Creek concentrated on its function to mediate between foreland and hinterland, with its own dhows and Beduin "ships of the desert" to maintain the transport infrastructure of its mixed maritime-terrestrial hinterland. Boats were also the mainstay of traffic within Dubai, with small *abras* linking both banks of the creek and lighters carrying goods and passengers to and from the steamers that had to anchor a few kilometres offshore. Satisfactory for dhow traffic, Dubai Creek was totally insufficient for the demands of the new era of global shipping in which vessels grew to gigantic proportions and cargo-handling

---

[21]Great Britain, Admiralty, Naval Intelligence Division, *Iraq and the Persian Gulf* (London, 1944), 136.

facilities were mechanised to ensure efficient turnaround. At the same time, the exponential growth of the oil industry swept the Gulf into a maelstrom of change in commercial and financial practice related to both the export of oil and the explosion of imports for consumption and investment projects. Rapid population growth and urbanisation were integral to the revolutionary modernisation that both engulfed and challenged all oil states, including Dubai. As its oil reserves were smaller and developed later than those of its neighbours, it was by building on its traditional strengths as a port and commercial city that Dubai was transformed into a thriving centre. In the course of the political changes and upheavals that turned the Gulf into one of the world's strategic hotspots, Dubai's leaders had to chart a course that guaranteed both survival and the freedom to maintain a free-wheeling outlook.

Although the first oil agreement had been signed by Shaikh Sa'id in 1937, Dubai had to wait until the mid-1960s until oil was discovered and 1969 before production actually started. During the preceding decades, when Saudi Arabia, Kuwait, Iran and Abu Dhabi began to receive huge revenues, Dubai had only its port city functions on which to build; as Michael Field put it, "Dubai pulled itself up by its own bootstraps...to become the most dynamic trading centre in the Arabian peninsula." Significantly, after Dubai became a producer (see table 1), its output remained modest and its rulers never regarded oil revenue as economically decisive; instead, they focussed on how to turn their city into the service centre for the eastern Gulf. Shipping, trade and finance remained the heart of Dubai's business, the priorities of its regime, and the core of its self-image. In the centre of all stood the port - which by 1950, unchanged from a century ago, meant Dubai Creek with eroding banks and a shallow bar offshore, hardly the material on which to base a vision for the future. During the next thirty-five years Dubai successively undertook four projects of harbour works: first, improving the creek and dredging the bar; then creating a modern harbour on the shoreside (Port Rashid, opened in 1972); next expanding Port Rashid from fifteen to thirty-seven berths; and finally building the world's largest man-made port at Jebel Ali, with seventy-four berths and a 10,000-hectare free-trade zone. In the process, Dubai changed from a traditional multi-cultural port city of 25,000 residents, with its traditional craft and narrow winding alleys that Thesiger visited in 1948, to a multi-function metropolis with 500,000 inhabitants, high-rise office blocks and international hotels.[22]

Table 1
Oil Production in Dubai, 1976-1991

Year	1976	1979	1982	1985	1989	1991
Production (million tonnes)	15.6	17.6	17.8	18.9	23.8	25.2
Share of Total Gulf Output (%)	1.43	1.65	2.75	3.64	2.64	2.79

Source: Peter Beaumont, *et al.*, *The Middle East. A Geographical Study* (2nd ed., London, 1988), 283; and Colbert C. Held, *Middle East Patterns. Places, Peoples, and Politics* (2nd ed., Boulder, CO, 1994), 121.

The modernisation and expansion of Dubai's port must be understood both for its intrinsic importance in underpinning the expansion of the city's maritime economy and as part of its general urban development. It thus fit into a broad pattern of measures that also included the establishment of the first overseas bank (the Imperial Bank of Iran, later the British Bank of the Middle East) in 1946, the transfer of the British Agency from Sharjah to Dubai in 1954, the establishment of a separate police force, the appointment of the shrewd (and wealthy) Mahdi al-Tajir as director of customs, the creation of the Dubai municipality, and the construction of a civilian airport in the late 1950s. Dubai's driving force was Shaikh Rashid bin-Sa'id, "known from Kuwait to Muscat as 'the fox of the Gulf,'" who had assumed effective power long before his actual succession in 1958.[23] To a remarkable extent he had learned the lessons of the *majlis* of 1938/1939 but combined these with a clear understanding of the need for big infrastructure projects to make Dubai the region's leading centre. Indeed, Port Rashid, Jebel Ali and some of his other projects were of such cost and dimensions - and came at a time that all Gulf states were frantically scrambling to create their own projects - that he was often

---

[22]Heard-Bey, *From Trucial States*, 252; Field, *Merchants*, 60; Christine Osborne, *The Gulf States and Oman* (London, 1977), 98; *Aramco World*, March-April 1992; Wilfred Thesiger, *Arabian Sands* (London, 1964), 275-276; and *Middle East Review 1997*, 161.

[23]Field, *Merchants*, 61. Osborne, *Gulf States*, 90, claimed that "even Lebanese businessmen hold him in awe."

regarded as a dreamer out of touch with reality and a major cause of the "seaport mania" in the region. In the final analysis, however, it appears that even if he built harbours in advance of demand, he laid the foundations for Dubai's rise to global status.

The first phase of Dubai's metamorphosis was triggered in the mid-1950s by exploration activities on the coast by the Petroleum Development Company, which required space and a proper wharfside for its heavy equipment. The importance of Rashid's initiative can be seen in the fact that the funds for the improvement of Dubai Creek were borrowed from Kuwait. A breakwater stabilised and helped deepen the entrance, while its banks were "bunded" into a solid waterfront. The dredged sand was used for land reclamation which repaid much of the expense. Completed by 1963, these works allowed boats and barges of up to 500 tons to enter the creek - which, in the longer term, was totally inadequate, as became evident once oil was discovered. In 1967 the construction of Mina (Port) Rashid, directly outside the creek, began. (It should be emphasised that Dubai's ports never handled any of the emirate's crude oil; shipments take place from facilities at its production field, Fateh, about fifty kilometres offshore.) Port development was paralleled by the further elaboration of local government and the state apparatus. Mahdi al-Tajir was appointed to head the Emiri Court as well as the Petroleum Department. Shaikh Rashid's sons were gradually introduced into public office and, as in contemporary Kuwait, the relationship between the ruling family and the business community was close. By contrast to Kuwait, it remained so after the death of Shaikh Rashid in 1990.

The productive symbiosis between the ruler and Dubai's mercantile oligarchy during the 1960s had a second, typically "Dubai" dimension: the extremely profitable dhow-based trade in gold to India, where the metal could be sold for more than double its value on the open world market.[24] The gold was flown in from London and Frankfurt, then transshipped by motorised dhow to Bombay. Although the import of gold into India was illegal, the trade boomed; at its height in 1970, Dubai handled 259 tons, about twenty percent of the non-communist world's production. All but a handful of Dubai's merchants were involved: the Galadari brothers, the Ghurair and Owais families, and many others. The meteoric

---

[24]See Field, *Merchants*, 61-63; John Bulloch, *The Gulf. A Portrait of Kuwait, Qatar, Bahrain and the UAE* (London, 1984), 122-123; and Osborne, *Gulf States*, 92-96, for graphical details of the "routine" of the trade.

price rise of the early 1970s and a vicious crackdown by Indira Gandhi's government caused a sudden end to the trade, but legal commercial relations with India and Pakistan, the source of most of the Gulf's cheap foreign labour force, flourished. Instead of gold, motor cars, consumer durables and wrist watches became the staples driving Dubai's entrepot trade, which covered the entire area from Saudi Arabia and Iran through the Emirates and Oman to South Asia. Imports soared from £3 million in 1958 to £42 million in 1967 and £200 million in the mid-1970s.

Two examples illustrate the commercial dynamism of the city's merchants. Saif Al-Ghurair, life president of the Dubai Chamber of Commerce, started life as a pearl diver before entering his father's shop in the 1950s. "Soon there was a string of shops, then a fleet of ships trading between the Gulf and East Africa in the old traditional way, taking dates on the outward voyage and bringing much-needed wood for the construction industry on the homeward run." His Bank of Oman was the first Gulf bank to open a branch in East Africa (Nairobi). Easa Saleh al-Gurg's parents migrated from Lingah to Dubai and he grew up bilingual in Arabic and Persian. As the assistant of the Dubai Post Office, established in 1943 by the British, he acquired English and after a few years at Bahrain joined the Dubai branch of the Imperial Bank of Iran. Striking out on his own, he built an impressive network of import agencies, acting for such companies as Siemens, Osram and Dunlop. His philosophy, "[o]il brings wealth to the nation, but trade takes it to its roots, to the man in the street," epitomised the consumerist political economy of Dubai as much as the *laissez-faire* policies of Shaikh Rashid.[25]

Central to Dubai's survival and the rise of its import and entrepot trades was the formation of the United Arab Emirates in the wake of the British withdrawal east of Suez. Once that was announced in 1967, the Gulf emirates and shaikhdoms realised that their futures as fully independent states depended on close cooperation. How close that cooperation was to be, and to what extent the interests of the various states could be harmonised, was hammered out in a series of meetings between the seven shaikhdoms of "Trucial Oman," Bahrain and Qatar. Ultimately, the latter two preferred to maintain their independence and the former joined the

[25]Bulloch, *The Gulf*, 123-124.

United Arab Emirates.[26] The UAE was to act for its members in the realms of foreign policy, defence and (originally not envisaged) sport representation. The UAE also became a member of OPEC and OAPEC but, significantly, the individual shaikhdoms retained full authority to determine their own levels of output - a freedom that Dubai did not hesitate to use. Economic policy in general also remained the domain of the members and, once again, Dubai retained full freedom of action. With its libertarian outlook it clearly was the least union-minded of all the shaikhdoms, yet with the great sense of *realpolitik* that characterised the Al-Maktoums, Rashid had made the formation of the UAE possible by not contesting Abu Dhabi's claim to its presidency. Instead, Dubai was allowed to nominate the Prime Minister, one of the two Deputy Prime Ministers, the Minister of Finance and Industry, and the Minister of Defence. While considerable scepticism existed about the viability of the UAE, the union has survived and in general has been politically stable.[27]

This is not the place to discuss the causes of that stability; what matters here is that the UAE, as the self-generated political answer to British withdrawal, created a political environment that enabled Dubai to continue its free-trade policies and ambitious development plans. The UAE did not regulate competition between its members or coordinate their development projects, as is shown, for example, by its excess of seaports. Indeed, it would not have been founded or survived if that had been the agenda of its initiators. To a certain extent, there was also a division of labour between the UAE's largest member, Abu Dhabi, and Dubai. Abu Dhabi was by far the largest oil producer, housed the capital and the bureaucracy, possessed the important inland oasis group of Al-Ain, and provided most of the financial support given to the minor shaikhdoms. Dubai, on the other hand, handled about seventy percent of the UAE's imports and general exports and strengthened its position as the union's commercial and financial centre.

---

[26]The formation of the UAE is the subject of many studies. In addition to the works of Heard-Bey and Abdullah, see, for example, A.O. Taryam, *The Establishment of the United Arab Emirates 1950-85* (London, 1987); Rosemary Said Zahlan, *The Origins of the United Arab Emirates* (New York, 1978); Ali Mohammed Khalifa, *The United Arab Emirates: Unity in Fragmentation* (Boulder, CO, 1979); Malcolm C. Peck, *The United Arab Emirates. A Venture in Unity* (Boulder, CO, 1986); and Liesl Graz, *The Turbulent Gulf* (London, 1990), 202-225.

[27]Said Zahlan, *Modern Gulf States*, 167; and *Middle East Review 1997*, 159.

Table 2
Major Gulf Ports, 1977

Port	Imports ('000 dwt)	Number of Berths
Dammam	6400	22
Bandar Shahpour	5616	12
Basrah	4455	18
Kuwait	4000	18
Dubai	3995	19
Khorromshahr	3780	14
Bandar Abbas	3074	8
Sharjah	1700	8
Abu Dhabi	1545	12
Doha	1217	9

Source: *Fairplay*, 14 December 1978, 29.

In 1972 Mina Rashid was opened, just before the great construction boom in the Gulf and Saudi Arabia began. Constructed at a cost of £24 million by the British firm Costain, it was the largest port in the Middle East.[28] Dubai's overseas shipping finally had the modern facilities necessary for efficient cargo handling; without them it would not have been able to maintain, let alone improve, its position, as other Gulf ports competed to attract the construction cargoes and consumer goods. As table 2 shows, the countries with the largest development projects - Saudi Arabia, Iran, Iraq and Kuwait - attracted the largest trade volumes, but Dubai's lead was pronounced and it was benefiting from its established entrepot functions; as Jonathan Raban put it, "the oil boom...simply intensified Dubai's traditional buzz of water traffic." At the heart of this entrepot trade still stood Dubai Creek, bustling as always, with the dhows looking like floating stores. The inventory of one, epitomising Al-Gurg's philosophy about trade bringing goods to the man in the street, included:

> six Korean refrigerators, four Japanese washing machines, three red Suzuki motorbikes, nine bicycles, five tricycles, a green garden wheelbarrow, sacks of steel wire, some mesh metting, a Buick, two dozen Taiwanese motor tyres and - Britain's only contribution - a case of

[28]Fred Halliday, *Arabia without Sultans* (Harmondsworth, 1974), 452.

> tempest hurricane lamps with much more that could not be identified.[29]

By 1977 the ports of Arabia and the Gulf were emerging from the chaos and congestion that had resulted from the sudden inflow of shipping; in May 1976 no fewer than fifty-eight ships waited for a berth off Dubai. Many new port projects were coming on stream throughout the region or were under construction. Dubai's response was to extend Mina Rashid from fifteen to thirty-seven berths. Shaikh Rashid, however, was not satisfied that even the enlarged port could ensure the continued growth of shipping, trade and prosperity of his shaikhdom, the population of which had skyrocketed from 59,000 in 1967 to 120,000 in 1973 and was to exceed 250,000 by the early 1980s. More wharf space and land for industrial and commercial purposes was needed to underpin Dubai's position. The first step in the strategy was taken in 1973 when he signed a £69 million contract to build a huge drydock complex, including one dock with the ability to lift a 1,000,000 dwt carrier (a tonnage that was, in fact never achieved, as the largest ULCCs ever built just exceeded 550,000 dwt). Significantly, like Port Rashid, the project was financed almost entirely with borrowed funds. Dubai Drydock, which opened in 1983, was regarded with the same scepticism as so many of Rashid's projects, but it attracted ample business and has earned reasonable profits. The drydock not only demonstrated Rashid's willingness to gamble on the future but also revealed another dimension of his economic policies, as he began construction after OAPEC decided to build its own dockyard at Bahrain. Although Dubai, through the UAE, held a small share in this facility, Rashid aimed to maximise the benefits of ship repair for his own state. The same independent spirit was evident in the construction of its own aluminium smelter and the founding of its own airline, Emirates, in direct competition with Gulf Air, jointly owned by Bahrain, Oman, Qatar and Abu Dhabi.[30]

---

[29]Jonathan Raban, *Arabia Through the Looking Glass* (1979; reprint, London, 1983), 179.

[30]Osborne, *Gulf States*, 98-99; Heard-Bey, *From Trucial States*, 263 and 269; *Dock & Harbour Authority*, May and September/October 1985; *Fairplay*, 22 November 1979 and 20 November 1986; *Seatrade Review*, March 1997; and Graz, *Turbulent*, 189.

Figure 2: Dubai, the Creek, Port Rashid, and the Dubai Drydocks, 1978.

Source: *Fairplay*, 14 December 1978.

Port Rashid and its drydock were by no means the end of Rashid's ambitions (see figure 2). By 1976 he had decided that Dubai's port-based economic growth needed to be lifted to an entirely higher plane, but he had to await the completion of these projects before he began the £800 million port complex of Jebel Ali, some thirty-five kilometres southwest of Dubai. When completed in 1985, it was - and still is - the largest man-made port in the world. At its heart stood no less than fifteen kilometres of waterfront with sixty-seven berths, equipped to deal with all kinds of liner and other traffic and intended to be the most efficient terminal yet. Three container berths with a total length of 900 metres and fourteen metres depth alongside were complemented by fifty hectares of stacking space. But as important as Jebel Ali's waterfront was its 10,000-hectare free- trade zone, including 42,000 square metres of cold storage. Here the most business-friendly regime, including permission for foreign companies to transfer all profits overseas, was to attract domestic and foreign investment for all possible industrial, manufacturing and commercial purposes. Rashid's vision was to provide the city-state with another non-oil pillar to support its economy, reinforce its shipping and entrepot functions, and turn Dubai into the future nucleus of the Gulf.[31]

The cornerstone of the new complex was Dubai's eighty-percent government-owned aluminium smelter, at $612 million the largest individual Gulf project to date. As with Dubai Drydocks, it was erected in direct competition with an established company, Aluminium Bahrain (ALBA). It will come as no surprise that many within and without the Gulf were critical of Dubai's economic ambitions, which were matched by the dimensions of its urban redevelopment, as the city built both a bridge over and a tunnel under Dubai Creek and took pride in having the tallest building in the Gulf. Many also saw Jebel Ali as a "pipedream," reflecting Gordon Jackson's comment on Grimsby's ambitions that a dock in itself does not make a port. Later developments, however, showed that Dubai was able to attract international companies such as Black & Decker, British Petroleum, Caltex, Citizen Watch, General Motors, Mitsubishi Motors, P&O Containers, Reebok, Rhone Poulenc, Schlumberger, Shell, Sony, Union Carbide and York Air Conditioners to the freeport; by late 1993 there were over 500 tenants. In advertisements it proudly boasted of its "state of the art communications, accommodations, hotels, hospitals, security and every modern amenity." Showing how in the course of time its Free Zone Authority expanded its horizons, in 1990 it could claim that "Jebel Ali is a unique opportunity for world markets," and that Dubai was "the Hong Kong of the Middle East."[32] It should be stressed that both Port Rashid and Jebel Ali, after their amalgamation into the Dubai Ports Authority (DPA), were under government control and were managed as part of the emirate's economic policy.

---

[31] *Fairplay*, 22 November 1979; and *Lloyd's Ports Bulletin International*, November 1986.

[32] Osborne, *Gulf States*, 99; J.B. Kelly, *Arabia, The Gulf and The West* (London, 1980), 197-198; Jackson, *Grimsby*, 8; *Lloyd's Maritime Asia*, November 1993; *Far Eastern Economic Review*, 26 April 1990; *Cargo Systems*, June 1996; and *Fairplay*, 13 April 1989.

Containerisation: From Port-of-Call to Global Hub

At the core of Dubai's diversifying economy was its identity as a port city, its ability to attract ships of all nations, and its boast that "[w]e have open skies and open seas." Most of its financial and commercial operations were directly related to the flow of goods through its ports. By 1976, Dubai had fifty overseas banks, against forty in Abu Dhabi and only fourteen in Saudi Arabia.[33] Still, the lifeblood of its prosperity was the more than 2000 ships per year that called at its ports. Many were bulk carriers and specialised vessels, but by far the most valuable were the cargo liners. Stability was returning to the Gulf by 1977 after the chaotic boom years as many fly-by-night operators left and ordinary liner services again became dominant, albeit with many new participants. The overall pattern of these services was hardly different from that of the previous fifty years; as no port was large enough to attract regular imports by the shipload, liners continued to call at a number of ports linked together by loops or strings. Major companies included most of the Gulf's larger ports but, because of their great number, individual vessels called at different strings, as table 3 shows.

There was never a complete return to the old order, however, as the height of the boom coincided with the container revolution reaching the Gulf. Containerisation had first been introduced on the North Atlantic in the second half of the 1960s and from there spread rapidly to the major east-west routes between the USA, Europe, East Asia and Australasia. Many observers initially believed it was not suitable for expansion into the less-developed countries because of their supposedly inadequate transport infrastructure. But they overlooked both the historical experience that technological change in shipping had always driven port change and the fact that during the 1970s the world was awash with petrodollars waiting to be used by international bankers and civil engineers for port and other infrastructure projects. Containerisation swept across the world's oceans. Arabia, the Gulf and Dubai were prime examples of the responsiveness of port authorities. In 1979 Jiddah was the world's seventeenth largest container port, with a turnover of almost 500,000 Twenty-Foot Equivalent Units (TEUs). In 1976 Dubai and its nearest rival, Sharjah, were the first

---

[33]Emirates' CEO Sheikh Ahmad bin-Said, quoted in *South*, April 1990; and Sandra Mackey, *The Saudis* (London, 1989), 175.

to install gantry cranes to handle the latest gearless container ships and to make suitable space available to park and stack containers.

Table 3
Nedlloyd's Gulf Service, Autumn 1977

Ship's Name	Ma-trah	Du-bai	Abu Dhabi	Do-ha	Bah-rain	Dam-mam	Bas-rah	Ku-wait
Nedlloyd Weser	yes	yes	yes	yes	-	yes	-	yes
Nedlloyd Sinoutskerk	-	-	yes	-	yes	yes	-	-
Neder Waal	yes	-	-	-	yes	yes	yes	-
Mississippi Lloyd	-	yes	-	yes	yes	yes	-	yes
Madison Lloyd	yes	-	yes	-	yes	yes	-	-

Source: *Maritieme Geschiedenis der Nederlanden*, IV (Bussum, 1978), 173.

Container shipping had an equally revolutionary impact on the world's ports and port systems. Three aspects in particular were related to the rise of Dubai to regional leadership. First, container shipping requires dedicated terminals. Second, infrastructure had to be created for the carriage of the containers to the port and from the port to their ultimate destination. In principle, there were no limits to the other modes of transport, but local and regional circumstances often dictated whether the predominant method would be rail, road, water or some combination. Whatever the method, the transfer from ship to train, truck, boat or ship needed to be as efficient and "seamless" as possible, the ideal being the railroad-based intermodalism of the USA. Third, containerisation has had an important, though sometimes contradictory, effect on the port systems of the world. On the one hand, because of the high cost of large container ships, companies want to make as few calls as possible on their mainline services; on the other hand, because it is difficult to fill a ship in one port, strings and loops have not disappeared. Port rivalry, moreover, has been fuelled considerably by the fact that civil engineers can build a container port at almost any site, whether as an extension to an existing port or in "green fields." In the major industrialised centres, like East Asia, Europe and the USA, all major companies, consortia and alliances call at four or more ports. Among the world's top 100 container ports for 1996, for example, were seven in Japan and eighteen in the USA. In other areas, by contrast, especially in enclosed systems like the Mediterranean and the Gulf, mainline services - especially after the initiation, in 1984/1985, of global and post-Panamax pendulum services between the east coast of North America, Europe and East Asia - increasingly tended to reduce their calls, often restricting themselves to one port only.[34] Such entrepots, or hubs, served their region through a network of feeder services. The quintessential regional hub is Singapore, whose hegemony in Southeast Asia is virtually incontestable, but in most regions a number of ports vie with each other as hubs. For Dubai, the Gulf and the western Indian Ocean, it was significant that from about 1980 two ports were developed in the UAE but outside the Straits of Hormuz: Fujairah (in the emirate of the same name) and Khor Fakkan, which belongs to Sharjah.[35] Ships calling at those ports rather than Dubai not only gained several days but also were able to avoid the Gulf war zone. Promoted by a number of the largest container companies, including APL, Seatrain and Sea-Land, the two ports attracted a number of major customers and took entrepot business away from Dubai. When APL in 1984 shifted to Fujairah, Dubai experienced its only, albeit miniscule, drop in TEU throughput.[36]

From the early 1980s containerisation transformed the Gulf from a system with string services to one which also contained competing hubs. The tendency toward hub formation was considerably strengthened when the Gulf a few years later became a "region-of-call" for the big west-east (and *vice versa*) mainline operators who wanted to reduce both the number of calls and time lost. Port concentration also received a powerful stimulus because it coincided with the rationalisation of shipping services in the

---

[34]On recent developments in container shipping, see Frank Broeze, "Containerization: The Globalization of Liner Shipping," in David J. Starkey and Gelina Harlaftis (eds.), *Global Markets: The Internationalization of Maritime Industries* (St. John's, 1998), 385-423. On the rapid increase of post-Panamax carriers, see *Containerisation International*, February 1997.

[35]*PDI*, September 1992; *Cargo Systems*, November 1994; *Docks & Harbour Authority* (January 1983), 302-303 and (December 1984/January 1985), 106; and *Fairplay*, 13 December 1984.

[36]*Fairplay*, 23 May 1985.

wake of the severe downturn of the Gulf economies caused by the collapse of oil prices and the outbreak of the Gulf War. Dubai benefited significantly from these circumstances, as it was able to capitalise on its long-standing historical experiences, expertise in the modern transshipment and entrepot business, and the facilities that Shaikh Rashid had constructed over the previous decade. With both Port Rashid and Jebel Ali – port and industrial free zone – equipped with the most modern facilities, it rapidly outdistanced all other Gulf ports and became the hub of not only the eastern but also the entire Gulf. The number of TEUs handled jumped from 200,000 in 1980 to 297,000 in 1983, 383,000 in 1986, 827,000 in 1989, and 1,428,000 in 1992, the first full year after Port Rashid and Jebel Ali had been administratively amalgamated. Growth continued and DPA throughput in 1996 reached 2,247,000 TEUs.[37] Dubai had steadily climbed the global port charts and reached thirteenth place, only 400,000 behind tenth-place Antwerp. In its own region, in 1996 the next ports were Khor Fakkan (708,000, 49th), Fujairah (556,000, 60th), and Dammam (307,000, 96th). The latter shared Saudi Arabia's imports with the "bride of the Red Sea," Jiddah (748,000, 47th).

Table 4
Top Container Ports in the Gulf, 1986-1994

Port	1994 rank/TEU	1990 rank/TEU	1986 rank/TEU	1982 rank/TEU
Dubai	1/1,881,990	1/916,363	1/529,262	2/323,676
Fujairah	2/694,452	2/414,353	5/138,558	n.a.
Khor Fakkan	3/433,806	5/162,260	4/183,000	n.a.
Dammam	4/287,206	3/232,456	3/206,707	1/344,062
Kuwait	5/220,724	7/69,800	2/220,599	3/284,029
Abu Dhabi	6/125,416	8/45,733	9/21,226	n.a.
Bandar Abbas	7/106,738	n.a.	n.a.	n.a.
Bahrain	8/103,162	6/ n.a.	7/80,363	4/92,963
Mina Qaboos	9/87,878	4/167,873	6/110,635	n.a.
Sharjah	10/57,320	9/24,208	8/53,657	5/57,385

Note: Dubai includes Port Rashid and Jebel Ali; and Kuwait includes Shuwaikh and Shuaiba. No figures were available for Bandar Abbas until 1991.

Source: *Containerisation International Yearbook*, 1983-1996.

---

[37] *Ibid.*, 24 April 1986 and 12 November 1987; *Dock & Harbour Authority*, February 1986, 236; *Containerisation International Yearbook*, various years; *PDI*, September 1992; *Cargo Systems*, April 1997; and *Cargo Today*, October 1997.

As table 4 shows, Dubai and the two new east coast ports, Fujairah and Khor Fakkan, far outdistanced all ports within the Gulf, such as Sharjah's Mina Khalid, Abu Dhabi's Mina Zayed, Bahrain's Mina Sultan, and also the early heavyweights, Kuwait and Dammam. The latter port in early 1997 counted only two companies as mainline callers; the rest of its business was all via feeders from Dubai.[38]

One interesting aspect of the shifting balance between the various Gulf ports lies in the operations and impact of the United Arab Shipping Company (UASC), another example of the cooperation among Arab states. Headquartered in Kuwait, it was jointly owned by the governments of Kuwait, Iraq, Saudi Arabia, Bahrain, Qatar and the UAE. Founded in 1976, by 1983 its fleet included fifty-nine cargo liners, including sixteen container ships. UASC had three major aims: to let the Arab countries share in the freight revenue generated by the economic boom; to lower freight rates; and to ensure that the major ports of all member states were served by lines to Europe, the USA and East Asia. In other words, UASC's mission was to prevent, or at least slow down, the rise of regional hubs like Dubai. During the depression in Gulf trade (1983-1988), when UASC stood under considerable financial pressure, such a policy was difficult to maintain. With extensive rationalisation came a significant shift in emphasis from project to container shipping and, ironically, a greater concentration on Dubai. As one insider commented, "[i]t is perhaps ironic that one of the visions of the most thoughtful of Arab port planners – that an efficient local distribution service and fewer main line termini – has at least in part come to pass as a consequence of the war and the economic condition." The occupation of Kuwait by Iraq stopped much of the upper Gulf traffic and necessitated the temporary transfer of the main office to Dubai. But as soon as the second Gulf War was over, UASC resumed many of its former string services. Its vessels from the USA, for example, called at Dubai (Port Rashid), Mina Qaboos, Dammam, Kuwait and Bahrain, with transshipment for Abu Dhabi, Sharjah and Doha at Dubai, while the service from Europe also included a call at Abu Dhabi and a second stop at Port Rashid. But it could not fight the trend toward concentration and in 1992 began reorganising its network in the Gulf from strings to hubs with, for example, its USA-Gulf service calling only at Khor Fakkan and Dubai. Its recently opened feeder

---

[38]*Seatrade Review*, March 1997; *Fairplay*, 8 April 1999.

from Khor Fakkan via Abu Dhabi and Dammam to Kuwait even by-passed Dubai.[39] It is likely that UASC's use of Khor Fakkan will increase as its cooperation with the DSR-Senator-Tricon-Hanjin consortium intensifies.

Dubai: Region and Rivals

The actual extent of Dubai's re-export trade is unknown, but estimates range from about fifty to seventy-five percent. Most of the upper Gulf is served by container ships, but Dubai's largest individual re-export market is Iran, where until recently much of the trade, both legal and smuggled, was carried by dhow. Dubai always maintained close links with Iran, even during the worst months of the Gulf War; the Iran Air Airbus that was shot down in July 1988 by the USS *Vincennes* had just started from Bandar Abbas for Dubai. In 1997 a fast catamaran service was opened between the two cities via Lingah. In recent years, however, a rising proportion of exports to Bandar Abbas has been containerised and is sent onward by truck and the recently opened "Silk Railroad" to the ex-Soviet Central Asian republics.[40] Dubai also reaches eastward, as containers from the USA and Europe are sent by feeders to Pakistan and India.

Another important aspect of Dubai's re-exports lies in an entirely different dimension, as from the 1980s it pioneered sea-air transshipment, especially in electrical and other high-value goods from East Asia for Europe. The interest of the Al-Maktoums in civil aviation was visible in their development and promotion of Dubai International Airport (which sports one of the world's most aggressively-marketed duty frees, "We go to any length to be within your reach"). Some of Dubai's initiatives were later taken up by others. A particularly interesting case is the recent

---

[39]United Arab Shipping Company (UASC), publicity brochure (Kuwait, [1983]); *Al-Mirsat Al-Arabiyah* (magazine of UASC), November 1989 and June 1990; Kingdom of Saudi Arabia, Saudi Ports Authority, *Annual Report 1988* (Riyadh, 1989), 23, 30-33, and 76-79; *Fairplay*, 12 November 1987 and 13 February 1992; and *Asian Shipping*, August 1997.

[40]*Seatrade Review*, January 1994; *Cargo Systems*, April 1997; *Lloyd's List*, 4 June 1997; *Lloyd's Maritime Asia*, September 1991; *South*, August 1988; and *Fairplay*, 25 August 1988 and 8 March 1990. For an interesting insight into the development of transport links between Iran and Central Asia, see Habib Chini, "The Islamic Republic of Iran Shipping Lines: Past Success and a Glance at the Future," *Payam-e-Darya* (Tehran), September 1996, 36-39 and *Fairplay*, 8 April 1999.

expansion of Sharjah International Airport for air freight, complete with a special free zone; within a few years its turnover has risen to 320,000 tonnes (against Dubai with 360,000), which included consignments originating in Dubai.[41]

A much greater challenge to Dubai, however, rests in the core of its business, the transshipment trade. Reconstruction after the Iraqi defeat in the second Gulf War and the effects of port industrialisation have strongly stimulated trade and led to more calls at other ports on services that have the Gulf as their terminus. Sea-Land and Maersk, for example, in 1997 revised their East Asia-Gulf service by including Muscat and Kuwait in the loop Jebel Ali–Kuwait–Dammam–Bahrain–Jebel Ali–Muscat. Dubai was not by-passed but some transshipment cargo was evidently lost. In many other services, though, Dubai remained the only port of call, as, for example, those of Kawasaki K-Line, Malaysian International Shipping Corporation, Nedlloyd and Mitsui OSK arriving from East Asia. But once Dubai's situation in the lower Gulf is considered in a broader context than the Gulf, it appears less favourable. For container ships on global or pendulum east-west mainline services, Dubai requires a considerable deviation from the shortest route between the Bab El-Mandeb to Colombo and beyond. The two external Gulf ports, with a joint turnover in 1996 of some 1.25 million TEUs, are more than a nuisance to Dubai. The development of Sharjah Airport with its free-trade zone has given Khor Fakkan an important additional advantage. The challenge to Dubai, however, lies not just in the entrepot trade to the Gulf but also in that to South Asia, in relation to which they also have a significant geographical advantage; steaming time from Fujairah to India is twelve hours less than from Dubai. Together, the three UAE rivals now play "a key role...Dubai, Khor Fakkan and Fujairah have become vital regional transshipment hubs, used by all the major carriers to serve destinations in the Middle East Gulf and Indian Sub-Continent."[42]

---

[41]*Fairplay*, 20 November 1986 and 25 August 1988; *Lloyd's Maritime Asia*, January 1993; *South*, April 1990; *Cargo Today*, October 1997; and *Lloyd's List*, 4 June 1997.

[42]*Containerisation International*, February and March 1996; *Lloyd's Maritime Asia*, November 1993 and November 1997; *PDI*, November 1994; and *Cargo Today*, October 1997.

Within the western Indian Ocean the three UAE ports possess one more dynamic rival and will soon have to face the challenge from two further container hubs. Almost from the beginning of containerisation Colombo has been the major hub into western India and has continuously expanded its container facilities. Its location, closer to Bombay and virtually on the main east-west route, gives it major advantages over its Arab rivals; in 1996 it turned over 1.4 million TEUs (ranked 26th), of which an estimated seventy-four percent was transshipment cargo. All ports mentioned were concerned about the opening in autumn 1998 of Mina Raysut, at Salalah in southern Oman, roughly halfway between Muscat and Aden. A joint venture of Sea-Land and the Omani government, its initiators claimed to have found the optimal location for a mainline port that would "enable East-West carriers to cover Middle Eastern markets without having to deviate to the Gulf." Others were sceptical about Salalah, which has no hinterland, and it is significant that both Sea-Land and its partner, Maersk, also cited the political risks of operating inside the Gulf as a prime reason for the move to Oman. Salalah's 900,000-TEU throughput capacity cannot but affect Dubai's position. The second new project is located in Aden, the traditional entrepot of sail and steam that during the People's Democratic Republic of Yemen had been cut off almost entirely from world shipping. Even more than at Salalah and the UAE ports, East Africa would enter into consideration, but in the Arabian business Jiddah rather than Dubai is likely to be affected. A final factor to be considered is that, as in the Gulf, through enlargement of trade volumes the causes of the transshipment trade may be undermined. As DPA chairman Sultan Sulayem expressed it, "[i]n the longer term, if India and Pakistan get their act together, then a lot of [DPA] business would be in jeopardy." The container world – ports as much as shipping – is in continuous flux. The huge companies, consortia and alliances that have resulted from concentration in the shipping industry and their Panamax and Post-Panamax carriers have the power to "make geography," not just by the lay-out of their mainline services but also by the creation of new ports. Rivalry never ceases, as all ports aim to be included in mainline services and to become regional hubs. What may come in the future is impossible to foresee, but the headlines indicate that Dubai stands at the crossroads. No port can ever rest on its laurels, least of all an entrepot like Dubai. Yet with its facilities and established position, it is possible to see why the DPA's sales manager could envisage "multi-national companies having logistical centres in three or four locations around the globe to handle their world wide distribution" and aim to make Dubai the hub of the Middle East.[43]

The Foundations of the Global Port City

As the previous paragraphs will have amply demonstrated, Dubai's rise has not been the automatic outcome of absolute advantages of its site and situation. Throughout its history Dubai's rulers, merchants and shipowners have had to use shrewd entrepreneurship, single-minded commercial policies and hard work to exploit opportunities. Site has had to be improved in stages in both the creek and the massive harbour works at Port Rashid and Jebel Ali, without which Dubai would never have risen above the rank of, for example, Ras Al-Khaimah. But each investment carried with it the risk of overcapitalisation and adding to the evident oversupply of facilities in the Gulf. The philosophy of Shaikh Rashid and his successors, however, was to supplement the potential advantages of Dubai's situation with a dedicated campaign to provide all "modern, reliable infrastructure of communications, finance and servicing...a symbiotic relationship between international banks, international corporations and local concerns that spells successful growth for all."[44] In particular, the Dubai government was keen to provide an optimal business climate, to attract "the world's leading hotels" and to create "a communications network that allows instantaneous access to all parts of the globe" and that would make "Dubai's infrastructure...comparable to that of New York, London or Singapore." This free-wheeling environment also entailed the widespread use of cheap immigrant labour (mainly from Pakistan and South Asia) and the total absence of trade unions.

The development of Dubai as a tourist destination and centre for major international sporting events was an extension of this self-promotional policy that was designed to create an image of Dubai as

---

[43]K. Dharmasena, "Bombay and Colombo 1948-1984: A Study in Port Development with Special Reference to Containerisation," *The Great Circle*, IX (1987), 119-133; *Cargo Systems*, June and October 1996, and April and June 1997; *Container Management*, September 1996: *Cargo Today*, October 1997; *Lloyd's Maritime Asia*, January 1993 and November 1997; *Fairplay*, 8 January 1998 and 8 April 1999; *PDI*, November 1994; and *Shipping Times Singapore*, 16 April 1999.

[44]Brochure, Port Rashid Authority, "Regional Distribution," n.d. [1988]; the following quotations have been taken from the same source.

a global city. But this economic and cultural diversification should not conceal the fact that the foundations of Dubai's prosperity remained its maritime economy. Of its GDP of some US $9 billion, ten percent was earned by shipping services; twenty percent by trade; ten percent by manufactures; and another eight percent by related utility services. Only twenty percent was generated by oil.[45]

Little of this could have been achieved without a commitment to quality as well as unfettered free enterprise. Dubai's "ultra-modern, deepwater ports of the latest generation" have always been in the forefront of port efficiency and the application of the latest cranes ("ranging from basic tangos to high-speed double trolley post-Panamax") and computer technology. The DPA has been a pioneer in the development of Differential Global Positioning Systems for the locating of containers. Port Rashid and Jebel Ali are renowned for their high productivity and Dubai Drydocks came out of the Gulf War with "an excellent reputation."[46] The DPA established training schemes for overseas ports and companies, which in late 1997 included a bizarre and controversial episode involving serving and former Australian soldiers being prepared for strikebreaking activities in Australian ports. As soon as the Dubai government realised that widespread opposition might jeopardise the smooth running of its ports, *realpolitik* determined that the scheme be terminated. In May 1999 the DPA followed the expansionary trend set by private port operators such as Hutchison's of Hong Kong and P&O Ports (Australia) by taking up the management of Sa'udi Arabia's leading container terminal at Jiddah.[47]

Dubai's fortunes, of course, were greatly assisted by the discovery of oil, which made huge additional funds available for investment and helped overcome periods of overcapacity, and the succession of wars in the Gulf between 1980 and 1991. As the upper Gulf was almost closed to traffic, Dubai received a massive boost to its entrepot business, bringing

---

[45]*The Australian Magazine*, 23-24 March 1996; *Time*, 23 April 1990 and 25 March 1996; *South*, April 1990; *The European*, 2-8 December 1994; and *GPS World*, September 1996.

[46]*Fairplay*, 20 November 1986 and 25 August 1988; *Docks & Harbour Authority*, May and November/December 1996; *Cargo Systems*, November 1995, April and June 1996; and *GPS World*, September 1996.

[47]*Fairplay*, 27 March 1999.

trade and investment to Mina Rashid and Jebel Ali. In particular, the collapse of the shipping of Basrah, Kuwait and Khorromshahr (later Bandar Khomeini) removed major props from the Gulf's loops-and-strings port system. But Dubai could not have capitalised on these opportunities had it not had the facilities, historical involvement and experience in the transshipment trade, confirming the validity of Jackson's observation that ports are communities of merchants.[48] In all these respects Dubai differed fundamentally from, for example, its bigger neighbour, Abu Dhabi. The rulers and people of Dubai traditionally viewed themselves as a maritime community and their city as a "Venice of Arabia."[49] The creek is still used by dhows, while its banks are the location of the financial and other service institutions that underpin Dubai's position as global city. The creek always was the gateway to overseas, even if, as Easa Al-Gurg recalled, in the 1940s Dubai's horizons did not yet stretch beyond the Straits of Hormuz.[50] Window to the world, Dubai Creek is both the cradle and heart of Arabia's global port city, linking past, present and future in the self-image of maritime ideas and interests which lie at the core of Dubai's identity.

---

[48]Jackson, *Grimsby*, 24.

[49]Osborne, *Gulf States*, 92.

[50]Bulloch, *The Gulf*, 123.

New York's German Suburb: The Creation of the Port of Bremerhaven, 1827-1918

Lars U. Scholl

> Nature can do a good deal, but not everything, to determine the success of a sea-port. Human initiative also accounts for something.
>
> (Robert Greenhalgh Albion)[1]

Introduction

In the preface to *The History and Archaeology of Ports*, Gordon Jackson deplored the fact that "despite the importance of trade to the British economy, relatively little has been written about the development of ports through which it passes, either in general or in particular."[2] His book attempted to "redress the balance a little" and in the process sparked a new scholarly interest in port history. In the intervening years, Jackson has continued to make important contributions.[3] In addition, Adrian Jarvis has produced a remarkable run of excellent publications on the Liverpool

[1]Robert Greenhalgh Albion, *The Rise of New York Port, 1815-1860* (New York, 1939), 16.

[2]Gordon Jackson, *The History and Archaeology of Ports* (Tadworth, 1983).

[3]See, for example, Gordon Jackson, "The Ports," in Derek H. Aldcroft and Michael J. Freeman (eds.), *Transport in the Industrial Revolution* (Manchester, 1983), 177-209; Jackson, "Do Docks Make Trade?: The Case of the Port of Great Grimsby," in Lewis R. Fischer (ed.), *From Wheel House to Counting House: Essays in Maritime Business History in Honour of Professor Peter Neville Davies* (St. John's, 1992), 17-41; Jackson, "The British Port System, c. 1850-1913," in A. Guimera and D. Romero (eds.). *Puertos y Sistemas Portuarios (siglos xvi-xx)* (Madrid, 1996), 77-97; and Jackson, "Ports, Ships and Government in the Nineteenth and Twentieth Centuries," in Paul C. van Royen, Lewis R. Fischer and David M. Williams (eds.), *Frutta di Mare: Evolution and Revolution in the Maritime World in the 19th and 20th Centuries* (Amsterdam, 1998), 161-175.

docks and their engineers.[4] Recently David Williams of Leicester University organized a session on port cities at the Fourth International Conference of Urban History in Venice.[5]

What Gordon Jackson said of the state of port history in Britain in the early 1980s could also be said with some justification about Germany at the end of the 1990s.[6] For this reason I want to concentrate on the foundation of a single port - Bremerhaven - with a special focus on the relationship between trade, the port and town development from the pre-industrial period through the decades when the industrial revolution transformed Germany in the second half of the nineteenth century.[7]

One striking feature of industrialization was the steady movement of people from rural areas into the rapidly-expanding towns.[8] Regardless of time or region, this phenomenon has been characteristic of eighteenth-century England, nineteenth-century Europe and North America, and twentieth-century East Asia. There were many reasons for leaving the countryside and foregoing the security of a tightly-knit social network. But the most important incentive was the expectation of participating in the new economic opportunities that were being created in industrial towns. Hoping to improve their lot, many people were prepared to suffer

---

[4]See, for example, Adrian Jarvis, *Liverpool Central Docks 1799-1905* (Stroud, 1991); and Jarvis, *The Liverpool Dock Engineers* (Stroud, 1996).

[5]An earlier version of this paper was among those originally delivered there.

[6]In the urban histories of port cities there is some information about the ports. But for Hamburg two port histories may be consulted: Arnold Kludas, *et al.*, *Hafen Hamburg. Geschichte des Hamburger Freihafens von den Anfängen bis zur Gegenwart* (Hamburg, 1988); and Dieter Maas, *Der Ausbau des Hamburger Hafens. 1840 bis 1910* (Hamburg, 1990).

[7]For examples of comparative port history in Germany, see Lars U. Scholl, "Marine und Hafen am Beispiel von Wilhelmshaven," in Jürgen Ellermeyer and Rainer Postel (eds.), *Stadt und Hafen. Hamburger Beiträge zur Geschichte von Handel und Häfen* (Hamburg 1986), 99-106; and Scholl, "Die Reichskriegshäfen Wilhelmshaven und Kiel," in Volker Plagemann (ed.), *Übersee. Seefahrt und Seemacht im Deutschen Kaiserreich* (München, 1988), 201-206.

[8]Hubert Kiesewetter, *Industrielle Revolution in Deutschland 1815-1914* (Frankfurt, 1989), 132-142.

hardship in towns that lacked the infrastructure to cope with the influx seeking employment in factories, trades or transport industries.

Towns have always been central points for the production of goods and for trade. Over the centuries, they have served as entrepots and have provided banking facilities; they have been centres of religious activity around churches and cathedrals; and rulers have located civil administration and military forces within their walls. All these functions remained unchanged when industrialization fundamentally altered urban life. If demands for space for housing and industry could not always be met within urban boundaries, existing villages were often absorbed. Cities of medieval origin soon grew beyond the old town walls and developed into agglomerations with hundreds of thousands of inhabitants. In the twentieth century such places have been superceded by the new giants, like Hong Kong, Singapore, Mexico City and Djakarta. Urban historians have pointed to the fact that the shift in population from rural to metropolitan districts only seems to halt when sixty to eighty percent of the population live in towns or suburbs near urban centres.[9]

While urbanization far transcended the physical restraints of towns, industrialization changed society as a whole, in the countryside as well as the city. Once unleashed, industrialization affected every aspect of human existence. Societies became industrialized mentally as well as economically, and in the process most people altered their traditional behaviour and adjusted their expectations to fit the new realities. At the same time, a minority began to protest against the negative effects of industrialization. The image of a particular town or region depended not only on its factories, chimneys and pollution but also on the way people lived and worked in those surroundings. Many observers were alternately fascinated, surprised and shocked by the industrial city. It was this ambiguity that led Asa Briggs to coin the phrase "shock city of the age" to describe Manchester in the 1820s.[10] Industrialization and associated urbanization in Germany affected existing towns, cities, and regions, especially in Upper Silesia or most strikingly in the Ruhr. Coal and iron formed the basis for developments that made contemporaries praise

---

[9]Hans-Jürgen Teuteberg (ed.), *Urbanisierung im 19. und 20. Jahrhundert. Historische und geographische Aspekte* (Köln, 1983); and Jürgen Reulecke, *Geschichte der Urbanisierung in Deutschland* (Frankfurt, 1985).

[10]Asa Briggs, *Victorian Cities* (New York, 1965), 87.

economic progress while at the same time quaking at the overcrowding, filth and social dislocation.

There were only three completely new towns created in Germany during the nineteenth century, and all were on rivers. Ludwigshafen on the Rhine was founded in 1842. A glance at the first map of 1853 reveals little more than a sheltered harbour and a few streets.[11] No recognizable town plan can be discerned, although in that year the first municipal elections were held and a local administration was established. Only after Badische Anilin and Soda-Fabrik (BASF) had been granted a concession to produce chemicals in 1865 did Ludwigshafen develop into an important industrial city. Similarly, Bremerhaven and Wilhelmshaven on the North Sea coast antedated industrialization. But both were very different than Ludwigshafen. Indeed, both ports can claim a certain uniqueness in the context of German urbanization in that development was determined to a great extent by circumstance rather than intent.

It was in the period prior to political unification that we find the explanation for why two German states moved their merchant and naval fleets to two new towns that on clear days were within visual range of each other. The bases for commercial and military purposes were established in foreign territory purchased from the Kingdom of Hanover and the Grand Duchy of Oldenburg. In both cases the purchasers wanted to move closer to the North Sea. But in neither case did the founders think they were creating new urban places. Both were built for one specific reason. In the case of Bremerhaven, the founders had a sort of colony in mind, while Prussia signed a contract with Oldenburg specifically ruling out the possibility that its new naval base would develop beyond a few barracks, sheds and quays.[12] But the contracts were signed in the early stages of German industrialization and well before the Franco-Prussian War resulted in the formation of the Kaiserreich in 1871. Thereafter, new strategic plans called for an enlarged navy that allegedly was necessary to

---

[11]Wilhelm Wortmann, *150 Jahre Bremerhaven. Der erste Schritt zur mehrpoligen Region Bremen/Unterweser* (Hannover, 1977), 23.

[12]Ingrid Dunger, *Wilhelmshaven 1870-1914, Staats-, Kommunal- und Parteipolitik im Jadegebiet zwischen Reichsgründung und Erstem Weltkrieg* (Wilhelmshaven, 1962); Rolf Uphoff, *"Hier laßt uns einen Hafen bau'n!" Entstehungsgeschichte der Stadt Wilhelmshaven. 1848-1890* (Oldenburg, 1995); and Axel Wiese, *Die Hafenarbeiter an der Jade. 1853-1871* (Oldenburg, 1998).

protect a rapidly-expanding merchant fleet. Once the technological construction for their function as ports had been completed, it soon became apparent that economic and military activities could not be undertaken without consequences for the locality where people worked and lived. By the beginning of the twentieth century two port cities had emerged that seemed to be prospering, although the First World War altered their fates totally. In this essay I shall examine the rationale that lay behind the foundation of Bremerhaven and look at the dynamic forces that sparked developments in the dock area and later in the adjoining community, which eventually gained municipal status. Finally, I will show how Bremerhaven developed an economy that left it highly vulnerable to events after 1918.

Bremen's "Colony" North of the River Geeste

At the beginning of the nineteenth century Germany was still largely agrarian. The territories which later formed the Deutsches Reich in 1871 counted little more than twenty million inhabitants in 1800, about ninety percent of whom lived in rural areas or small towns of less than 5000 people. Fifteen percent of the remainder lived in cities. Up to 1850 not much had changed.[13] In the span between 1816 and 1885 the population doubled, while at the same time more than four million emigrants left Germany, mainly for North America.[14] This period witnessed the early stages of industrialization, as many people moved into towns and industrializing regions. But early in the century only Berlin and Hamburg had more than 100,000 inhabitants, and fifty years later only Breslau and Munich had joined them.[15] The future giant in the Ruhr basin, Essen, had only 9000 residents, and Dortmund and Duisburg were still small hamlets

[13]Hermann Kellenbenz, *Deutsche Wirtschaftsgeschichte. Vol. II. Vom Ausgang des 18. Jahrhunderts bis zum Ende des Zweiten Weltkriegs* (München, 1981), 26-31.

[14]Peter Marschalck, *Bevölkerungsgeschichte Deutschlands im 19. und 20. Jahrhundert* (Frankfurt, 1984), 27-45 and 145-146.

[15]Hans-Ulrich Wehler, *Deutsche Gesellschaftsgeschichte 1815-1845/49* (Munich, 1987), 18.

in the 1850s. Then an enormous population boom commenced.[16] Hamburg's Hanseatic sister on the river Weser, Bremen, housed only 52,000 people in 1852. Despite being a much smaller merchant city than Hamburg, Bremen's shipping companies were able to recover more quickly from the Napoleonic wars because they seized the opportunities of trade with North America, while Hamburg concentrated its transatlantic activities on Latin America after the Spanish and Portuguese colonies became independent.[17]

Both Hanseatic merchant fleets had experienced dramatic declines because of the Napoleon's imposition of a continental blockade in 1806, after a period of growth during the Franco-British struggle for supremacy at sea. Hamburg's fleet comprised 248 sailing vessels (about 47,000 tons) in 1798, but by 1822 it had contracted to eighty-eight vessels (about 13,000 tons). Bremen's fleet was reduced from 179 sailing vessels (about 29,000 tons) in 1799 to 127 vessels (about 13,000 tons) in 1816, and fell to sixty-eight vessels by 1826.[18] The first signs of recovery came in the late 1820s when trade with North America expanded after the inauguration of regular packet service between Bremen and New York, New Orleans and Philadelphia. Between 1820 and 1827 goods worth US $14.5 million were shipped to the US and cargo worth US $18 million arrived in German ports, mainly Bremen. More then seventy percent of the cargo unloaded in Bremen was shipped on American vessels between 1815 and 1829. In the 1830s, however, this figure was reversed: in 1832 fewer than half the vessels calling at Bremen flew the American flag and by the beginning of the 1840s more than eighty percent of the ships in the trade between Bremen and the US were registered in the Hanseatic port.[19] While Baltimore was the most prominent port of call for ships from Bremen up

---

[16]André Armengaud, "Population in Europe 1700-1914," in Carlo M. Cipolla (ed.), *The Fontana Economic History of Europe. Vol. III. The Industrial Revolution* (London, 1973), 33-34.

[17]Otto Mathies, "Hamburgs Seeschiffahrt und Seehandel," in Kurt Wiedenfeld (ed.), *Die deutsche Wirtschaft und ihre Führer. Vol. 5* (Gotha, 1928), 9-10.

[18]Hermann Wätjen, *Aus der Zeit des Nordatlantikverkehrs* (Leipzig, 1932), 7-23.

[19]Franz Josef Pitsch, *Die wirtschaftlichen Beziehungen Bremens zu den Vereinigten Staaten von Amerika bis zur Mitte des 19. Jahrhunderts* (Bremen, 1974), 99-109.

to 1836, it was gradually superceded by New York because of the improved connections to the hinterland once the Erie Canal had been built. Vessels from Bremen were fourth behind ships from America, Britain and Sweden in New York's harbour statistics in 1837.[20]

Baltimore had already been the target of merchants from Bremen in the eighteenth century because it was a natural outlet for tobacco. Indeed, some German merchants even founded branches in Baltimore. The most important commodities exported from the US to Bremen were tobacco, cotton and to a lesser extent rice and train oil.[21] As German exports of manufactured products were not sufficient to provide full cargoes on westbound legs, Bremen seized the opportunity to enter the emigrant trade, which eventually sparked a boom in the town's shipping. The political relations between Bremen and the US were strengthened by a trade agreement signed in 1827 and by the appointment of an American consul in Bremen; in turn, Bremen established consulates in New York (1815), Baltimore (1818), Philadelphia (1827) and New Orleans (1840).[22]

There was, however, a serious threat to these positive trends that was by no means new to the merchants in Bremen. As early as the seventeenth century the Weser had become so shallow that larger ships were no longer able to reach Bremen. In an early attempt to prevent being cut off from seaborne trade, the outport of Vegesack (now part of Bremen) was founded several miles upriver between 1619 and 1622.[23] Barges and horse-drawn vehicles transshipped the cargo to Bremen, where the merchant houses continued to maintain their operations. Besides the fact that the problem of silting remained unsolved, it was not long before the ships became too large even to reach Vegesack. Cargo for Bremen had to be shipped to Brake, a port belonging to the Grand Duchy of Oldenburg,

---

[20]Many of the Swedish vessels were of course Norwegian; before Norway became fully independent in 1905, American authorities frequently confused the two.

[21]Hermann Entholt, "Bremens Handel, Schiffahrt und Industrie im 19. Jahrhundert (1815-1914)," in Kurt Wiedenfeld (ed.), *Die deutsche Wirtschaft und ihre Führer, Vol. 5* (Gotha, 1928), 135.

[22]Pitsch, *Wirtschaftliche Beziehungen*, 78-86.

[23]Herbert Schwarzwälder, *Geschichte der Freien Hansestadt Bremen. Vol I. Von den Anfängen bis zur Franzosenzeit [1810]* (Bremen, 1995), 300; and Sophie Hollanders, *Vegesack. Alte Bilder einer Hafenstadt* (Bremen, 1984), 11-12.

where the goods were unloaded and shipped in smaller river craft to Bremen. In 1824 Oldenburg even tried to have Bremen replaced by Brake in the shipping documents that indicated the point of destination or departure.[24]

The delicate situation that endangered Bremen's future as a seaport and the commercial centre of the Lower Weser called for action. In previous centuries plans to create a new port closer to the North Sea coast had been discussed, but only in 1825 did Bremen's mayor, Johann Smidt, decide to put some ideas into practice by having a dock built north of the river Geeste, some sixty kilometres down the river. Since the territory belonged to the Kingdom of Hanover, Smidt had to negotiate the purchase of a strip of land with the authorities, who of course were anxious to safeguard their interests south of the Geeste, although there was then only a little village in existence. Only after long negotiations and assurances in the preamble of the contract that the new project would serve not only Bremen's but also Hanover's commercial interests did the parties agree to sign the final agreement on 11 January 1827. Bremen paid 74,000 *taler* for the land and in addition promised to invest 200,000 *taler* within the next three years. In May the territory was officially handed over to Bremen, along with nineteen Hanoverian subjects who became the first inhabitants of the new town of Bremerhaven.[25]

The same month a senior clerk was appointed to administer a strip of land that was to house the new harbour. As there was no available German experienced in dock building, a Dutch engineer who had acted as a consultant and who had drafted a preliminary plan in 1826 was invited to construct a basin that could give shelter to ships of at least 180 registered tons. Johannes Jacobus van Ronzelen (1800-1865), whose design of the dock was approved in Bremen, found Dutch contractors who estimated the cost at 416,000 *tale*r. The project attracted hundreds of Dutch construction workers. Since no houses existed, they had to live in hastily-constructed reed huts. More than 900 workers were temporarily employed, two-thirds of whom commuted daily from nearby villages. On 1 September 1830 the dock, which was 752 metres long, fifty-eight metres

---

[24]Herbert Schwarzwälder, *Geschichte der Freien Hansestadt Bremen. Vol. II. Von der Franzosenzeit bis zum Ersten Weltkrieg [1810-1918]* (Bremen, 1995), 122-123.

[25]Rita Kellner-Stoll, *Bremerhaven 1827-1888. Politische, wirtschaftliche und soziale Probleme einer Stadtgründung* (Bremerhaven, 1982), 45-54.

wide, and 5.5 metres deep, was completed. The chamber lock was forty-two metres long and twenty-six metres wide. Eleven days later the American schooner *Draper* became the first vessel to enter the new "Hafen Bassin."[26] Dock and town did not develop simultaneously. The main object was the outport; the adjoining settlement was of secondary importance.

While van Ronzelen was busy constructing the dock basin, the authorities in Bremen faced the problem that running such a complex enterprise was not feasible with labourers from nearby agrarian communities who lacked the necessary qualifications and experience. Many different craftsmen had to be attracted to the new port and they had to have premises for their trade and houses for their families. Based on van Ronzelen's original plan, a civil engineer produced a map with a rigid gridiron street system and a marketplace. A total of 232 building sites were provided, but although the authorities in Bremen advertised widely, only eight were sold by the end of the year.

It was not the social needs of the population that governed the decision-making process in Bremen but rather the needs of trade and commerce. Nevertheless, Bremerhaven was not popular among merchants, shipowners and craftsmen whose business was supposed to benefit most. By the end of 1830 only five foreign and twelve Bremen-registered ships had entered the harbour. Most vessels deliberately avoided the new port. In 1831, only ninety-five ships bound for Bremen called at Bremerhaven, while more than 900 sailed to Bremen or Brake. The authorities in Oldenburg suddenly welcomed ships unloading freight for Bremen in Brake, thus stirring emotions in Bremen against the new outport. Merchants began to complain that more than half a million *taler* had been wasted and spoke disparagingly about the new port. Indeed, many wanted the "puddle" to be filled with sand, and there were merchants who even moaned that the creation of Bremerhaven was the most deplorable event to hit Bremen since the French occupation during the Napoleonic wars.[27] In April 1831 the parliament in Bremen stopped further financial aid until

---

[26]Burchard Scheper, *Die jüngste Geschichte der Stadt Bremerhaven* (Bremerhaven, 1977), 48-64.

[27]Kellner-Stoll, *Bremerhaven*, 52-54; and Georg Bessell, *Geschichte Bremerhavens* (Bremerhaven, 1927), 244-246.

an investigation headed by civil servants from Oldenburg proved that the money had been spent with the utmost care.

By the end of 1831, 602,000 *taler* had been expended, three times as much as originally planned. Merchants and shipowners never considered moving their businesses or their families to Bremerhaven. Firmly rooted in the urban surroundings in Bremen, few fancied living in a place that lacked all the amenities of bourgeois life in the old Hanseatic city. Under these circumstances it is not surprising that only real pioneers were prepared to start a new life in Bremerhaven. Once roads, railways and telecommunications had come into being much later, there were even fewer reasons to move to a place populated mostly by the working-class. By the end of 1831 there were only sixteen houses in Bremerhaven, owned by the harbourmaster, a carpenter, a smith, a baker, a pub owner, and a shopkeeper. Food for the workers was imported from surrounding villages. In 1833 the first two shipbuilders, Wencke and Lange, rented sites on the Geeste for shipyards, and in 1835 the first seagoing vessel built in Bremerhaven was launched.

Despite short-sighted reservations and hostilities against the "colony," Mayor Smidt and his administrators had no doubts about the future development of Bremerhaven. As soon as the maritime economy improved, further town planning would surely follow. Without hesitation Smidt continued to pursue his project. Politicians in Bremen and Hanover knew that Smidt's visionary ideas would lead to more than just a dock and a few houses. In the 1827 contract there were several passages that showed clearly that both states accepted that Bremerhaven was most likely more than a puddle in which a few ships could moor. Provisions for settling colonists and for establishing consulates, agencies and brokers were made. Hanover consented to the inclusion of Bremerhaven in trade agreements and to the levying of customs duties and taxes.

The economic revival of Bremen's shipping business silenced all the critics. In 1832 about 170 vessels called at the new outport and more than ten thousand emigrants left Germany via Bremerhaven. Still, in 1833 there were only twenty-seven houses, so we can hardly speak of even a village six years after the foundation of Bremerhaven. But a hard winter in 1834/1835 had a decisive effect on the future. Heavy ice interrupted shipping on the river between Brake and Bremen; for months only Bremerhaven's basin was accessible. The existence of an ice-free passage into a safe harbour finally silenced the critics. The advantages of the new port were now evident. "Ice" literally broke the ice.[28] Thereafter, ships called regularly at Bremerhaven. In 1836 more than 400 vessels used the facilities in the new port and growth to mid-century was impressive (see table 1). The number of houses had risen to 186, a hotel had been erected, most streets had been paved, and Bremerhaven had 1460 inhabitants. More than half the houses were inhabited by low-paid workers and craftsmen and their families, who could only afford one-storey buildings. The warehouses around the dock, however, were several storeys high.

Table 1
Ships Calling at Bremerhaven, 1830-1850

Year	Number of Vessels
1830	18
1835	286
1840	624
1845	650
1850	850

Source: Rita Kellner-Stoll, *Bremerhaven 1827-1888. Politische, wirtschaftliche und soziale Probleme einer Stadtgründung* (Bremerhaven, 1982), 79.

The tobacco and emigrant trades began to pay off. In 1843 Bremen's fleet comprised twenty-three large sailing vessels of more than 450 tons, six times as many as in all of France. The Senator and merchant Arnold Duckwitz proudly announced that the German merchant fleet was the second largest in Europe. In 1837 he had already boasted that Bremen's market for tobacco was "without doubt the most important in Europe."[29] As early as 1832 Bremen had outstripped the Dutch in the American tobacco trade, when the merchants on the Weser imported 26,500 barrels of tobacco compared to 24,000 barrels at Rotterdam and Amsterdam combined. In 1841 the American consul Derkheim reported to Washington that "with respect to this article generally, especially such of the growth of the United States, this market is the most extensive of the

[28]Kellner-Stoll, *Bremerhaven*, 79-81.

[29]Bessell, *Geschichte Bremerhavens*, 259.

continent."[30] In the next few years the German city stretched its lead (see table 2).

Table 2
Barrels of North American Tobacco Sold, 1834-1844

Year	Bremen	Amsterdam/ Rotterdam	Antwerp
1834	25,077	11,426	6,957
1841	33,338	22,049	8,396
1844	37,752	29,498	7,313

Source: Franz Josef Pitsch, *Die wirtschaftlichen Beziehungen Bremens zu den Vereinigten Staaten von Amerika bis zur Mitte des 19. Jahrhunderts* (Bremen, 1974), 151.

Table 3
German Emigration, 1816-1849

Years	Emigrants	Years	Emigrants
1816-1819	25,000	1816-1844	303,200
1820-1829	22,500	1845-1849	308,200
1830-1839	145,100		
1840-1849	418,800	1816-1847	583,800

Source: Hans-Ulrich Wehler, *Deutsche Gesellschaftsgeschichte 1815-1845/49* (Munich, 1987), 17.

The other pillar on which Bremen's economy rested was emigration. From 1816 to 1848 almost 600,000 Germans left the old country, pushed by famines, crop failures and the general fear of poverty and pulled across the Atlantic by economic opportunities (see table 3).[31] In the quinquennium 1845-1849, economic crisis and revolutionary developments led 310,000 Germans to turn to the New World. Bremerhaven gained immensely from this exodus. While many Germans

---

[30]Pitsch, *Wirtschaftliche Beziehungen*, 150.

[31]Knut Borchardt, "The Industrial Revolution in Germany 1700-1914," in Carlo M. Cipolla (ed.), *The Fontana Economic History of Europe. Vol. IV. The Emergence of Industrial Societies* (London, 1972), 51. Borchardt's figures for the period 1821-1850 are 637,000. The statistics for German emigration first become reasonably reliable after political unification in 1871, when a yearly *Reichsstatistik* was published.

chose other ports, like Le Havre, Antwerp, the Dutch ports or Hamburg for their departure, a large number left via Bremen's outpost (see table 4).

Table 4
German Emigration, 1843-1849

Port	1843	1845	1847	1849
Le Havre	8,600	23,500	39,400	33,800
Antwerp	2,800	4,500	14,600	10,300
Amsterdam/ Rotterdam	1,700	5,100	13,100	8,700
Hamburg	1,800	2,400	8,600	7,600
Bremen	9,800	31,800	33,700	28,600
Total	23,000	67,200	109,500	89,100

Source: Rolf Engelsing, *Bremen als Auswandererhafen* (Bremen, 1961), 63-64.

Before the first provisional municipal code was issued by the government in Bremen in 1837, a senior clerk who took instructions from Bremen functioned as a communal officer responsible for the police, road and dyke construction, public hygiene, the fire brigade, the water supply, and the schools. Until 1836 no taxes were paid by Bremerhaven's inhabitants, who were still generally poor labourers with no influence or means of participating in the administration. The new municipal code allowed elections for a council, which took place in November 1837. Eighty-nine men, or 5.6% of the populace, had the right to vote, but the dock itself remained under direct rule by the authorities in Bremen. The good intentions, however, did not come to fruition: eleven years later Senator Heineken had to admit that next to nothing with regard to municipal self-rule had been achieved.[32] Still, in 1839 all 232 building sites had been sold and several private schools founded (the first public elementary school opened in 1843). The first newspapers appeared, and in 1842 the Bremen parliament provided a site for Bremerhaven's first church.

When the Kingdom of Hanover became aware of the economic progress of Bremen's colony north of the Geeste, it decided to develop a settlement on the south side of the river, taking up old plans centred

---

[32]Bessell, *Geschichte Bremerhavens*, 289.

around the existing emergency harbour.[33] While the village was only intended to serve as a Hanoverian suburb of Bremerhaven, the rationale for founding Geestemünde in the mid-1840s was altered in an attempt to participate in the new traffic on the Weser.[34] Naturally, the political climate between Bremen and Hanover deteriorated until several controversial issues had been settled. Bremen had to seek an understanding because it needed the Hanoverians to consent to new dock construction that was essential to Bremerhaven's future as a port.[35]

The outport across from Geestemünde fared well economically in the 1840s. Despite an order by the Bremen government that merchants who owned, for example, a shipping company, brokerage firm or emigration agency had to have their headquarters in Bremen "lest the 'colony Bremerhaven' should come into the possession of a line of trade to which the City of Bremen is entitled to," several shipbuilders moved to Bremerhaven.[36] The big sailing vessels no longer attempted to reach Brake or Bremen and preferred to unload in Bremerhaven, with the cargo then shipped upriver by barges or lighters. Although the main road to Bremen was completed in 1832, most travellers preferred to use the Weser between Bremen and Bremerhaven.

Economic Growth and Urban Development

In many respects the late 1840s marked a turning point in Bremerhaven's history. Not only was the foundation of Geestemünde an indication of economic progress along the Lower Weser but also the emigrant trade had become a consistent element in Bremen's shipping, with tens of thousands

---

[33]For a new interpretation of Geestemünde's origins, see Hartmut Bickelmann, "Hafenbau, Verkehrswege und Stadtgestalt. Räumliche Aspekte der frühen Stadt- und Hafengründung an der Geestemündung," *Jahrbuch der Männer vom Morgenstern*, LXXVI (1997), 99-160.

[34]Lars U. Scholl, "Die Gründung Geestemündes oder wie das Königreich Hannover am wirtschaftlichen Aufschwung Bremerhavens teilnehmen wollte," *Jahrbuch der Männer vom Morgenstern*, LXIV (1984), 183-196.

[35]Kellner-Stoll, *Bremerhaven*, 81-105.

[36]Harry Gabcke, *et al.*, *Bremerhaven in zwei Jahrhunderten. Vol. I. 1827-1918* (Bremerhaven, 1989), 41.

departing from Bremerhaven each year. The infrastructure in the hinterland was improved considerably in 1847 when a railway linked Bremen and Hanover, which meant also that connections to Berlin and the east and to Cologne and the west and south were cemented. The extension of the line to Geestemünde and Bremerhaven was completed in 1862. In January 1847 the optical telegraph between Bremerhaven and Bremen, which was only just installed, was replaced by an electromagnetic telegraph, the first of its kind in Germany.[37]

Perhaps the most important positive change was the result of a diplomatic coup by Bremen's negotiators in the US, who snatched from Rotterdam, Antwerp, Le Havre, Bordeaux and Lisbon the first regular post and passenger liner service between the US and Europe.[38] The Cunard Line, which was subsidised by the British government, dominated transatlantic steam shipping between Europe and America until Americans began to call for alternatives to reduce the dependence on a single line and to speed up distribution for less money. Bremen and other German states not only raised US $300,000 - in addition to the American contribution of US $350,000 - to found the Ocean Steam Navigation Company (OSNC) but also offered to lower transit duties for American goods in Germany, improve navigation on the Weser, speed up railway construction in Northwest Germany and, most important, build a new dock with a wider lock so that paddle steamers had access to the new harbour. When the OSNC's paddle steamer *Washington* opened regular services in June 1847, it had to moor in the river because the lock on the first dock was too small.[39] Four years later the new dock (230 metres long and eighty-five metres wide), built north of the existing one, was completed. The twenty-two-metre-wide lock allowed large paddle steamers to enter the "Neuer Hafen."

---

[37]Lars U. Scholl, "The Global Communications Industry and its Impact on International Shipping before 1914," in David J. Starkey and Gelina Harlaftis (eds.), *Global Markets: The Internationalization of the Sea Transport Industries since 1850* (St. John's, 1998), 199.

[38]Pierre Henri Laurent, "Antwerp versus Bremen: Transatlantic Steamship Diplomacy and European Port Rivalry, 1939-1846," *Journal of World History*, IX (1966), 939-952.

[39]Rolf Böttcher, *Die Ankunft des Raddampfers Washington in Bremerhaven 1847* (Bremerhaven, 1997).

Bremen in effect became America's continental post office. In 1848 the OSNC carried 80,000 letters to Bremen; five years later the number had risen to 350,000.[40] While the paddle steamers had facilities for passengers, emigrants continued to use sailing vessels because the price for the passage was much lower. A large hostel had been built in 1850 to provide up to 2000 emigrants with shelter while they were awaiting departure. Over the next decade about fifty-seven percent of emigrants made use of the hostel. In the early 1860s more ships became available to carry passengers, who gradually began to favour the increasingly more punctual steamers. After the opening of the railway between Bremen and Geestemünde, the flow of emigrants from the hinterland became more predictable and the hostel became less important.[41]

Following the termination of the postal contract in June 1857, the OSNC was no longer viable and the shareholders agreed to liquidation. In its place, the American shipowner Cornelius Vanderbilt received approval from the US Postmaster General to offer the same services. As other shipping companies were also prepared to carry the mail from America to various continental ports, the political dimension of the 1847 agreement - to end the Cunard monopoly - was superceded by economics: who could do the job at the least cost? Since 1847 the feasibility of liner services had been demonstrated and merchants in Bremen were prepared to take additional risks, especially after the termination of the Crimean War. On the initiative of Hermann Henrich Meyer, the North German Lloyd (NDL) was founded as a limited company in Bremen in 1857. While there may have been several turning points in the history of Bremerhaven, this was arguably the most important. The story of this successful company does not need to be repeated here, but suffice it to say that the NDL became the engine of Bremerhaven's economic growth and that it also had repercussions on municipal developments.[42]

---

[40]F. Graue, "Die Gründung der ersten deutsch-amerikanischen Postdampfschiffslinie," *Archiv für Post und Telegraphie*, V (1903), 129-183.

[41]Kellner-Stoll, *Bremerhaven*, 256-264.

[42]Georg Bessell, *1857-1957. Norddeutscher Lloyd. Geschichte einer Reederei* (Bremen, 1957). For the rise of merchant shipping prior to 1871, see Lars U. Scholl, "Shipping Business in Germany in the Nineteenth and Twentieth Centuries," in Tsunehiko Yui and Keiichiro Nakagawa, *Business History of Shipping. Strategy and Structure* (Tokyo, 1985), 185-193.

In 1851 the status of the colony was revised and redefined. Following the provisional municipal code, from 1837 the administration had remained in Bremen. But now Bremerhaven was granted a municipal constitution. One of the most important new powers given the town was the right to levy taxes. The first budget, which was amended in Bremen, imposed taxes on pubs and clubs; games like billiard and skittles; advertisements; dogs; pigeons; and nightingales.[43] The final political responsibility, however, remained with the Senate in Bremen. All financial matters had to be approved there and Bremen's administrator in Bremerhaven was always able to overrule local decisions if the "state's interests" were affected. Still, Bremerhaven had partial control over the well-being of its 4290 inhabitants. And it was granted the right to call itself a town, as long as "no inappropriate claims were put forward because of that title."[44]

Between 1851 and 1879, when its municipal status was revised once more, Bremerhaven experienced constant growth. More land had to be bought from Prussia in 1869 (the Kingdom of Hanover had become a Prussian province in 1866). In 1872 the Senate agreed to spend seven million marks for a third dock, "Kaiserhafen I," which opened in 1875, after the first dock (1862) and the second dock (1858 and 1862/1863) had been enlarged several times. While the "Alter" and "Neuer Hafen" remained distinct, a canal was built between the latter and Kaiserhafen. The new lock was only seventeen metres wide because paddle wheelers had been replaced by narrower screw steamers on the North Atlantic.[45] When in the 1880s the NDL began to order so-called "express steamers," Kaiserhafen I soon proved too small and the NDL sought remedy in Nordenham on the other side of the river. It was quickly decided in Bremen to build a new lock, to deepen the dock entrance and to enlarge Kaiserhafen. The new lock (223 metres long and forty-five metres wide, with the lock gates opening twenty-eight metres) was completed in 1897, when the next generation of passenger vessels, exemplified by the four-

---

[43]Gabcke, *Bremerhaven*, 64.

[44]Manfred Ernst, *50 Jahre Buchhandlung Mügge - Gedanken zu einem urbanen Zentrum* (Bremerhaven, 1998). Ernst is preparing a constitutional history of Bremerhaven.

[45]Bessell, *Geschichte Bremerhavens*, 446-481.

funnel steamer *Kaiser Wilhelm der Grosse*, came into service.[46] On its maiden voyage it became the first German vessel to win the prestigious Blue Riband. Congestion was often experienced in the Kaiserhafen, so further extensions were necessary and Kaiserhafen II and III were built between 1906 and 1909. The NDL returned to Bremerhaven and in 1913 a record 660,000 passengers and 4.1 million tons of cargo were carried by NDL vessels.[47]

Although the ferry across the Geeste was replaced by a solid bridge in 1857, Bremerhaven as a port and port city only expanded to the north despite several new docks in Geestemünde. After acquiring 88.7 hectares in 1827 for the first dock, Bremen had to buy more land in 1830, 1861, 1869, 1892 and 1905 to serve the needs of shipping. In 1905 Bremerhaven's territory comprised 879 hectares.[48] Along with the new docks, the town itself moved north. The developments ran parallel to each other because responsibilities for the port lay in Bremen while the town looked after its own affairs. Alterations of Bremerhaven's municipal status in 1879 led to a far-reaching independence within the framework of the constitutions of the state of Bremen and the Reich. Apart from these overriding political limitations, Bremerhaven was given full authority over municipal life and was granted the right to decide all local matters without Bremen's consent. The second town constitution abolished the supervisory position of Bremen's senior administrator in Bremerhaven. The thirty aldermen of the town council, elected by citizens belonging to the three classes who qualified for voting by sex, age and financial status, chose a body of eight councillors to form the executive, headed by a town clerk, that was responsible for Bremerhaven's administration. Up to 1914 Bremerhaven benefited enormously from Germany's attempt to become a prominent sea power. The maritime industries dominated local economic development.

Two more important decisions were made in Bremen in the 1880s. After decades of hesitation, Bremen eventually joined the German Customs Union. Only the dock area remained outside the Union and

---

[46]Arnold Kludas, *Die Geschichte der Deutschen Passagierschiffahrt. Vol. I. Die Pionierjahre von 1850 bis 1890* (Hamburg, 1986), 122-147.

[47]Bessell, *Geschichte Bremerhavens*, 558-561.

[48]Gabcke, *Bremerhaven*, 178.

shipping continued to be exempted from duties. Between 1887 and 1895 the Weser was deepened to enable larger ships with draughts up to five metres to reach the free port in Bremen. While some shipping again bypassed Bremerhaven, these measures helped to safeguard the economic survival of the Hanseatic city.[49] A large part of several million emigrants, increasingly comprised in the later years of the nineteenth century by Eastern Europeans, made use of Bremerhaven's facilities on their way to the US. While German emigration from Bremerhaven peaked in 1881, when 221,000 people left via the port, after 1900 about ninety percent of emigrants were non-German. The peak years were 1907 and 1913, when 234,000 and 239,000 people, respectively, emigrated through Bremerhaven.[50]

Table 5
German Emigration Overseas by Decade

1851-1860	1,075,000	1881-1890	1,342,400
1861-1870	832,700,000	1891-1900	529,900
1871-1880	626,000,000	1901-1910	279,600

Source: Knut Borchard, "The Industrial Revolution in Germany 1700-1914," in Carlo M. Caipolla, *The Fontana Economic History of Europe, Vol. 4: The Emergence of Industrial Societies* (London, 1972), 51.

The NDL was the largest Bremen-based shipping company, operating forty lines in 1914. The fleet consisted of 135 steamers of 907,996 gross register tons, a total surpassed only by the Hamburg-America Line. Bremen's fleet had quintupled since 1871, and one-third of the German merchant marine flew Bremen's flag in 1914. Bremerhaven's share of this traffic rose to over seventy-five percent from the 1870s. In 1875, for example, 2809 ships of 755,188 net register tons left Bremerhaven, while in 1913 almost 6400 ships of 5.2 million register tons departed. Expanding maritime traffic attracted more shipyards to Bremerhaven and Geestemünde. Some yards, like Rickmers and Tecklenborg, had to move from Bremerhaven to south of the Geeste because of lack of space. The number of shipyard workers also grew dramatically, and in 1864 they felt strong enough to stage their first strike

---

[49]Kellner-Stoll, *Bremerhaven*, 200-206.

[50]Entholt, "Bremens Handel," 217-225.

for higher wages. The next strike in 1867 involved 500-700 workers on both sides of the Geeste.[51] The dispute ended after four months in total defeat for the workers, but in the following years the labour movement was strengthened by a huge influx of labourers from Mecklenburg and Silesia. The population of Bremerhaven was almost 14,000 in 1880, while 22,000 more lived in nearby Lehe and Geestemünde/Geestendorf. At the outbreak of the First World War, the population of Bremerhaven and the Lower Weser region was just below 100,000.

Bremerhaven was well on its way to achieving unparalleled success when World War I erupted in 1914. Four years later the town was hard hit by the defeat of Germany and the resulting Treaty of Versailles, which forced the country to hand over its merchant and naval fleets to the Allies. Apart from being stripped of the tools for military aggression, the motivation was also economic. But as harsh as this was for Bremerhaven, at least the town was spared the fate of Wilhelmshaven, where all naval institutions and facilities had to be dismantled. For the most part, Bremerhaven was left with the infrastructure that was to be crucial to its economic re-birth in the interwar years.

Conclusion

Bremerhaven owed its existence to a specific commercial concern. The intention was for the town to serve as an outport for Bremen and attempts were made to limit it to this function. That it became more than this was largely the result of circumstance. There is no doubt that Mayor Smidt had more complex intentions when he purchased a strip of land north of the Geeste than just having a dock built, but the area acquired was not big enough for both dock and harbour space, on the one hand, and major town development on the other. One factor that crippled Bremerhaven in the early years was the lack of a broad political and economic vision for the whole region on both sides of the Geeste. Limitations imposed by geography and politics were never seriously questioned, which meant that only uninhabited land to the north was available for future expansion. During the nineteenth and early twentieth centuries the urban agglomeration of Bremerhaven, Geestemünde and Lehe continued to flourish without

---

[51]Rudolf Herbig, *Wirtschaft, Arbeit, Streik, Aussperrung an der Unterweser* (Wolframs-Eschenbach, 1979), 50-87.

any master plan. Even when a dictatorial state decided to merge all three towns into the Prussian city of Wesermünde in November 1939, the National Socialists did not alter the status of the docks in Bremerhaven, which continued to be administered by the city of Bremen.

The entire economy of the Lower Weser region depended on the sea and most of the population earned their living from maritime industries. Indeed, the general prosperity was directly related to activities in the port. Shipping and trade, fishing and shipbuilding, and a wide variety of service industries dominated life in Bremerhaven and its sister towns. Deficiencies, such as the fact that so many major mercantile firms never contemplated moving from Bremen, could be ignored as long as Germany's economic expansion seemed like it would never end. The narrow economic base and the absence of a strong merchant elite caused few problems when times were good. But in 1918, when the NDL fleet no longer existed; when the fishing fleet had been decimated by the war; and when money to invest in shipping and shipbuilding was scarce, the negative side of the economic structure became painfully apparent.

In this century Bremerhaven has been unable to shed its economic dependence on maritime industries. A short boom in the 1930s collapsed after 1945. After the war, shipbuilding was forbidden, but from the mid-1950s a new, if smaller, fleet came into being. Nonetheless shipbuilding, along with fishing, continued to decline and are almost non-existent today, so the city is left with an unemployment rate of twenty percent and more, well above the national average. Maritime industries cannot provide enough employment and there are few alternatives. Even the booming container terminal, where the turnover of 1.8 million TEUs in 1998 placed Bremerhaven for the first time among the world's top twenty container ports, never created the number of jobs that politicians had envisaged.[52] With an annual increase in traffic of seven percent, growth in the port fails to match the growth rates of competitors like Antwerp (10.1%), Rotterdam (10.8%) or Hamburg (7.8%). From this perspective, there seem few easy solutions for hard-hit port cities like Bremerhaven.[53]

---

[52]Lars U. Scholl, "The Container Terminals in Bremerhaven and Bremen," in Poul Holm and John Edwards (eds.), *North Sea Ports and Harbours. Adaptions to Change* (Esbjerg, 1992), 159-183.

[53]A so-called "Ocean Park" project around the defunct Alter and Neuer Hafen is the topic of a highly controversial discussion in Bremerhaven at this time.

Capital and Labour in the Port Town of Esbjerg, 1945-1999

Poul Holm

Throughout the twentieth century employment has contracted in most port towns in Western Europe and inhabitants accordingly have lost much of their dependence on maritime businesses. Key technological factors underlying this process have been mechanisation and containerisation, which together have enabled a shrinking work force to shift more cargo with increasing speed. The consequence of the development of liner shipping and containerisation has been to concentrate half the world's container handling in no more than twenty ports world-wide, leaving the remainder to survive as feeder terminals or to transform their infrastructure into marinas and business parks.[1] Likewise, resource depletion and concentration have caused many fishing ports to surrender their traditional ways and seek new leases of life as tourist destinations or residential areas. Needless to say, the ports that did not make the transformation, or which lacked the natural beauty, have often been left as desolate industrial sites.[2]

At a conference on port history held in Esbjerg in 1991, Gordon Jackson remarked that "ports are living organisms" that have to adapt to changing demands and an often shifting commercial environment.[3] Adaptation may take various forms, from hostility to eager acceptance. While any decision on the allocation of capital plays a decisive role in the fate of a port town, the flexibility of the local labour market, or the willingness of individuals to adapt to change, should not be overlooked.

[1]F. Broeze, "Containerization and the Globalization of Liner Shipping," in D.J. Starkey and G. Harlaftis (eds.), *Global Markets: The Internationalization of of the Sea Transport Industries since 1850* (St. John's, 1998), 413.

[2]G. Jackson, *The History and Archaeology of Ports* (Tadworth, 1983).

[3]Quoted by D.M. Williams, "Conference Summary," in P. Holm and J. Edwards (eds.), *North Sea Ports and Harbours - Adaptations to Change* (Esbjerg, 1992), 226.

Especially after 1965, rationalisation and automation caused the demand for manual labour to decrease steadily, and in many ports this process was accompanied by wildcat strikes and public outcry over empty quays. The effects of this change led in many port towns to a social trauma which will likely always remain with the generation that lived through them.

The problem for many ports in coping with change was the scarcity of capital. Investments came mainly from outside the port city, and when its competitive advantage vanished there was little incentive for outside investors to risk their capital. Old maritime centres in north-western Europe, such as Bremerhaven and Liverpool, were scarred by the loss of capital and jobs from the 1970s.[4] In other ports, however, labour was shifted relatively easily into other industrial sectors. Gothenburg offers one example where capital from outside the maritime sector (automobile manufacturing) was able to profit from the availability of skilled metal workers from the collapsed shipyard industry.

In this paper I shall investigate the experience of a port which managed to adapt by harnessing both its own and outside maritime capital. The medium-size port of Esbjerg on the Danish North Sea coast has survived dramatic changes over the past two generations as the importance of primary maritime activities has diminished. Key to this transition was the fact that a generation of highly successful fishermen, who had acquired considerable amounts of capital, decided to invest in their home town. While in recent years the town also benefited from outside investments in oil extraction, the analysis will show that the labour market was highly dependent on local capital. Investment decisions originally were focussed on developing the port's primary and secondary maritime industries, but in later years they have shifted to non-maritime activities situated to the east of the town, away from the port. Recently, however, politicians and businessmen have begun to reemphasize the town's origins and to focus on revitalising the port.

Demography and Port Activity

In the twentieth century Esbjerg's population has grown at a rate consistently above the Danish average. Indeed, between 1900 and 1940 Esbjerg

---

[4]Tony Lane, *Liverpool. City of the Sea* (Liverpool, 1995); and Lars U. Scholl, "The Container Terminals in Bremerhaven and Bremen," in Holm and Edwards (eds.), *North Sea Ports and Harbours*, 159-184.

was the fastest growing urban place in Denmark and was the fifth largest city by 1932.[5] From 1911 to 1997 Esbjerg's numbers swelled four- fold while the Danish population as a whole barely doubled. Difficult spells of relatively short duration were experienced during the First World War; the depression of the 1930s; and the early 1960s. After 1975 population growth slowed to close to the national average (see table 1).

Table 1
Average Annual Growth of Population per Decade, Esbjerg, 1901-1997

	Esbjerg	Annual Growth %	Denmark, Annual Growth %
1901	14800		
1906	17625	3.82	1.14
1911	20860	3.67	1.3
1916	22100	1.19	1.19
1921	24961	2.59	2.38
1926	28941	3.19	1.02
1930	33350	3.81	0.67
1935	36505	1.89	0.88
1940	38930	1.33	0.75
1945	43241	2.21	1.04
1950	N/A	-	1.17
1955	50921	1.78	0.78
1960	54989	1.6	0.62
1965	55882	0.32	0.8
1970	62568	2.39	0.71
1976	69688	2.28	
1980	N/A	-	0.37
1990	71962	0.23	
1997	73149	0.24	0.15

Note: Esbjerg includes the municipalities of Esbjerg and Jerne, which were joined in 1944.

Source: *Danmarks statistik*, relevant years.

Demographic growth was clearly related to economic prosperity, which in Esbjerg was primarily in harbour-related businesses. Figure 1 shows the population trend and two main indicators for port activity:

---

[5]A full treatment of the population statistics may be found in V. Bruhn and P. Holm, *Esbjergs historie. Vol. III: 1910-1998. Havneby og storkommune* (Esbjerg, 1998), 8-14.

incoming and outgoing cargoes and landings of fish. The figure highlights that fishing and shipping alternated in underpinning Esbjerg's economy. For employment in a port town the value of traded goods is not the primary factor: no matter its value, to shift a sack of potatoes still requires a certain amount of labour. Or rather this was the relationship until the 1950s, when pallets and cranes were introduced, and the 1960s, when containers revolutionised the work process and displaced a good deal of labour. Similarly, a tonne of fish required a certain amount of labour on board the ships, on the quays and in the fish merchants' shops, until the mid-1960s when the fisheries were thoroughly rationalised by the introduction of larger ships, freezers and automated fileting. In short, in the last thirty years direct maritime employment has declined despite a stable turnover of goods and fish. Yet even as figure 1 shows the relationship between a healthy port and population growth, it does not give a full explanation behind the demographic trends. And at any rate, after 1970 the connection between tonnage and population was broken. Stagnation in the port masked a dramatic decline in actual employment as a consequence of technological change.

Figure 1

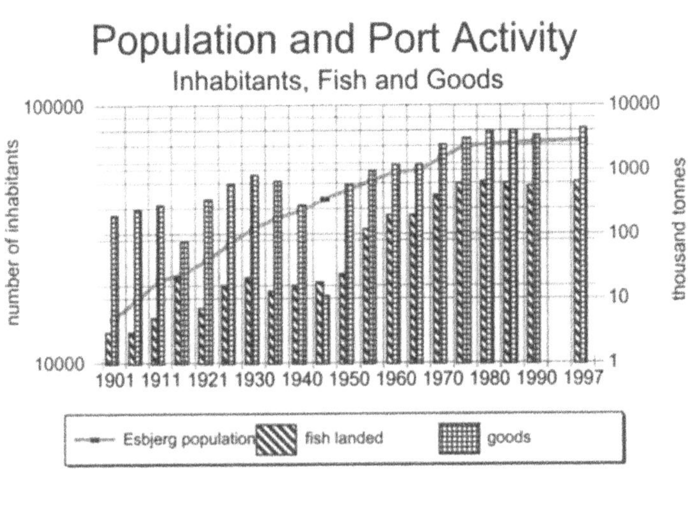

Source: See text.

Capital and Labour Markets in the "Agricultural Port Town" of the 1930s

Figure 1 shows the marked growth in the fisheries between 1905 and 1919. When the German market collapsed in the early 1920s, general cargoes enjoyed a strong recovery. The economic depression of the 1930s and the Second World War hit shipping hard, while the fisheries were able to stave off the effects of low prices by increasing landings. During World War II landings fell again but high prices brought unprecedented prosperity to the fishing community. The population statistics followed these trends closely, with, for example, slow growth in the 1930s and a remarkable wartime increase unparalleled in the rest of the country.[6]

In 1939 the total number employed in Esbjerg stood at around 17,000. Roughly one-third, or 4800-5300 of the jobs, were directly related to the port: 1500-2000 in shipbuilding, port services and port-related trades; 1500 in slaughterhouses, cargo-handling and shipping; 1300 in fishing; and 500 in fish merchanting and processing. The main portion of the jobs, some 6600-7100, was outside the port on the railways; in tobacco sheds and textile factories; and in many small companies. The remainder were at the town council as clerks and teachers or in private households as housemaids.

Esbjerg was focussed on the port. The economic cycles of the slaughterhouses and most machine industries were correlated with the health of the town's shipping industry, which in turn reflected the state of its premier market, the United Kingdom. Esbjerg existed mainly to serve the export needs of the Danish agricultural sector and may fairly be described as an "agricultural port town." Moreover, most of the businesses were owned by companies based in Copenhagen. Shipping, for example, was dominated by DFDS, which had a *de facto* monopoly on the vital liner operations to Britain, while the slaughterhouses and the single large non-port-oriented business, the tobacco company, were also owned by outside interests. In the case of the tobacco company, the town council only countered a threat to close the facilities by giving the company a free lease for a new factory building. The lack of local capital was a very real problem for a town which rightly perceived itself as a "branch economy."

---

[6]This section is based on Bruhn and Holm, *Esbjergs historie*, III, 55-102.

Most people who thought about the problem realised that the town needed new non-port related industries. Indeed, this was the prime rationale for the Esbjerg Business Centre, which was established by the town and the local business association in 1937. The Second World War, however, soon brought an end to this strategy; if anything, the war strengthened the dependence of the town on the port.

The Capital and Labour Market of the Fishing Port Town, 1940-1975

Growth in the three and one-half decades after 1940 was mostly related to the port, and especially to the fish processing industries which benefited from a large pool of female labour. Although access to the major fishing grounds was restricted because of offshore activities, high prices and an insatiable demand in Germany ensured that Esbjerg's fish merchants and skippers were extremely prosperous by the end of the Second World War. The exceptional boom in the fisheries during the war years attracted many people who wanted to share in the prosperity. By 1946 the town had 2147 fishermen and a local fleet which had grown from 347 vessels in 1939 to 488 in 1945 (the new vessels were also much larger than the old). A town report in the autumn of 1945 stated that the fishermen "undoubtedly have made considerable savings from their big wartime incomes." This capital would determine the direction of development in the next few decades.[7]

World War II was a watershed: where previously agricultural exports had been the leading sector, now it was the fisheries which occupied this role. Fishing and shipping, however, stagnated due to weaknesses in the traditional markets in Germany and Britain and the main sea lanes off Esbjerg were mined and fully cleared only in 1950. When the liner service to Britain returned from their temporary centre in Århus, rationalisation of cargo-handling and meat-packing technology precluded Esbjerg from again becoming an agricultural port. In the interim, capital accumulated by the fishermen was invested in a number of "experimental" fisheries, especially for North Sea herring. This fishery became extremely successful once it was discovered that the fish could be used for fish meal and oil rather than merely for human consumption. Indeed, this industry was one of the fastest growing in the 1950s, achieving consistent growth rates of twenty percent of net sales and attracting new migrants to the

[7] *Ibid.*, III, 171-195.

town. As a result, Esbjerg became even more dependent on port-related activities between 1945 and 1975. Landings continued to increase until 1968, when over one-half million tonnes were landed for industrial uses. Despite some intermittent price weaknesses, income tended to rise.

In these years Esbjerg was one of the largest fishing ports in Europe. By 1970, 3800 people were directly employed in the industry, half in fish processing and trading. Esbjerg's population had grown to 63,000, of whom 27,000 were employed. While ten percent of all jobs had been in the fisheries in 1940, thirty years later the proportion had risen by fifty percent. More than one person in seven was directly employed in the fishing industry.

At the same time, the provision of services to the industry and its workers became increasingly important. It is difficult to assess the spin-offs accurately; contemporaries often guessed at a ratio of three to five jobs for every fisherman, but these were probably exaggerated. A 1994 report, for example, calculated the multiplier effect of the fish meal industry at 2.32 jobs per employee, compared with 0.5 per employee in the fisheries for human consumption. Although the ratios may have been higher in 1970 when there was less automation, if we accept these later assessments the fishery created at least 5150 ancillary jobs, meaning that total direct and indirect employment from the fisheries was in the range of 8900. In short, at least one-third of all jobs in Esbjerg depended on activities related to the fishing harbour.

Income from the port accounted for half of all private-sector wages in the late 1950s. In fact, the figure may have been higher, because not all landings or income were reported. Of 217 million kroner in wages in Esbjerg in 1958, 166 million came from private employers. Fifty-four million kroner were derived directly from the fishery, twenty-five million from the port's "agricultural sector" (slaughterhouses, food companies, stevedoring firms, etc.), and eighteen million from building companies. If not a pure fishing town, Esbjerg certainly was increasingly dependent on its fishery between 1950 and 1970.

At its centenary in 1968 the port faced radically new challenges. Over the next few years the fisheries would encounter severe difficulties, while containerisation would begin to cause redundancies in cargo-handling operations.

Structural Changes in Port Labour

In the 1970s shipping and fishing lost their dominant positions. Rationalisation of work processes hit general cargo handling first. Containers for butter and bacon exports to the UK market were introduced as early as 1967, and large parts of the older docks were soon converted into a container terminal. The number of dockers declined, and by the 1990s was only one-fifth as high as forty years earlier.

Table 2
Number of Fishing Vessels and GRT, Fishing Port of Esbjerg, 1910-1997

Year	Number	GRT	Average Size GRT
1910	125	4183	33
1930	324	8359	26
1950	462	16095	35
1969	601	27684	46
1990	198	28324	143
1997	94	19500	207

Source: V. Bruhn and P. Holm, *Esbjergs historie. Vol. III: 1910-1998. Havneby og storkommune* (Esbjerg, 1998), 189.

Throughout most of the twentieth century, growth in the fishing sector came from adding more units to the fleet. The typical fishing boat of the 1950s and 1960s was a wooden vessel of thirty to fifty gross registered tons (grt), with a few as large as 100 grt. The fleet peaked in numbers in 1969 with 601 units. The early 1970s were highly profitable, and large steel vessels replaced many of the old boats, bringing fleet tonnage to a peak at 38,000 grt in 1976. The years after 1976 were very difficult as overfishing, the imposition of EEC quotas, and a moratorium on herring led to a sharp rise in bankruptcies. The decline was almost continuous until the mid-1990s, when the fleet stabilised at ninety-four vessels of 19,500 grt (see table 2). Despite reductions in vessels and crew, the catch levels of the late 1960s were maintained and at times surpassed. The industrial fishery survived and even increased its relative share by specialising in sand eels and Norwegian pout.

Table 3
Employment in Esbjerg, 1970-1997

	Direct Employment	Derived Employment	Total Fishing-related Employment	Total Employment Esbjerg	Percentage of Fishing-related Employment of Total
1970	3800	5150	8900	27000	33
1997	1200	930	2130	46000	5

Source: Bruhn and Holm, *Esbjergs historie*, III, 194.

Formerly, most work at the fishing harbour took place in the open and was visible to passers-by. Today, however, maintenance is taken care of by special companies and the fishermen have time for themselves when in port. The fish processing and service companies also keep their businesses out of the sight of casual observers. This development is often misconstrued as indicating that the harbour is declining. The activities are still occurring, although the number of workers has been drastically reduced. By the end of 1997 there were about 425 fishermen, or one-fifth the number in 1970 (see table 3). While every seventh Esbjerg citizen was employed in the fishery in 1970, only 2.6% were in 1997. The multiplier effect increased the number dependent on the fishery to five percent, but this too represented a dramatic decrease. Fish processing only employed one-third the number of thirty years before. The total number of jobs directly or indirectly connected to the fisheries was down to about 2130. Since the number of employed people had over the same period risen from 27,000 to 46,000, growth obviously had occurred in other sectors.

Strikers' Town

In the 1970s and 1980s the port of Esbjerg was known for its many labour disputes. In this respect it resembled many other harbours around the world that were undergoing rationalisation and modernisation.[8] The system of casual labour meant that conflict flared up easily at times of peak demand, such as when the suction equipment malfunctioned while unloading a cargo of grain. The dockers would typically call their foreman

[8] *Ibid.*, III, 228-230.

to report that they could not stick to the agreed contract. Until a negotiated settlement was reached, work would come to a halt. After a bitter strike in 1972, related to the introduction of container and ro/ro handling, DFDS avoided future problems by hiring its own permanent staff to handle agricultural exports. But the problems continued in the general cargo sector. Many conflicts had political overtones, although they usually were caused by economic disputes. The recurrent theme for almost ten years was the right of dockers to claim supplementary unemployment benefits for hours when they were not contracted. When both social democratic and centre-right governments cut benefits, the effects were felt throughout the general labour market, but the Esbjerg dockers were the first and most important opponents of these reforms. As the dispute continued, the dockers became more isolated, and in February 1983 a series of arson attacks at the ports of Horsens, Aabenraa and Esbjerg led to public revulsion that finally broke the power of the dockers. In the offshore sector, the operating company Danbor threatened in 1983 to move the base for Danish North Sea operations to Holland or Scotland. In the end, the solution was to adopt the DFDS model.

Troubles in the docks spilled over to many of Esbjerg's larger workplaces. There were constant threats to divert traffic from the port because of strikes and inflexible labour agreements. Some contracts with Esbjerg companies were made conditional on goods being delivered by lorry to Hamburg for shipment by sea. At the fishing port, under-reporting of catches and physical confrontations with fishery inspectors were common. Esbjerg became known as a "red" town where ordinary work-related disputes exceeded normal bounds. Many confrontations were led by Communists, and an informal ring of trade unionists coordinated strikes against major employers like the Vestfrost Company and even the town council. But rising unemployment from 1987 lessened the power of wildcat strikes, and in the 1990s a more individualistic generation was less willing to embrace collective action. Nonetheless, as late as 1995 a nine-month strike by bus drivers spawned sympathy strikes, which were brought to a halt only when Danbor again threatened to move its operations to Den Helder. Significantly, dockers no longer had the power to bring the port to a standstill.

There can be no doubt that labour relations were fundamentally strained during the 1970s and 1980s because of the seemingly endless shedding of labour in all the manual trades. Powerless to respond to the real cause of the problem – technological change – labourers struck to retain old manning agreements and piecework contracts. The strikes were often directed against both employers and government. While many were successful in raising wages, in the long run the workers still lost, as technology rendered their labour unnecessary.

The Labour Market of the Industrial Port Town

There is little in this portrait of Esbjerg which will be unfamiliar to those familiar with other port towns in the modern world.[9] During the same years, however, significant changes also occurred in trades which were less dependent on the docks, yet which derived both capital and labour from the same pools. Decisive changes in the townscape were occurring to the northeast, a good distance from the port. Esbjerg was changing from a national port town to a regional trades and service centre.[10]

Internationalisation of trade and especially the Danish decision in 1972 to join the Common Market gave Esbjerg new access to European markets. What limited industry the town had before, apart from the slaughterhouses, was almost entirely based on the domestic market, and much of it disappeared with increased competition. The expansion of Esbjerg's employment was thus left almost entirely to new companies.

In the 1950s the town had little success in attracting new businesses. One of the few that came, the "Dan" motor company, moved from Copenhagen to be closer to its main customers in the fishing fleet. But the town also needed companies that were not so reliant on a single sector. When the fish meal industry suffered a temporary downturn in 1960, for example, the repercussions for the town were very severe. When attempts to attract outside capital proved disappointing, a few hardy souls began to look to local capital. Over time, in fact, the largest companies were created by local people using capital predominantly derived from port businesses. Although some of the new companies were not port-related, their owners proved very conscious of their origins.

One notable industry resulted from experiments in the mid-1950s by an owner of several fishing vessels. Claus Sørensen founded a firm that developed a revolutionary inflatable rubber boat which proved to have a

---

[9]See, for example, M. Tull, *A Community Enterprise: The History of the Port of Fremantle, 1897 to 1997* (St. John's, 1997).

[10]Bruhn and Holm, *Esbjergs historie*, III, 213-223.

huge market for a variety of maritime purposes. The company became known as Viking Life-Saving Equipment, and eventually had a presence in 300 ports around the globe. By 1998 the company employed 625 people and was the third largest employer in the town. The largest employer, a producer of refrigerators and freezers called Vestfrost, is another example of how industries grew from the expertise and capital generated in the fisheries. The company, started in 1960, grew under the leadership of Arne Højvig, a former fisherman, who obtained financial support from a former colleague, skipper Chr. Muff Iversen, and Tage Sørensen, general manager of a fish meal company and a son of Claus Sørensen. Tage Sørenson was also a director of several ice companies for the fish trade and thus brought not only capital but also knowledge in freezing technology. The fishing connection was underlined again when in 1975 Erling Damkjær became managing director. He was a fisherman's son who had worked in the fish trade, including some years in Grimsby. The products were originally intended for the home market but were soon also directed to Britain, Sweden and Norway; when customs barriers to the Common Market were lifted, sales began an almost continuous upward trend. By 1986 the company had more than 1000 employees, and when Eastern European markets opened after 1989, Vestfrost was able to expand its staff to 1700 by 1998. The third large company is Arovit Pet Food, incorporated in 1957 by Johan P. Hoffmann, a descendant of the founder of a construction company which earned its first money in the extension of Esbjerg's quays. Hoffman was also a nephew of a producer of motors for fishing vessels. By 1998 the company had 600 employees. The two common denominators for these and the many other small- and medium-sized companies are their origins in the fishing port of the 1950s and 1960s and the fact that they were able to grow on the large unskilled, but hard-working, labour force made redundant in the early 1970s on the docks and the fishing industry.

A number of smaller companies had the same origins. Grumsens Maskinfabrik, which produced hydraulic tools with some seventy-five employees, was started with money borrowed from two skippers in 1946, while IRAS was started by a fisherman and a smith who developed a crane to unload fish holds. Others, like KJ Maskinfabrikken and Granly, are also linear descendants of the port, although both to varying degrees have developed other markets. Many of these businesses are still located in the fishing port although only a small part of their business is derived from fishing. A report into the "dead docks of the fishing harbour" in 1998 revealed as many as 1500 jobs in companies unrelated to fishing.[11]

It is a testimony of the success of this industrial transition that when a fish processing company opened a new production line in 1997 it was unable to recruit any of the hundreds of experienced fish gutters who had been made redundant in the early 1990s, when in one year three major plants closed. The town job centre confirmed that workers in the fish industry had either taken early retirement or obtained new employment outside fishing. The fish gutters had reputations for efficiency and stamina, traits that were much desired by other industries. Unemployment, which had been around twelve percent in the worst years of the late 1980s, was by 1999 down to 4.6%. It may not be surprising that Danish producers find it hard to make fish processing profitable at minimum wages of £8 per hour compared to British competitors who pay half this rate.[12] The remarkable thing, however, is that this wage differential has not caused a downward spiral of wages but has rather shifted labour into more promising secondary industries.

Offshore Town

Despite the emergence of a host of new companies, Esbjerg would have faced a recession by the early 1980s like so many other Western European fishing ports if North Sea oil and gas had not come to the rescue. Work on the Gorm field in 1980-1983 led to a deluge of investments and subsequently to a wide array of job opportunities, not only for geologists, engineers and helicopter pilots but also for thousands of sailors, fishermen, blacksmiths, caterers, cleaners and secretaries. By 1983, 800-900 people were employed in offshore work, and when Danbor moved its onshore operations to Esbjerg in 1991 it brought a host of highly-trained people. By 1992 the oil business provided about 2500 jobs in the Esbjerg

---

[11]Center for Maritim og Regional Historie, *Nyt Liv på Esbjerg Fiskerihavn* (Esbjerg, 1998).

[12]Craig Lazenby, "Change and Adaptation in European Fishing Communities 1970-1997," in P. Holm and D.J. Starkey (eds.), *Studia Atlantica 3* (Esbjerg, 1999), forthcoming.

region and an estimated eight percent of tax revenues.[13] About 500 direct and indirect jobs came from the oil sector.[14] The offshore thus provided an important boost to the town's economy at a time when the fishing industry was in trouble.

As important as oil is, it will probably run out around 2020, while gas may continue to flow until about 2040. It is therefore vital that the town and port generate some lasting benefit from it. Thus far, there has been only one large local company created to serve the offshore, Esbjerg Oilfield Services A/S, founded by Henning Kruse in 1979. It has become one of the town's largest companies, with several hundred people working both offshore and in the yard, which builds mainly oil-related structures.

Local Versus Branch Economy

This essay has stressed the importance of local capital. Unfortunately, almost nothing is known about local financial institutions. The town's own bank, Varde Bank, was publicly regarded as one the most solid financial institutions in Denmark until it collapsed spectacularly in 1991-1992. Shortly before this, Varde Bank had taken over the other local bank, Esbjerg Bank. Varde had speculated in a hazardous Spanish building venture and large sums had been lost. Spurred on by local sentiments a group of local entrepreneurs, many of who were owners of the companies mentioned above, rallied to rescue the regional bank and made a sizable investment. In a few months the new money was also lost, and Esbjerg lost its main financial institution. Still, the closure caused no noticeable losses to the community, and while fears were high that outside banks would be less understanding of the needs of the community, there seems to be no evidence of this happening.[15]

If Esbjerg used to be considered a "branch economy" because of the few businesses owned locally, the reality has changed. Table 4 lists larger companies located in major Danish provincial towns. The number is compared to population to establish an index. While Esbjerg clearly lags

---

[13]Bruhn and Holm, *Esbjergs historie*, III, 224-227.

[14]Villy Søgaard and Inge Sofie Sørensen, *Offshoreaktiviteter i Nordsøen og basebyen Esbjerg* (Århus, 1983).

[15]Bruhn and Holm, *Esbjergs historie*, III, 230-232.

behind Randers and Odense, it has done better than either Aalborg or Århus. Although the index is flawed somewhat because domicile need not be synonymous with either origin or ownership, it is at least an indication that Esbjerg has become "normalised" and has the share of companies to be expected in a large Danish provincial town.

Table 4
Larger Companies Based in Danish Provincial Towns

Home Town	More than 200 Employees	50-199 Employees	Total	Per 1,000 Inhabitants
Århus	29	110	139	0.5
Odense	44	154	198	1.1
Aalborg	29	90	119	0.8
Esbjerg	17	61	76	0.9
Randers	19	52	71	1.2

Source: Krak online database of Danish coporate industries: http://www.krak.dk.

While in the 1990s Esbjerg had a far broader business foundation than ever before, the port continued to play a dominant role. Five thousand jobs were directly or indirectly the effect of offshore developmen; 2200 were related to the fisheries; while 1200 sailors and a more uncertain figure of another 1000-2000 were related to the shipping harbour. All in all, the port provided one in five of the town's 46,000 employees. The port had lost some grip relative to earlier times but Esbjerg could still not afford to ignore it. As a new act of parliament is expected by the end of 1999 to devolve ownership of the port to the municipality, there is every reason to believe that town and port will continue the historical pattern of shared destinies.

Conclusion

Esbjerg's experience over the past few decades resembled many other ports. Rationalisation in cargo handling and fish processing cost thousands of jobs. Structural changes in the labour market caused severe industrial unrest through the 1970s and 1980s, and in some ways the town lost its traditional bustling quayside life. Yet the port town survived mainly due to two factors: the windfall discovery of oil in the North Sea and the fact that fishing profits were plowed back into the town's industrial base. The majority of these new businesses thrived on the town's maritime past and developed an expertise in secondary maritime industries.

The importance of local sentiments for the development of a port town's industrial base may be doubted. Yet there is little doubt that Esbjerg would have ended up as an unemployment trap in the 1980s if the profits accrued during the heyday of fishing had not been reinvested locally. Almost no outside investment was attracted in that decade, apart from offshore positions which were geared mainly towards specialists with higher degrees. Esbjerg was characterised by a high proportion of manual labour which had always found jobs on the docks. One conclusion is that local industries were able to expand due to the availability of this labour. The other is that had local capital not been available, there would have been little choice for most workers but to leave or go on the dole. One telling example of the importance of local capital was a call in the spring of 1999 for the creation of an investment company to assist prospective skippers faced with impossible capital demands if they want to take over or build a modern trawler. In a couple of weeks, the company raised fifty million kroner from local investors, who may have seen some business possibilities in the scheme but clearly were rallied to the venture by sentiment for the old port.

The main purpose of this essay was to highlight a phase of structural change which touched port towns all over the world. The paper will have served a purpose if it can contribute to a comparative study of this process.

Port Policies: Seaport Planning around the North Atlantic, 1850-1939

Lewis R. Fischer

In most nations around the North Atlantic littoral, the suggestion that it would be advisable to engage in long-term economic planning has generally met an icy reception. Indeed, despite a good deal of self-serving rhetoric, few countries have ever engaged in this exercise even in the short term, and most of those that have are located in Scandinavia.[1] The generalization that planning has been ignored also applies to Canada where, notwithstanding the advocacy of this idea on the right by bodies such as the Science Council and on the left by the New Democratic Party, more centrist (and, dare I say it, more "central") groups have consistently argued successfully against such a "heresy."[2]

There is a maritime equivalent to the idea of opposing economic planning: the argument that it is a bad idea to have any kind of national ports policy. In the seminal *History and Archaeology of Ports*, Gordon Jackson noted that there has never been a ports policy in Britain - and he could have added that this was also the case virtually everywhere else.[3] But what is significant is that Canada, which has never been an apostle of

---

[1]See, for example, the discussions in Fritz Hodne, *The Norwegian Economy, 1920-1980* (London, 1983); Gregg M. Olsen, *The Struggle for Economic Democracy in Sweden* (Aldershot, 1992); Hans-Chr. Johansen, *The Danish Economy in the Twentieth Century* (London, 1987); and *Growth Policies in a Nordic Perspective* (Helsinki, 1987). For an interesting perspective on the slightly different Finnish case, see Christian Bordes, *et al.*, *Three Assessments of Finland's Economic Crisis and Economic Policy* (Helsinki, 1993).

[2]The classic Science Council of Canada call for a national industrial policy is *The Politics of an Industrial Policy* (Ottawa, 1979). But see also *Forging the Links: A Technology Policy for Canada* (Ottawa, 1979); and *Enabling Technologies: Springboard for a Competitive Future* (Ottawa, 1989).

[3]Gordon Jackson, *The History and Archaeology of Ports* (Tadworth, 1983).

planning of any sort, actually came close in the interwar period to being the exception that proved the rule.

This brief essay describes the abortive proposals for a national ports policy in Canada and offers an explanation for why in the end it was never enacted. In order to place the Canadian experience in some kind of context, it also offers a very broad overview of developments elsewhere around the North Atlantic, concentrating mainly on the period from 1850 to the outbreak of the Second World War. Taken as a whole, the experiences of North Atlantic nations suggest strongly that Gordon Jackson's generalization can profitably be extended beyond the British Isles, albeit with some caution.

The second half of the nineteenth century was in maritime terms really quite a remarkable era. When it began, the economic doctrine of mercantilism was just beginning to be superseded around the North Atlantic by the new dogma of free trade. The former, of course, held that the best way for a nation to achieve wealth was to plant colonies. The argument came to be understood to mean that colonies would provide raw materials and markets, while the mother country would produce manufactured goods. The magic of value-added being what it is, the relationship was in some ways rather one-sided. But in other ways it was symbiotic, a fact demonstrated, at least in part, by the existence of a prosperous country like Canada, which spent its adolescence in the protective bosom of the British Empire.[4]

One of the advantages of mercantilism was that it provided an impetus to maritime investment, if only because most of the more interesting - not to mention available - places to colonize were inconveniently separated from the metropolitan lands by broad stretches of ocean. Indeed, what Walt Rostow called "the take-off stage" for the the Canadian Maritime provinces (although not in the same way for Newfoundland) makes the point explicitly. The Maritimes were fairly stagnant in both population and output until Napoleon decided to introduce his "Continental Policy," which was designed to isolate Britain by placing an embargo on its trade with Europe. Since timber for both the Royal Navy and the British merchant marine by the first decade of the nineteenth century came largely from nations located around the shores of the Baltic, this occa-

---

[4]The most accessible discussion of this background is A.G. Kenwood and A.L. Lougheed, *The Growth of the International Economy, 1820-1990* (3rd ed., New York, 1992).

sioned a fair amount of panic at Westminster – until it was remembered that travellers to British North America had reported the existence of large stands of suitable timber in Nova Scotia, New Brunswick and Lower Canada. Using prosaic tools like tariffs, Parliament literally called forth a timber industry from the eastern Canadian wilderness. But all this lovely timber was useless unless it could be transported across the Atlantic. If you realize that this meant that there was money to be made in building ships, you would have done well as an entrepreneur in, say, Saint John, New Brunswick or Pictou, Nova Scotia, at the time, for that is precisely what many of the more thoughtful inhabitants concluded. The result was a world-class shipbuilding industry, and eventually a shipping industry that at its peak in the early 1870s made Atlantic Canadians the proud owners of the third largest fleet of sailing vessels in the entire world.[5]

While this brief tale might make it seem as though mercantilism was, in maritime terms, a totally positive doctrine, the reality was a bit more complex. Although mercantilism's emphasis on empire made nations like the Netherlands, Spain, Portugal and France, along with Britain, major maritime powers, its incentives for maritime investment were really fairly small compared to what was to come after Britain led the rest of Europe into the verdant sunlight of free trade. This is because, by creating a system based upon the notion of comparative advantage, free trade led to increasing interdependency and, eventually, to the creation of what some historians like to refer to grandly as the "international economy." Ushered in by the repeal of various protective duties and the proscriptive Navigation Acts, the hallmark of free trade became rapidly increasing commerce, especially of the intercontinental variety. Indeed, the volume of trade between continents grew by more than fifteen-fold between 1850 and 1914. And all this inter-continental trade – and a good deal of intra-continental commerce, as well – required ships. Not surprisingly, investment in shipping increased by about eleven times over the same period. But if we measure this in terms of value, it grew even faster, which reminds us that at the same time that trade was increasing, the

---

[5]The Rostow model was first articulated in W.W. Rostow, *The Stages of Economic Growth* (Cambridge, 1960); and further elaborated in Rostow, *The World Economy: History and Prospect* (Austin, TX, 1978). The best study of Atlantic Canadian shipping is Eric W. Sager with Gerald E. Panting, *Maritime Capital: The Shipping Industry in Atlantic Canada, 1820-1914* (Montréal, 1990).

shipping industry underwent a breathtaking technological transformation: the transition from sail to steam.[6]

The cliché that the pace of change has become more rapid the closer we get to the present is as true for maritime industries as for any other type of human endeavour. If the six and one-half decades after 1850 were characterized by the transition from sail to steam, the twenty years between the end of the Great War and the outbreak of World War II was marked by two major transitions: the introduction of the diesel-powered motorship and the widespread acceptance of the tanker. Both remade the shipping industry as surely as had the earlier technological transition.[7]

All right then: the period from 1850 to 1939 was marked by a series of technological changes in the maritime sector. But what did this have to do with ports? The answer is at the same time both obvious and slightly less apparent. The obvious answer is that as ships got bigger - and as the amount of capital invested in them grew - new demands were made on ports. The sheer size of some of these vessels often required entirely new facilities. Some older ports, like Liverpool and Antwerp in Europe, or Halifax and New York on the other side of the Atlantic, were relatively successful at adapting. But others, many of which had been vitally important during the "golden age of sail," fell by the wayside. This list of doomed ports included places like Québec, Bremen and Amsterdam. And sometimes the technological revolution led to the creation of new ports. Rotterdam was only a fairly minor port even within the Netherlands in

---

[6]A brief introduction to the North Atlantic maritime context in the second half of the nineteenth century is Lewis R. Fischer and Helge W. Nordvik, "Maritime Transport and the Integration of the North Atlantic Economy, 1850-1914," in Wolfram Fischer, R. Marvin McInnis and Jürgen Schneider (eds.), *The Emergence of a World Economy, 1500-1914* (Weisbaden, 1986), 519-544. For a very different view, however, see Paul Butel, *The Atlantic* (London, 1999).

[7]The best brief introductions to these trends are Ewan Corlett, *The Revolution in Merchant Shipping, 1950-1980* (London, 1981), which also does a reasonable job on the interwar years; and Robert Gardiner (ed.), *The Golden Age of Shipping 1900-1960* (London, 1994). For one still useful context into which to situate this technological change, see S.G. Sturmey, *British Shipping and World Competition* (London, 1962).

1850; by 1900, it was the most important port in the world measured by the volume of cargo handled.[8]

In short, changes in shipping and trade begat a host of challenges for ports. Perhaps predictably, ports in general were singularly unprepared to confront these new conditions. In part, this was because virtually anywhere one looked around the Atlantic rim, ports were treated by key decision-makers almost as afterthoughts. Perhaps nowhere was there such a bewildering variety of port organization as in Britain, where in the late nineteenth century there were at least six different forms of port ownership - private, public dock companies, railway, municipal, canal companies, and trusts. And within each of these types there was an equally confusing set of variations as to how the port was actually operated.[9] But perhaps the greatest vogue in Britain in the late nineteenth century was for the "harbour trust." The most obvious model was the Mersey Docks and Docks and Harbour Board, which operated the docks in Liverpool. In the first decade of this century, when declining revenues coupled with increasing demand brought about the collapse of most of the major dock companies in London, Britain's largest port was also converted to a trust. By World War, it had become accepted wisdom among professional port managers that the harbour trust was almost divinely ordained. Empire being what it was, British expatriates spread the gospel around the globe.[10]

---

[8]On non-Canadian ports see, for example, Robert G. Albion, *The Rise of New York Port, 1815-1860* (Cambridge, MA, 1939); Francis E. Hyde, *Liverpool and the Mersey: An Economic History of a Port, 1700-1970* (Newton Abbot, 1971); F. Suykens, *et al.*, *Antwerp: A Port for All Seasons* (Antwerp, 1986); and L.M. Akveld and J.R. Bruijn (eds.), *Shipping Companies and Authorities in the 19th and 20th Centuries: Their Common Interest in the Development of Port Facilities* (Den Haag, 1989). The only decent modern history of any of the Canadian ports east of Québec is Elizabeth W. McGahan, *The Port of Saint John: From Confederation to Nationalization, 1867-1927* (Saint John, 1982).

[9]On UK "ports policy," see Jackson, *History and Archaeology*, chapter 6. British policy is put into context in Lewis R. Fischer and Helge W. Nordvik, "Subsidy and Protection in National Shipping Industries around the North Sea since World War II," in Randi Skotheim (ed.), *Business and Finance in Maritime Industries around the North Sea* (Stavanger, 1999), forthcoming.

[10]For a fuller discussion, see Adrian Jarvis, "Managing Change: The Organisation of Port Authorities at the Turn of the Twentieth Century," *The Northern Mariner/Le Marin du nord*, VI, No. 2 (April 1996), 31-42.

Yet if there was something approaching a consensus on port policy in Britain, it is important to note that there was still lots of room for debate. Indeed, even at the height of the mania for harbour trusts, municipally-owned ports like Manchester and railway ports like Southampton were constructed. Moreover, only a minority of British ports ever adopted the trust format. But this unfortunate reality did little to cool the ardour of its apostles. It is thus worth asking what these individuals saw as the principal advantages of trust ports.[11]

To its advocates, the most important advantage that trust-owned ports had was that they represented the interests of virtually everyone who might conceivably benefit from their services, including shipowners, merchants, marine artisans, and a whole host of maritime actors of one stripe or another. Members of trusts were frequently lauded as "gentlemen of high character and ability," typically because many accepted no salaries or direct payments for their services. But "indirect payments" were ubiquitous, a fact that certainly did nothing to elevate either the civic culture or ethical standards of the various port towns. And once it became clear after 1919 that many of the trust ports were in serious financial difficulties, the notion that this type of organization was one of the lost Commandments became less prevalent. In short, anyone who looked at the British experience in this period would, after piercing the rhetorical veil, notice quickly that there was nothing remotely resembling a national ports policy between 1850 and 1939.[12]

I think I can anticipate the next question: why would anyone expect that Britain would have had a national ports policy in this period? After all, was this not the golden age of *laissez-faire*, and was Britain not its foremost champion? Both of these shibboleths are pure poppycock: the British government constantly intervened in the economy, and in no sector was *laissez-faire* more honoured in principle but ignored in practice than shipping. Put simply, British policy-makers recognized the importance of maritime industries to the nation and were hardly believers in "leaving

---

[11]See, for example, D.L. Williams, *Southampton* (London, 1984); and D.A. Farnie, *The Manchester Ship Canal and the Rise of the Port of Manchester 1894-1975* (Manchester, 1980).

[12]See the discussion in Adrian Jarvis, "The Members of the Mersey Docks and Harbour Board and Their Way of Doing Business, 1858-1905," *International Journal of Maritime History*, VI, No. 1 (June 1994), 123-139.

things alone." Indeed, there was no set of industries that were as regulated as those related to shipping. It is precisely because government was so interested in overseeing virtually every other aspect of shipping that the absence of a ports policy is so noticeable.[13]

But to argue that it seems strange that Britain lacked a ports policy is not the same thing as contending that the United Kingdom was somehow unique, for it was not. Throughout Western Europe there was nothing approaching a well-articulated policy on ports. Take the case of Spain as an example. While the choice of Spain might seem somewhat strange, it in fact makes a good deal of sense – in the second half of the nineteenth century, Spain was an innovator in various aspects of maritime affairs. Indeed, no nation save Belgium made the transition from sail to steam as rapidly. And in thinking about national ports policies, Spain was also in the vanguard. In the mid-1850s the country even adopted a policy of sorts, with the passage of a law that standardized port administration and provided special levies to pay for port improvements. It all sounded nice and logical, except for the fact that most of the funds available for port improvements either disappeared through fraud; were diverted to other purposes; or were never collected in a misguided attempt at introducing "competition" through reduced port duties. By 1878, the government was forced to repeal the earlier laws and, in effect, to allow ports to adopt any form of organization that they wished. Some ports with close ties to Britain, like the northern harbours of Bilbao and Santander, quickly set up harbour trusts, while a few of the largest ports, most noticeably Barcelona, sunk into chaos. By the outbreak of World War I, the idea of a national ports policy had become shrouded in the fogs of time. And the turmoil that marked Spain in the interwar years ensured that ports would be ignored thereafter.[14]

---

[13]One of the most obvious lacunae in British maritime history is the lack of an adequate modern study of shipping policy. But the general outline can be pieced together by reading A.W. Kirkaldy, *British Shipping: Its History, Organisation and Importance* (London, 1914); Sturmey, *British Shipping*; and Ronald Hope, *A New History of British Shipping* (London, 1990). An especially useful study, although restricted thematically and temporally, is A.N. Porter, *Victorian Shipping, Business, and Imperial Policy: Donald Currie, the Castle Line, and Southern Africa* (London, 1986).

[14]See Natividad de la Puerta Rueda, *El puerto de Bilbao como reflejo del desarollo industrial de Vizcaya, 1857-1913* (Bilbao, 1994); and de la Puerta Rueda, "Management and Finance in Nineteenth-Century Spanish Ports," *The Northern*

Perhaps an even more logical nation to compare to Britain was Norway. After all, by 1914 Norway trailed only Britain and Germany in the volume of shipping owned in Europe. And no nation (save perhaps Finland) was as dependent upon maritime employment; almost ten percent of the Norwegian population worked directly in the shipping or shipbuilding industries. Moreover, Norway was an export-dependent nation – and most of its exports were shipped by sea. In short, at least on the surface, one might expect Norway to have been interested in creating a national ports policy.[15]

Such expectations, however, would have been wrong. Those of us who have studied Norwegian shipping ought not be surprised: no nation that depended so much on shipping was as reluctant in the nineteenth and early twentieth centuries to interfere in the industry. Even Canada, which in general also failed either to regulate or to stimulate shipping in the nineteenth century, bestirred itself every now and then to pass a law that impinged upon maritime industries. But not Norway, where there were no subsidies offered to shipowners or shipbuilders, and prospective liner operators who hoped to emulate British practices by winning postal subventions to subsidize new services came away disappointed. In terms of its historical experience, then, Norway was an unlikely candidate to have a ports policy, at least until after the forging of a social democratic consensus in the 1930s. But that is another story.[16]

In fact, the Norwegian experience came much closer to the second than to the first set of expectations. The operation of ports for the most part was left either to municipalities, as at Stavanger or Bergen, or to private interests, as in most of the timber ports along the Oslofjord and the south coast. Indeed, not until about 1905 (conveniently, also the year of Norwegian independence from Sweden) did the national government take jurisdiction over a port. This involved the northern port of Narvik, which came into being when a railway connecting the small town with the

Mariner/Le Marin du nord, VII, No. 3 (July 1997), 41-49.

[15]See the discussion in Lewis R. Fischer and Helge W. Nordvik, "Floating Capital: Investment in the Canadian and Norwegian Merchant Marines in Comparative Perspective, 1850-1914," *Scandinavian-Canadian Studies*, III (1988), 17-42.

[16]See the discussion on this point in Fischer and Nordvik, "Subsidy and Intervention," forthcoming.

Swedish iron mines was opened. But it was a very reluctant government that agreed to oversee the port, and the Norwegian Parliament made it very clear that it did not see this as a precedent. While many of the ports were nationalized during the First World War, this was a temporary expedient to allow a neutral Norway to maximize its earnings (and to protect its security) in the short-term. By early 1919, all the ports save Narvik went back to antebellum operations. Indeed, there was even a movement to turn Narvik over to private interests, but this was eventually rejected on strategic grounds. Even in 1919, Norwegians were suspicious of the awakening Soviet bear with which it shared a lengthy border; as the nation's most northerly commercial port, Narvik was considered too close to the USSR to be allowed to operate in the best interests of anything but the Norwegian state.[17]

If there was nothing resembling a ports policy in Europe, what about in North America - and especially in the United States, a country with a decidedly mixed attitude toward the sea? In the middle of the nineteenth century, Americans owned the second largest merchant fleet in the world, and more than one optimistic observer even predicted that the US was destined in a relatively short time to surpass Britain as "Lord of the Seas." While I never wish to cast aspersions on other people's crystal balls, in this case the predictions proved totally without substance. By the late 1850s the size of the US merchant fleet was beginning to decline, and during the Civil War about one-third of the US fleet was either lost to enemy actions or sold to new owners abroad. Significantly, there were fairly few public expressions of grief over this outside the shipowning community.[18]

If the initial decline in the fortunes of the US merchant fleet was a reasonably accurate reflection of the way Americans thought about the sea, the final nail in the coffin of the US shipping industry was a direct

---

[17]For a lengthier discussion, see Lewis R. Fischer and Helge W. Nordvik, "The Evolution of the Norwegian Export Ports," in Lars U. Scholl, *et al.* (eds.), *The North Sea: Resources and Sea Way* (Aberdeen, 1996), 11-55.

[18]The most sensible introduction to American shipping in this period is Jeffrey J. Safford, "The Decline of the American Merchant Marine, 1850-1914," in Lewis R. Fischer and Gerald E. Panting (eds.), *Change and Adaptation in Maritime History: The North Atlantic Fleets in the Nineteenth Century* (St. John's, 1985), 51-85. But see also Bemjamin W. Labaree, *et al.*, *America and the Sea: A Maritime History* (Mystic, CT, 1998), especially chapter 10.

result of government actions. In 1868 a major Merchant Shipping Act required American owners who wanted their vessels to be listed on the domestic registry to buy only vessels built in America. With the single stroke of a pen, the short and medium-term fortunes of American shipping were sealed, since high-cost American-built ships automatically saddled domestic owners with a huge competitive disadvantage. Of course, there was nothing that required Americans to use their own registry - even before the days of flags of convenience, there were dozens of nations that would have been only too happy to earn the fees associated with registering US-owned vessels offshore. Congress recognized the possibility, however, and attached to the Merchant Shipping Act an important rider which reserved the rich US coastal trade to vessels on US registry. In other words, those who chose to register their vessels abroad paid a very heavy price for doing so.[19]

The experience with shipping demonstrated that the US, like most North Atlantic nations, had very complex and often contradictory ideas about shipping. On one hand, the prevailing ideology was something akin to *laissez-faire*, and it is unquestionably the case that the frontier exerted a greater place in the American imagination than did the sea. Yet, on the other hand, the American government proved at least as capable as any other jurisdiction of intervening in maritime industries when it so desired. And perhaps in no sector had American governments demonstrated such a willingness to intercede as in ports. The first session of Congress after the adoption of the Constitution debated the desirability of a ports policy to stimulate the economy. Moreover, the on-going debate over canals and railways was most often linked to ports. In arguing for the Erie Canal, for example, New York politicians were forever promising that investments in internal improvements would make New York City the most important port in America - and asserting that this mattered.[20] In the next three decades, local boosters proclaimed that the same advantages would accrue if canals or railways were built to connect Boston, Philadelphia, Baltimore and even Charleston to their hinterlands. New Orleans promoters,

---

[19]See John G.B. Hutchins, *The American Maritime Industries and Public Policy, 1789-1914* (Cambridge, MA, 1941).

[20]This argument is elaborated in Albion, *Rise of New York Port*. But see also the important (and convincing) revisionist perspective in Jean Heffer, *Le port de New York et le commerce extérieur américain, 1860-1900* (Paris, 1986).

recognizing that their home port sat near the mouth of a magnificent riverine system that drained two-thirds of the land mass of the continental United States, constantly lobbied - often successfully for improvements to the Mississippi, Missouri and Ohio Rivers, as well as for their tributaries. And when they were successful, it was only a small jump to argue that governments needed to pay for improvements to the ports themselves, in order to maximize the benefits to be derived from previous government-sponsored public works.[21]

In short, despite protestations to the contrary, the US had a long history of government involvement with ports. And no amount of rhapsodizing over the metaphysical attributes of the frontier could disguise the fact that between about 1865 and the outbreak of the First World War, the US economy was transformed by what was up to that point in time the largest, most sustained export boom in the history of the world. Of course, exports never exceeded five percent of American Gross Domestic Product (compared to the thirty-five to forty percent of GDP normally accounted for by Canadian exports), but most Americans were at least aware that exports contributed to their prosperity - and that more or less efficient ports were important if the export boom were to be sustained.

But did this lead to agitation for any kind of national ports policy? Not on your life! Instead, Americans adopted an ideological position on the issue: ports were local (or sometimes state) entities that could, if they wished, lobby for federal aid, but would likely serve the nation better if they competed rather than worked together. Moreover, the Constitution did not enumerate ports as a federal responsibility, and every American knew that if the Founding Fathers had not reserved jurisdiction for the federal government, control rested with the states. While "foreign trade" and "interstate commerce" were in fact federal responsibilities, there was a general (if not completely logical) consensus that ports were not.

The ultimate extension of this policy of local control of ports came in New York, where the harbour crossed state boundaries. Until the end of World War I, to speak of "port governance" in New York Harbour would have been to stretch the plausible meaning of the term. Suffice it to say that jurisdictional disputes made the port as ungovernable as any such entity in the world. Some progress was made in 1921, when the Port of

---

[21]This point is dealt with nicely in René de la Pedraja, *The Rise and Decline of U.S. Merchant Shipping in the Twentieth Century* (New York, 1992), chapter 1. See also Harold Sinclair, *The Port of New Orleans* (Garden City, NY, 1942).

New York Authority was created with support from both New York and New Jersey, but well into the post-World War II era, disputes over jurisdiction made the efficient operation of the port virtually impossible.

While New York was obviously in several ways exceptional, in other ways it reflected fairly accurately the American attitude to ports. The weight of public opinion held that ports were really local problems – and that these local entities could best be improved by a leaving reform to Adam Smith's sure and steady "hidden hand." As long as the public believed that unfettered competition between ports was a good idea, the likelihood that a national ports policy would develop was nil.[22]

This brings us – finally – to Canada. Despite the oft-repeated homily that Canada and the United States are closer culturally than any two nations in the world, their historical experiences have been very different. Nowhere is this more apparent than in the field of transportation. While Americans accepted some forms of government intervention – especially subsidization – by and large they believed that the private sector could be counted on to meet the nation's transport needs. The Canadian experience, however, was substantially different. In a huge and under-populated country like Canada, the reasoning went, the state had an obligation to play a positive role in creating transport infrastructure.

Take the building of transcontinental railways as a an example. While each of the four US transcontinentals built before World War I traversed lengthy stretches where small populations were unlikely to generate much traffic, all of them at least connected populated places to other populated places. But this was not true in Canada. There was no American equivalent to the desolate passage across the Canadian Shield. The Great Plains had a substantial settled population before any of the transcontinentals were built, but the same could not be said for the Canadian Prairies. San Francisco was a boom town when the Central Pacific began construction, but Vancouver, which was served by two of the Canadian transcontinentals, was hardly in the same league. And one of the Canadian transcontinentals was planned to terminate in a west coast city that did not even exist when the first rails were laid. Given all this,

---

[22]The preceding section was based mainly on my own research in progress. But many of the key points are discussed in A.J. Sargent, *Seaports and Hinterlands* (London, 1938), especially 71-95; and American Association of Port Authorities, *Ports of the Americas: History and Development* (New York, 1961), 123-125.

the role of government in railway building had to have been different than in the United States.

During the debates that led up to Confederation, it is noteworthy that there was little dispute over the idea that ports ought to be a federal responsibility. And right from the start the federal government in fact operated most Canadian ports. By the early 1930s, of the nation's 399 designated ports, 319 were operated in one form or another by the federal government. Without exception, those that were not were generally little more than undeveloped anchorages with little or no regular trade.[23]

The fact that Canadians have had different experiences than Americans in developing transportation infrastructure, combined with the fact that ports were a federal rather than a local responsibility, meant that it was possible in Canada to talk about a "National Transportation System" with a straight face. Indeed, this is precisely what Sir Alexander Gibb did when he drafted his *National Ports Survey* in 1932 in response to a request from the Prime Minister of the day, R.B. Bennett. While Bennett was interested principally in advice on specific topics, such as efficiency, facilities and administration, the terms of reference he provided Gibb were sufficiently broad that the Commissioner could proceed to devise a prospective national ports policy without going beyond his mandate. Indeed, Gibb's integrated set of recommendations could potentially have formed the basis for the only national ports policy around the North Atlantic rim prior to World War II.[24]

I have discussed Gibb's recommendations in detail elsewhere.[25] But it is not the details that make Gibb's plans noteworthy; instead it is the broad conception and how the parts fit together. Canadian ports, argued Gibb, "are an inherent and vital unit in a national system of transportation." Moreover, "national ports," he believed, had a duty "to serve more than local interests." Indeed, since the Dominion's ports were not "created and developed by merchant or shipping interests" but rather existed

---

[23]Sir Alexander Gibb, *National Ports Survey, 1931-32* (Ottawa, 1932), part 1.

[24]Lewis R. Fischer, "Any Port in a Storm: The Development of North Atlantic Harbours, 1850-1914," in Peter T. Haydon and Gregory L. Witol (eds.), *An Oceans Management Strategy for the Northwest Atlantic in the 21st Century* (Ottawa, 1998), 85-99.

[25]See Lewis R. Fischer, "Ports and Managers: A Comparative Examination of the Historical Development of Port Management in Australia and Canada, 1850-1970," in David J. Starkey (ed.), *Steam at Sea* (Hull, 1999), forthcoming.

"primarily as the connection between land and sea in the long route that the exports of Canada must take to reach their market," they had to be "directed on national lines and in accordance with a definite, coordinated policy." In addition, he contended that ports were too important to be left solely to the whims of "business and economics. For these reasons," he concluded, "they must be subject to a considerable amount of federal control."[26]

Having disposed of the philosophical arguments, Gibb proceeded to sketch how these ports ought to be operated, which was in a coordinated way to serve the entire country rather than local or regional interests. He believed that in the first instance government ought to abolish harbour boards where they existed, which was in about fourteen ports at the time. Instead, he recommended that operating authority be vested principally in a Port Manager appointed by Parliament. This was one of his more contentious arguments, since it smacked firmly of centralization and went against regional and local self-interests. Yet if we accept that ports play national rather than local roles, the old bromide that local control is always better loses much of its power. While local people might well have a greater knowledge of local conditions and needs, this becomes less relevant if ports are conceived of as part of a national web.[27]

Gibb also railed strongly against the duplication of facilities. If local self-interest were the sole criterion, he admitted, it might make sense to expend substantial improving the infrastructure in the port of Québec so that it could compete with its larger neighbour, Montréal, but if national interests were deemed more important, this became less desirable. A similar problem existed on the east coast, where Saint John and Halifax competed for what was essentially the same traffic. And on the Great Lakes, a host of small ports harboured ambitions to challenge Thunder Bay and Toronto. In every case, Gibb came down on the side of national rather than local interests.[28]

Lest you think that Gibb was proposing the ultimate in "big brother" administration, I should also point out that since in his view "adequate representation of local interests and port users...is essential,"

---

[26]*Ibid.*, 4.

[27]*Ibid.*, especially 12-16 and 26-30.

[28]See, for example, *ibid.*, 108-111 and 140-144.

ultimately all ports should have "a strong local Harbour Council" where warranted. He left the decision on whether to create such boards chiefly to local sentiment and local interests, and urged the federal government to create them wherever and whenever they were requested.[29]

Fleshed out with a series of specific recommendations about individual ports, Gibb's report provided a solid base for the evolution of a national ports policy. But this is different than saying that the report led to the creation of such a policy. By the time that the Bennett government received the report, Canada was at the nadir of the depression. And given Bennett's reluctance to see public works as a solution to the related problems of unemployment and deflation, it is hardly surprising that he put the report on the back burner. Yet in 1934, Bennett's outlook changed. Whether this was caused by the constitutional requirement to hold an election, as cynics would have it, or because the harshness of the depression had radicalized him, as his more ardent supporters would have it, remains a open question. But we do know that among the programmes traditionally lumped together as "Bennett's New Deal" were several that used public works to create jobs. None, however, involved ports, although there is some tangential evidence that just before he left office he was beginning to think about such investments.[30]

If the Gibb Report languished under the Conservatives, it was completely ignored by the Liberal administration presided over by Mackenzie King. Judged by longevity, King may well have been one of Canada's greatest Prime Ministers. But if the criterion is shifted to compassion, his ranking would be much closer to the bottom. We know, for example, that he submitted Bennett's most progressive programmes to the Supreme Court, which quickly ruled them unconstitutional. As perhaps Canada's most cautious Prime Minister, it should occasion no surprise that his inclination was to ignore the Gibb Report. When Canada entered the Second World War in 1939, even the limited number of ardent proponents of Gibb's recommendations dropped the issue for the duration. This suited King just fine.

That Gibb's recommendations fell victim to caution and political ennui is in my view unfortunate. It is unfortunate because by ignoring his recommendations, Canada was left with an inefficient port system. I have

---

[29]*Ibid.*, 26.

[30]This is all discussed more fully in Fischer, "Ports and Managers."

written about this in other places, and I have no desire here to repeat myself. But suffice it to say that by most criteria, Canadian deep-sea ports by the 1930s were among the least efficient in the world. While there are no guarantees that the Gibb Plan would by itself have transformed Canadian harbours into paragons of efficiency, the sheer logic of what he suggested should at the very least have made our ports more efficient. It is today a virtual cliché among historians that Canada's ports performed "brilliantly" in World War II, but a closer examination of ports like Halifax demonstrates that this was simply not true. Canada played a major role in World War II in spite of its ports - not because of them.[31]

And had Canada's leaders paid more heed to Alexander Gibb's recommendations, many of the follies of post-1945 port developments might have been avoided. What is even more certain, I suspect, is that Canada would not today be facing the lunacy of devolution, in which a "downsizing" (or "fiscally prudent," if you like the term better) federal government is attempting to pawn off responsibility for most ports to local authorities. If you are prepared to believe that ports ought to serve primarily local functions, and that ports have no real national responsibilities, then you might well be a cheerleader for this approach. But if you share the larger vision propounded by Gibb - and if you have examined the waste that is part and parcel of not having a national ports policy - you may well conclude the opposite. Ports, as I have tried to argue, have traditionally been among the least managed sectors of the North Atlantic maritime economy. But as Sir Alexander Gibb so eloquently reminded us two-thirds of a century ago, it did not have to be this way. There were - and are - alternatives, if only we can muster the imagination, common sense and will to grasp them.

---

[31] I have examined the performance of Halifax quantitatively in Lewis R. Fischer, "A Losing Battle: The Struggle for Efficiency in Australian, Canadian, and American Ports, 1919-1945," Paper presented to the Ports Projects V symposium, University of Leeds, May 1997.

Gordon Jackson: A Bibliography

Compiled by Lewis R. Fischer

Books

Grimsby and the Haven Company, 1796-1846. Grimsby: Grimsby Libraries Committee, 1971.

Hull in the Eighteenth Century. London: Oxford University Press, 1972. Paperback reprint, Hull: Hull University Press, 1988.

The Trade and Shipping of Eighteenth Century Hull. York: East Yorkshire Local History Society, 1975.

The British Whaling Trade. London: Adam and Charles Black, 1978.

The History and Archaeology of Ports. Tadworth: World's Work, 1983.

The Trade and Shipping of Dundee, 1780-1850. Dundee: Abertay Historical Society, 1991 (with Kate Kinnear).

Edited Books

The Port of Montrose: A History of Its Harbour, Trade and Shipping. Tayport: Hutton Press, 1993 (with S.G.E. Lythe).

Glasgow, Volume 1. Manchester: Manchester University Press, 1995 (with T.M. Devine).

Shipping, Technology and Imperialism. Aldershot: Scolar Press, 1996 (with D.M. Williams).

Chapters in Books

"Government Bounties and the Establishment of the Scottish Whaling Trade, 1750-1800." In J. Butt and J.T. Ward (eds.). *Scottish Themes: Essays in Honour of Professor S.G.E. Lythe*. Edinburgh: Scottish Academic Press, 1976, 46-66.

"Trade and Shipping." In J.R. Jones (ed.). *The Restored Monarchy*. London: Macmillan, 1979, 136-154.

"Port Competition on the Humber: Docks, Railways and Steamships in the Early Nineteenth Century." In E. Sigsworth (ed.). *Ports and Resorts in the Regions*. Hull: Hull College of Higher Education, 1981, 45-58.

"Scottish Shipping, 1775-1805." In P.L. Cottrell and D.H. Aldcroft (eds.). *Shipping, Trade and Commerce: Essays in Memory of Ralph Davis*. Leicester: Leicester University Press, 1981, 117-136.

"The Rise and Fall of English Whaling in the Seventeenth Century." In A.G.F. van Holk (ed.). *Early European Exploration of the North Atlantic, 800-1700*. Groningen: University of Groningen Press, 1981, 55-68.

"The Ports." In D.H. Aldcroft and M. Freeman (eds.). *Transport in the Industrial Revolution*. Manchester: Manchester University Press, 1983, 177-209.

"Charles Henry Wilson and Arthur Wilson, Shipowners." In D. Jeremy (ed.), *Dictionary of Business Biography*. London: Butterworths, 1986.

"Sea Trade." In J. Langton and J. Morris (eds.). *Atlas of Industrializing Britain, 1780-1814*. London: Methuen, 1986, 94-105.

"The Ports." In M.J. Freeman and D.H. Aldcroft (eds.). *Transport in Victorian Britain*. Manchester: Manchester University Press, 1988, 218-252.

"The Shipping Industry." In M.J. Freeman and D.H. Aldcroft (eds.). *Transport in Victorian Britain*. Manchester: Manchester University Press, 1988, 253-283.

"Whaling." In *Encyclopaedia Britannica*, 1989 edition.

"Shipowners and Private Dock Companies: The Case of Hull, 1770-1970." In L.M. Akveld and J.R. Bruijn (eds.). *Shipping Companies and Authorities in the 19th and 20th Centuries: Their Common Interest in the Development of Port Facilities*. Den Haag: Nederlandse Vereniging voor Zeegeschiedenis, 1989, 47-61.

"Anglo-Dutch Trade, 1660-1760." In C. Wilson and D. Proctor (eds.). *The Seaborne Alliance and Diplomatic Revolution*. Greenwich: National Maritime Museum, 1989.

"The Changing Structure of British Trade, Shipping and Ports, 1700-1850." In J. Bruijn and W.F.J. Mörzer Bruyns (eds.). *Anglo-Dutch Mercantile Marine Relations, 1700-1850*. Amsterdam: Rijksmuseum Scheepvaart Museum, 1991, 43-57.

"'Do Docks Make Trade?' The Case of the Port of Great Grimsby." In L.R. Fischer (ed.). *From Wheel House to Counting House: Essays in Maritime Business History in Honour of Professor Peter N. Davies*. St. John's: International Maritime Economic History Association, Research in Maritime History No. 2, 1992, 17-41.

"Operational Problems of the Transfer to Steam: Dundee, Perth & London Shipping Company, 1820-1845." In T.C. Smout (ed.), *Scotland and the Sea*. Edinburgh: J. Donald, 1992, 154-181.

"Introduction." In G. Jackson and S.G.E. Lythe (eds.). *The Port of Montrose: A History of Its Harbour, Trade and Shipping*. Tayport: Hutton Press, 1993, xviv-xxix.

"The Battle with the Arctic: Montrose Whaling, 1785-1839." In G. Jackson and S.G.E. Lythe (eds.). *The Port of Montrose: A History of Its Harbour, Trade and Shipping*. Tayport: Hutton Press, 1993, 220-224.

"Why Did the British Not Catch Rorquals in the Nineteenth Century?" In B.L. Basberg, J.E. Ringstad and E. Wexelsen (eds.). *Whaling and History: Perspectives on the Evolution of the Industry*. Sandefjord: Kommandør Chr. Christensens Hvalfangstmuseum, 1993, 111-119.

"The Rise and Fall of the Trade in Edible Whale Products." In K. Friedland (ed.). *Maritime Food Transport*. Köln: Böhlau Verlag, 1994, 433-448.

"Glasgow in Transition, 1660-1740." In T.M. Devine and G. Jackson (eds.). *Glasgow, Volume 1*. Manchester: Manchester University Press, 1995, 63-105.

"New Horizons in Trade, 1780-1830." In T.M. Devine and G. Jackson (eds.). *Glasgow, Volume 1*. Manchester: Manchester University Press, 1995, 214-238.

"The British Port System, c. 1850-1913." In A. Guimera and D. Romero (eds.). *Puertos y Sistemas Portuarios (siglos xvi-xx)*. Madrid: Ministerio de Fomento, 1996, 77-97.

"Introduction." In G. Jackson and D.M. Williams (eds.). *Shipping, Technology and Imperialism*. Aldershot: Scolar Press, 1996, 1-30.

"Trade, Commerce and Finance." In W.H. Fraser and I. Maver (eds.). *Glasgow, Volume 2*. Manchester: Manchester University Press, 1996, 52-95 (with C.W. Munn).

"Competition or Collaboration? Technical Change in the North Sea Countries." In J. Edwards and L. Scholl (eds.). *The North Sea – Resources and Seaways*. Aberdeen: North Sea Society, 1996, 419-445.

"Docks and Railways: An Overview." In P. Rees (ed.). *Docks, Railways and the Movement of Goods*. Liverpool: National Museums and Galleries on Merseyside and the University of Liverpool, 1996, 5-16.

"Ports, Ships and Government in the Nineteenth and Twentieth Centuries." In P.C. van Royen, L.R. Fischer and D.M. Williams (eds.). *Frutta di Mare: Evolution and Revolution in the Maritime World in the 19th and 20th Centuries*. Amsterdam: Batavian Lion International, 1998, 161-175.

"Big Ships and Small Harbours: The Evolution of Dock Facilities c. 1700-1840." In A. Jarvis and K. Smith (eds.). *Albert Dock Trade and Technology*. Liverpool: National Museums and Galleries on Merseyside and the University of Liverpool, 1999, forthcoming.

Articles

"Cary Elwes, Lord of Brigg." *Lincolnshire Historian*, I, No. 12 (1965), 1-13.

"The Struggle for the First Hull Dock." *Transport History*, I, No. 1 (1968), 21-47.

"The Foundation of Trinity House School: An Experiment in Marine Education." *Durham Research Review*, XXI (1968), 313-323.

"Marine Insurance Frauds in Scotland, 1796-1821. Cases of Deliberate Shipwreck Tried in the Scottish Court of Vice Admiralty." *Mariner's Mirror*, LVII, No. 3 (1971), 307-322.

"Port Building on the Humber, c. 1770-1850: A Survey of Local Motivation." *Bulletin of Economic Research*, XXIII, No. 1 (1971), 67-81.

"The Claytons of Grimsby: Local Trade and Politics in the Eighteenth and Early Nineteenth Centuries." *Lincolnshire History and Archaeology*, IX (1974), 43-51.

"Records for Scottish Maritime History, c. 1780-1830." *Scottish Records Association Conference Report No. 15* (1992), 1-5.

"Overview: Some Problems of Decision-Making in a Changing World." *International Journal of Maritime History*, VI, No. 2 (December 1994), 260-277.

Printed and bound by CPI Group (UK) Ltd, Croydon, CR0 4YY
16/09/2026
14963469-0004